Qualitative
Data
Analysis
Using a
Dialogical Approach

SAGE has been part of the global academic community since 1965, supporting high quality research and learning that transforms society and our understanding of individuals, groups, and cultures. SAGE is the independent, innovative, natural home for authors, editors and societies who share our commitment and passion for the social sciences.

Find out more at: **www.sagepublications.com**

Qualitative Data Analysis

Using a

Dialogical Approach

Paul Sullivan

Los Angeles | London | New Delhi
Singapore | Washington DC

SAGE Publications Ltd
1 Oliver's Yard
55 City Road
London EC1Y 1SP

SAGE Publications Inc.
2455 Teller Road
Thousand Oaks, California 91320

SAGE Publications India Pvt Ltd
B 1/I 1 Mohan Cooperative Industrial Area
Mathura Road
New Delhi 110 044

SAGE Publications Asia-Pacific Pte Ltd
33 Pekin Street #02-01
Far East Square
Singapore 048763

Library of Congress Control Number: 2011925497

British Library Cataloguing in Publication data

A catalogue record for this book is available from the British Library

ISBN 978-1-84920-609-9
ISBN 978-1-84920-610-5 (pbk)

Typeset by C&M Digitals (P) Ltd, Chennai, India
Printed and bound by CPI Group (UK) Ltd, Croydon, CRO 4YY
Printed on paper from sustainable resources

For my parents, Pat and Carol

BRIEF CONTENTS

About the Author   xi
Preface   xii
Acknowledgements   xiii

1   Introducing Dialogue to Qualitative Analysis   1

2   Analysing Subjectivity in Qualitative Research   21

3   Using Dialogue to Explore Subjectivity   43

4   Data Preparation and Analysis   64

5   Writing up an Analysis   81

6   Double-Voiced Discourse and Focus Group Data   103

7   Analysing Commentaries on Subjectivity   123

8   Evaluation   143

9   Discussion   165

Bibliography   180
Index   187

CONTENTS

About the Author   xi
Preface   xii
Acknowledgements   xiii

1. **Introducing Dialogue to Qualitative Analysis**   **1**
   What is a dialogue?   2
   Who was Bakhtin?   6
   Trust and suspicion in qualitative research   8
   The dialogical contribution to qualitative methods   13
   Some other methodological readings of dialogue   17
   About this book   18

2. **Analysing Subjectivity in Qualitative Research**   **21**
   Blank subjectivity   22
   Complex subjectivity   30
   Uncomplicated subjectivity   37
   Discussion: towards a complex, conscious subjectivity   41

3. **Using Dialogue to Explore Subjectivity**   **43**
   Discourse viewed aesthetically   43
   Epic and 'outside-in' discourse   48
   Parody and 'inside-out' discourse   50
   'Outside-in' and 'inside-out' struggles   53
   The novel and the shaping of subjectivity   60
   In summary and moving on   61

4. **Data Preparation and Analysis**   **64**
   Bureaucracy and charisma in qualitative research   64
   Bureaucracy in a dialogical approach   67
   The charismatic side of dialogical research   78
   Discussion   80

5. **Writing up an Analysis**   **81**
   Gaining an overview of the analysis   82
   Writing about a major genre   84
   Dialogue with another genre   93
   Discussion   100

6. **Double-Voiced Discourse and Focus Group Data**   **103**
   A folk psychology genre   105
   A carnival genre in double-voiced discourse   111
   Discussion   119

7. **Analysing Commentaries on Subjectivity**   **123**
   Intertextuality   123
   Analysis of two commentaries on subjectivity   125
   Discussion   140

8. **Evaluation**   **143**
   Traditional evaluation criteria   144
   Evaluation criteria in qualitative research   146
   Evaluation criteria for a dialogical approach   150
   Discussion   162

9. **Discussion**   **165**
   Theoretical reflection   165
   Reflections on method   172
   Future directions   176

Bibliography   180
Index   187

ABOUT THE AUTHOR

Dr Paul Sullivan lectures in psychology at the University of Bradford. His research is concerned with the significance of dialogue in understanding interpersonal as well as intrapersonal relationships and its applications for doing qualitative psychology. He is the 2009 winner of the Qualitative Methods in Psychology Section Prize for 'Outstanding Early Career Scholar'.

PREFACE

This book is intended for a broad range of academics, practitioners and students interested in the turn to dialogue in the social sciences and how it may be used as a qualitative methodology. A dialogical analysis, inspired by the philosopher and literary critic, Mikhail Bakhtin (1895–1975) is particularly appropriate for students of subjectivity; those who are interested in how the thoughts, feelings and emotions of the author intone language and are open to analysis. The author is very much alive and well in this kind of approach but is interpreted as a searching author, seeking to give shape to others as well as to self through language. Discourse, rhetoric and ambivalent experience are united under a view of dialogue that is primarily aesthetic in spirit.

A dialogical approach to data analysis is worked out, in part, through engaging seriously with existing qualitative methodologies. These include grounded theory, narrative analysis, phenomenological analysis and discourse analysis. These qualitative methodologies are approached in terms of their practices rather than theory alone. So, for instance, their relevance to dialogue is examined from the point of view of the attitude they bring to the text (trust and suspicion), how they deal with subjectivity, the guidelines they propose (bureaucratic and charismatic) and the view of time and space that they suggest. Against the light of these practices, it is possible to assess a dialogical approach to the text.

Great effort has been expended in trying to make this a readable and usable book. Overly technical terms and convoluted phraseology is avoided as far as possible. Summary tables at the end of most sections are included for easy navigation. Case studies and examples are regularly examined as a means of testing what a dialogical approach can bring to the table. A further reading list is provided at the end of every chapter.

I hope that these efforts pay off for the reader and that a dialogue with the methodology will be rewarding.

Paul Sullivan
December 2010

ACKNOWLEDGEMENTS

I would like to thank the University of Bradford for permitting me to take study leave to complete this book.

I have been incredibly fortunate with the quality of comment and support I have received at every single stage of the writing. Without the enthusiasm and support of expert friends, this book would not have been written. John McCarthy from University College Cork has provided constructive and challenging suggestions. I am very grateful to John for his enthusiasm, remarkable insight and capacity to push forward the frontiers of ideas and the horizon of idea-heroes. Many heartfelt thanks also to Anna Madill from the University of Leeds. Anna has provided numerous constructive, thoughtful, challenging comments and has opened up exciting new worlds of possibility for engaging with the text. I also would like to extend a very big thank you to Ian Burkitt at the University of Bradford. Ian, with characteristic generosity and intellectual curiosity, has discussed ideas and given very helpful comments on chapters from the book.

There are others who have also made important contributions to this book. Patrick Brindle and David Hodge from Sage have also been very generous with their time and critical feedback. Without Patrick and David reminding me of the reader, the book would be lost. Many thanks also to Lucy Goldsmith and Timothy Gomersall for their valuable comments and dialogue with the work.

Finally, I have been engaged in an intense dialogue with myself and the 'hidden' addressees who help shape the book. Many thanks to my wife, Val, for her support, good humour and energy in rescuing me from the worst excesses of this dialogue and creating another world outside this particular text.

1

INTRODUCING DIALOGUE TO
QUALITATIVE ANALYSIS

In the busy marketplace of qualitative methodologies, this book sets out the stall for a dialogical approach to qualitative analysis. A dialogical approach provides tools for the methodological analysis of subjectivity in qualitative data. Subjectivity is theorised as changing and responsive to others. This will be useful for those who have collected interviews or done focus groups or selected material for analysis and are wondering where to go next amidst a bewildering array of qualitative methods. If the data is concerned with subjectivity, then it may be worthwhile shepherding it into the arms of a dialogical methodology.

Questions that may be associated with subjectivity include: what is it like to struggle against others, what is the significance of absorption or alienation in any given activity, what are the circumstances under which transformative moments are experienced, how do participants articulate intimate encounters, how is power experienced and how is it resisted and/or embraced? A dialogical approach is particularly suitable for these kinds of questions.

Existing qualitative methodologies, however, are also interested in subjectivity and lived experience. Grounded theory (e.g., Glaser and Strauss, 1967; Charmaz, 2006), interpretive phenomenological analysis (e.g., Smith, 1996), narrative analysis (e.g., Crossley, 2000; Bamberg, 2006) and varieties of discourse analysis (e.g., Potter and Wetherell, 1987; Fairclough, 1992, 2003) also provide methodological tools for the analysis of subjectivity. From this point of view, the field is a little crowded and I anticipate some objections may start along the lines of 'but x analysis already does this!'

Considering the crowded field, this chapter introduces what is meant by 'dialogue' and outlines what it has to offer qualitative analysis. I do this over three steps. First, I introduce some features of 'dialogue' by turning to the philosopher and literary critic – Mikhail Mikhailovich Bakhtin (1895–1975).

While a significant figure in Russia since at least 1929, in the West, Bakhtin has moved from a peripheral to a central position across the humanities and social sciences since some significant translations in the 1980s and 1990s. Secondly, I summarise existing qualitative methodologies by classifying them according to the attitudes of 'trust' and 'suspicion' they bring to the data. I then bring these two strands of the chapter together in a section on 'the dialogical contribution to qualitative methods'. Here I outline the key contributions as well as distinctiveness of a dialogical approach to qualitative analysis.

This overview is also a preview of the rest of the book. For this reason, it may be a bit sketchy in feel or appear to jump the gun, in assuming knowledge, in places for some readers. Hopefully, however, it will give enough information and be sufficiently stimulating to encourage a turn to the subsequent chapters where the more labour-intensive building of the stall begins.

What is a dialogue?

In this section, I introduce what I mean by dialogue. There are many interpretations of dialogue. A dialogue, in an academic sense, is much more than the give and take of a conversation. That is the more everyday understanding of the term. In fact, there are many ways to describe a 'dialogue' and much academic debate around what constitutes one. Theorists of 'dialogue' include Martin Buber (e.g., 1970), Jürgen Habermas (e.g., 1984) and Hans Georg Gadamer (e.g., 1989).

In this book, however, I will be arguing for a view of dialogue that emerges from my reading of Bakhtin. There are many overlaps and differences between his work and other theorists of dialogue (see Michael Gardiner, 1992, for more detail). The reason I focus on Bakhtin, rather than these other theorists, however, is because his view of dialogue is very practical and usable. It sews the seeds for qualitative tools that explicitly link the thinking, feeling subject to language. It is to Bakhtin's particular usage of 'dialogue' that we now turn.

In a dialogue, as Bakhtin describes it, ideas are exchanged but ideas are actually lived rather than abstract and are full of personal values and judgements. So, for example, the idea of 'death' can be understood in an abstract way as something that calls an end to life as we know it, but we gain an understanding of a different side of death when somebody close to us dies – a more visceral understanding of the tragedy of the idea. This is a somewhat easier distinction to make in Russian where there is a word for 'truth as lived' (*pravda*) and 'truth as abstract' (*istina*). Bakhtin (1993) makes much of these distinctions as signifying different sides of the same idea. These different sides of the idea may even be contradictory, consisting of the 'logos' or the proposition and the 'anti-logos' or the oppositional other side of the idea (see also, Michael Billig, 1987).

There are many everyday examples of the distinction between abstract and lived truth. To experience somebody as attractive or as funny, for instance, depends on both our abstract ideas of what these qualities are and our immediate experience of these in the specific encounter with another. If someone laughs at our joke, we may feel funny; or flirts with us, we may feel attractive; or appears interested in what we have to say, we may feel interesting. Crucially, these are sides to our idea of ourselves to which other people may have better access than we do ourselves. In Bakhtin's (1990) words, someone bestows these qualities upon us as a 'gift'. Famously optimistic in his youthful earlier works, he tends to emphasise positive qualities although, equally, we may experience negative, heavy values that we may struggle against – e.g., to be called stupid or boring or ugly.

What is particularly interesting about this view of 'self' and 'other' is that these are not just straightforward expressions of bodies separated in space, e.g., 'my body is myself'; 'the other is any other body', but self and other are also marked by a relationship between an 'author' (self) who gives a value to a 'hero' (other). We anticipate and react to how others may author us or do author us. We try to author our own identities (becoming an 'other' to ourselves), perhaps in anticipation of how someone else should 'author' us, or want to see us. This leads to a complicated sense of identity where 'I-for-myself' is simultaneously in dialogue with 'I-for-others' and 'others-for-me'.

The different sides of selfhood may lead to a set of reflexive dialogues – e.g., 'I am my body in life but transcend it in death', 'I am attractive to one person, but anticipate being a bore to the next' and so on. In this view, there is a multiplicity of dialogues between self and other which means that our sense of these is open to change through experience, that they can refer to different levels of investment in activity ('I am alienated from my body at work') and can be somewhat unknown to the participants in the activity – e.g., 'is this who I really am?'

What then are the ingredients of authorship that give it form-shaping power? One vital ingredient is the emotional register and intonation of language. So, for instance, a child learns to relate the muscular-skeletal dimension of its body as being precious and important from the loving tones of those around it – their hand is not just a 'hand', for example, it is a 'precious handie'. This doubles our pain when hurt – there is the pain of the wound and the tragedy that it is 'my precious handie' that is wounded. The value we give ourselves comes from these outside values. Alternatively, particularly as adults, we may find that the loving gaze of another is too complete and defining of who we are, robbing us of any mystery, and react badly against this loving construction.

Bakhtin's favourite analogy for this kind of fraught emotional shaping of other people is art. We give each other a form out of the raw material of an encounter. We may embrace this form or struggle against it. Moreover, we can live our life as a work of art – organising it and shaping it so that it is consistent with social ideas that we invest in it – e.g., to be intellectual at all times, to be a loving parent or to transcend the earthly world in spirituality. This can be an ongoing project as we strive to 'improve' the self or make sense of different, contradictory experiences to what we believed – e.g., denouncing infidelity in general only to end up being unfaithful. As such, dialogue may involve a process of feeling the different shapes and sounds of that idea (its intonation) through life.

Contrary to a common-sense view of dialogue where it automatically involves a zone of special equality between self and other, the form-shaping view of dialogue suggests that dialogue is born out of inequality between self and other (where one has the power to complete the other) and equality, if present at all, translates as an onus on both self and other, to use this inequality to enrich each other. This introduces a prescriptive and ethical dimension to dialogue. We ought to linger over otherness attentively so that the personality we 'bestow' upon the other emerges out of a deep understanding of their particularity (see Deborah Hicks, 2000, for more on this).

Some points around epistemology and ontology

On a technical level, it is worth noting that 'dialogue' is an epistemology (Holquist, 2002). An epistemology is a theory of knowledge. This sounds a little circular but what it means is that there are different theories for how we can get at 'true' knowledge. In contrast to theorists who say we can only get at true knowledge by a scientific method or by removing our personal interests out of the picture, for Bakhtin, true knowledge of the most important issues – is there a God, what does it mean to live authentically – only comes from a personal participation. That personal participation is a dialogue with ideas of others – sometimes dogmatic ideas that admit no dispute and sometimes with more open ideas. While we may not articulate life in these terms, through our activities, we are expressing our background assumptions of what it is to live a good life (whether this is to get married and have children, or make loads of money, or have loads of gratuitous sex and so on) and perhaps even revising them from time to time if and when they go wrong or enter into conflict with each other.

Dialogue is also an 'ontology' or a theory of being as well as a theory of knowing. As an ontology, it suggests that people are born 'needy', as they depend on others for values or embodied ideas to give a clear sense of who they are. They also have a sense of the creative potential of the future. At its root, Bakhtin assumes a needy, desiring subject that sensuously engages with others. Nonetheless, this engagement is a language, even if pre-verbal, as much as music or dance is a language, in so far as it involves a sensuous, touching exchange and a grammar through which it can take place.

In the sense of giving us 'foundational' starting points for identity, Bakhtin's theory of dialogue sits uneasily with strong forms of social constructionism that deny any foundational dimension to subjectivity – even if it is as general as 'neediness' or 'indigency'. However, the concept of a 'needy' author giving shape to the other through dialogue does resonate with weaker forms of social constructionism. As John Shotter (1993) explicates, in contrast to 'strong' forms of social constructionism, weaker forms admit to vague feelings and indeterminate experiences that are ordered and made sense of through communication. We bring thoughts, feelings and values to each other's attention. Consciousness, viewed as awareness, is very important in weaker forms of social constructionism.

I should point out, however, that while many commentators have noted a strand of weak social constructionism in dialogue (e.g., Clark and Holquist, 1984; Shotter, 1993; Bernard-Donals, 1994; Roberts, 2004), this is not the only reading of dialogue. This is particularly the case when one considers the wider 'Bakhtin Circle' – encompassing Valentin Voloshinov, Pavel Medvedev and Ivan Kanaev. These were contemporaries of Bakhtin, more clearly rooted in a sociological tradition. However, there is some debate over whether Bakhtin may have been involved in authoring some of their work. When one considers the 'Bakhtin Circle', an interpretation of 'critical realism' and 'Marxism' is also possible in dialogue (see Michael Roberts, 2004, for an in-depth discussion).

In 'critical realism', developed by Roy Bhaskar, Rom Harré and Mary Hesse, language depends on practices, institutions and structures that a scientist, following a methodology, can have access to. These structures and practices are conceptualised as providing the material through which people make sense out of their lives (such as medical knowledge, for example) and in making sense, people reciprocally interact with these structures and practices.

In looking at deep structures and practices that provide the material for experience, critical realism shares an affinity with Marxism. The emphasis in Marxism is on 'false consciousness' or how economic (e.g., inheritance of capital) and ideological relations (e.g., religion) can deceive people into being comfortable in their own oppression.

This brief description of Critical Realism and Marxism loses the complexity and subtlety of these frameworks. Suffice is to say, however, I shy away from extending the interpretation of dialogue into the wider Bakhtin Circle and critical realist and Marxist readings. Instead, I am drawn to Bakhtin's emphasis on consciousness in terms of its aesthetic potential for qualitative methodologies (as we shall see). Structures and processes are very relevant to this but only in terms of how they are intoned or appropriated by the participants of a study. In other words, emotional intonation, with its occasional ambivalence and capacity to give value to what is being said, is of interest in this approach.

More generally, although Critical Realism, Marxism and other philosophical traditions have had a significant impact on qualitative methodologies, I situate dialogue among qualitative methods by looking at the practices of these different approaches, rather than debating which epistemology best describes a qualitative methodology. This is partly because it is possible to read the same qualitative method in different epistemological guises (as we can see also with dialogue). It is also because the variety of epistemologies is very diverse and sometimes they have fuzzy boundaries (see Madill, 2010, for a description).

In a Wittgensteinian vein, I argue that when we look at methodological 'practices', we can more clearly delineate the contours of a method. In this book, for instance (as will become clearer as the chapters progress), I examine the relationship between dialogue and other qualitative methods in terms of the attitudes of trust and suspicion they adopt, how they deal with subjectivity, the bureaucratic and charismatic aspects of the methods and the various configurations of time and space with which they are associated.

Who was Bakhtin?

In this section, I briefly outline Bakhtin's biography. Considering that so many of the ideas in the book depend on this man's ideas, I feel that it is important to get a sense not only of what he thought and wrote, but also how he lived.

Bakhtin was born in Orel, south of Moscow, in 1895. His father was a bank executive. He lived in Nivel and Vitebsk from 1918 to 1924 and here, along with the aforementioned Voloshinov and Medvedev, he was involved in underground intellectual discussion groups. These had links to banned groups of Orthodox believers. Indeed, there is a curious and interesting vein of religious thinking that runs through much of his work (for example, he refers to the 'I-for-myself' relationship as 'spirit' and the 'I-for-other/other-for-me' as 'soul').

In 1924, he moved to Petrograd/Leningrad, where, due to his political and religious associations, he was unemployed (his wife made stuffed animals to help eke out a living) but very productive in his writing (see bibliography). Although never charged with anything, he was exiled in 1929 to Kazakhstan. Here, he taught bookkeeping until 1936. In the 1940s he taught literature in Saransk and in 1947 controversially had his dissertation on Rabelais rejected for the degree of Doctor but was awarded a lower degree of 'Candidate' (Bakhtin presented a more 'earthy' view of the Russian peasant in Rabelais than the idealised Soviet view of the glorious peasant). We also know that he lived in chronic pain, suffering osteomyelitis (an infection of bone marrow) since the early 1920s and eventually had a leg amputated in 1938. He died from emphysema in 1975.

As Ken Hirschkop (1999) makes clear, there are also many mythologies that surround his biography (e.g., that he carelessly smoked away his precious writings due to a shortage of cigarette paper). There is an intense debate around the authorship of some of his texts, with Bakhtin claiming that he had a significant role in the authorship of his friends' work, Kanaev, Voloshinov and Medvedev (an introduction to the debates can be found in Katerina Clark and Michael Holquist, 1984, and Ken Hirschkop, 1999). There is also some confusion about some of the details of his life with Bakhtin's own testimony apparently borrowing more from his brother, Nikolai's, memoirs. There is also a hint of unacknowledged referencing of Ernst Cassirer in his work on carnival (Poole, 1998).

Perhaps most importantly, however, we know that he dedicated his academic life, despite adversity and anonymity, to trying to understand the relationship between language and subjectivity. Considering his suffering at the hands of bureaucracy, politics and biology, this exploration appears to remarkably non-political and non-systemic but very personal and ethical – although there is of course debate about this as well (see Caryl Emerson, 1994). He freely took and gave ideas to others, but arguing all the while that ideas 'sound different' when they are passed through different voices (what he describes as 'polyphony').

At this point, it may be useful to summarise, in rough terms, my interpretation of Bakhtin's dialogism. This will help in later sections when we seek to draw out in more detail the implications of dialogue for qualitative analysis. This summary is shown in Table 1.1.

Table 1.1   General overview of dialogue

Self as:	Other as:	Language involves	Truth involves
'Author'. Needy. Tests out ideas with life.	'Hero' Sensing subject of authorship.	Intonation. Anticipated replies of others. Aesthetic potential. Embodiment.	Adventurous participation (*pravda*). Knowledge from cognitive reflection (*istina*).

Now that I have outlined the basics of Bakhtin's dialogical approach, the next step is to point out how his work is relevant to qualitative methodologies. To do this, however, we must first outline some of the particularly popular qualitative methodologies out there. Considering Bakhtin's emphasis on emotion, a good way of approaching this summary is in terms of the emotional attitude that various qualitative methodologies bring to the text. From here, I will then outline the methodological implications of dialogism for qualitative analysis.

Trust and suspicion in qualitative research

This section is concerned with summarising qualitative analysis by looking at the emotional attitudes to the data that different qualitative methodologies assume. In focusing on the emotional attitude of different methodologies, it is a summary that starts off on a dialogical footing.

Qualitative analysis is broadly concerned with systematically interpreting what people say and do. Within this broadness, there is a contrast between qualitative approaches that examine the content of talk as a gateway into lived experience (most notably varieties of grounded theory, phenomenology and some forms of narrative analysis) and those that look at the form that this talk takes as reflective of power relations and the local negotiation of identity (most notably varieties of discourse analysis and some forms of narrative analysis).

An example may help clarify the different styles of interpretation that these methods bring to the text (such as an interview transcript). If someone in your transcript data says 'I am in pain all the time', you can look at the meaning of this statement with the aim of gaining access to a strange and unusual world. This is also a traditional aim of anthropology. In this approach, you would try to understand how a person's world is managed when it is full of pain, what the different levels of pain are like and how other people are perceived from within this world of pain. At the risk of generalising, this tends to be the approach of phenomenological and grounded theory methodologies. There is a certain spirit of adventurous anthropology in these methods.

Alternatively, it is possible to focus on what this statement is trying to achieve. Is it trying to evoke sympathy? Is it contradicted by a later statement? What position does it create for the participant – e.g., helpless, enabled? What is the history of pain in that particular cultural context? Are there particular institutions (such as pharmaceutical companies) that have a vested interest in the experience and management of pain? This tends to be the approach of discursive methodologies. Such methods are interested in the world revealed in the data but from a critical point of view. The analysis is done in a spirit of critical anthropology; gaining access to how the world is constructed rather than what it feels like to be in it.

Finally, from a narrative point of view, the interpretation would focus on the structure of the statement 'I am in pain all the time'. The analyst may ask: What genre does it articulate – e.g., tragedy? What is the style of the text, e.g., dramatic and/or poignant, and where does the statement fit in a wider plot? At the same time, however, the reader may empathise with the reference of the text and the world that it signifies – i.e., the difficulties of living with this kind of pain and the possibly productive ways of organising the experience. The analysts' response opens up a world that derives from the data. In this sense, the analysis is done in a spirit of adventurous anthropology, although from a critical distance.

These are not rigid distinctions, with researchers sometimes combining and comparing these approaches (e.g., Burck, 2005; Starks, 2007; Langdridge, 2007). Nonetheless, their different aims and attitudes present something of a dilemma for the student and practitioner who want to 'do some interviews' and 'analyse' them. Here, I would like to speculate on what exactly this dilemma involves and the possibilities that it affords a dialogical approach.

The dilemma that I detect lies between a 'hermeneutics of suspicion' and a 'hermeneutics of trust'. Hermeneutics means a style of interpretation. The distinction between 'trust' or 'empathy' and 'suspicion' is drawn by Paul Ricoeur (1981) to refer to the differences between methods that seek to adopt a critical distance from the content of the text (in qualitative research this includes varieties of discourse analysis) and methods that seek to remain open to the truths of the content (varieties of phenomenology and grounded theory). Narrative analyses, although varying widely and wildly, tend to combine these attitudes in different ways. As the names of these hermeneutic styles indicate, they involve a value-orientation on the part of the investigator – suspicion and trust.

While there are many different varieties of discourse analysis, most tend to be suspicious of the purpose that the talk serves. In some varieties of discourse analysis, this translates as a suspicion of what truth-claims achieve as 'warranting devices' rather than what they reveal about the author's experience (e.g., Potter and Wetherell, 1987). To help in the exposure of this use of language, discourse analysts turn to theories of rhetoric and social action, including, but not exhausting, John Austin's (1962) theory of language as well as Erving Goffman's (1959) version of symbolic interaction. Here, there is an armoury of terms to describe the strategic positioning and footing that may take place through language. I will examine these in more detail in Chapter 2.

In other varieties of discourse analysis, the temptation is to uncover the power dynamics, including unconscious, social and historical power dynamics, which are responsible for the organisation of truth-claims in discourses (e.g., Fairclough, 1992; Parker, 1992; Walkerdine, 1987). Much of this suspicion of the truth-claims of the talk derives from French philosophy, including Jacque Lacan, Ferdinand de Saussure, Roland Barthes and Michel Foucault (see Kress, 2001). They argue that the author is one who reproduces and adds to social meanings but whose intentions are largely irrelevant to the organisation and study of the talk.

In both these varieties of discourse analysis, the text is an object of suspicion and the author is ambivalently spoken of as either a strategic agent or ultimately irrelevant to the production of the text in the first place (see also Anna Madill and Kathy Doherty, 1994). The aim is to expose the various kinds of interests and power that construct a particular world.

In methodological terms, there is much variation in terms of how a text is initially coded in varieties of discourse analysis. Nonetheless, there is a general concern with coding the data in terms of: (1) the function of the talk; (2) contradictions in talk; (3) variation between accounts. This practice leads to different results within each framework (e.g., codes that signal historical power relations and/or as the moment-to-moment production of an identity) and are elaborated through the identification of different features exclusive to different frameworks (e.g., 'interpretive repertoire', 'defence mechanisms', 'historical discourses').

In contrast to the suspicion around the function of talk in varieties of discourse analysis, varieties of grounded theory and phenomenology tend to adopt a more trusting attitude towards the talk. That is, the talk is seen to give clues to another world. These approaches are less interested in the function of the talk in its relationship to a particular context and more interested in what the content itself reveals about the author's experience, including their thoughts and feelings, and potentially about others who have similar experiences. In this sense, grounded theory and phenomenology are anthropological, trusting and exploratory in spirit while forms of discourse analysis are more suspicious, critical and analytic in spirit.

There are many differences within 'trusting' approaches. In some versions of grounded theory (e.g., Glaser and Strauss, 1967) and in some forms of phenomenology (e.g., Giorgi, 1985), the researcher is theorised as being able to understand the strangeness of the participant's world simply by going through the gates of what they say, following a systematic method. In the case of grounded theory, this involves line by line coding, memo-writing and the triangulation of results. In Amedeo Giorgi's (1985) form of phenomenological analysis (the Duquesne school of phenomenological analysis), this involves starting by reading the whole text, then identifying 'meaning units', then expressing the psychological significance of these and finally producing a structural summary of the experience. They trust that the lived experience of the participants can be extracted from the text through this method.

More recent advocates of grounded theory, such as Charmaz (2006), and phenomenology, such as Smith's (1996) 'interpretive phenomenological analysis', tend to emphasise the reflexive, constructive and critical interaction between the researcher and the text. Instead of discovering meaning, meaning is more explicitly seen as emerging from the interaction between the data and the researcher. They do not simply enter into the participants' world but they are at least partly responsible for its creation in the first place by virtue of asking particular questions, having particular interests and having different styles of analysis (Madill, Jordan and Shirley, 2000; Smith, Flowers and Larkin, 2009).

Such methods adventurously explore the world of lived experience, and trust that the participant is making sense of a profound experience, even though this may be contradictory. The codes that are generated seek to describe as well as reveal the participants' experience, including their thoughts, feelings and emotions. This is in contrast to an attitude of suspicion to the text. Here, the text is coded for function, variation and contradiction with the aim of exploring how experience is created and shaped by different sets of power relations within the text (e.g., rhetorical strategies, economic relations, psychodynamic conflicts).

So far, I have outlined the trusting approach of phenomenological and grounded theory type approaches to qualitative analysis. Before finishing the section, however, it is worth briefly discussing Ricoeur's (1981) turn to narrative as a form of bringing together a critical, distancing suspicious attitude with a more trusting attitude.

Ricoeur's aim is to interpret a text (qualitative data) in terms of a possible world that it discloses rather than the original intended meaning of the author. In other words, the qualitative analyst should be more concerned with the potential benefit of the analysis for the reader rather than recovering the author's intended meaning. Such a response may mean, for instance, creating theory, formulating a policy response, and contradicting and adding to previous research. One does this, however, by looking at the text from a distance. This is possible because once a text is written down it becomes separate from the original time and place of utterance. This allows an in-depth interrogation of the structure of the text.

Ricoeur is particularly interested in the narrative structure of the text, including the genres, symbols and style that it articulates. Outside Ricoeur, there are many narrative theorists who analyse the structure of the text. Vladimir Propp (1968) analysed the structure of fairy tales to look at the function that each character serves; Misia Landau (1991) has looked at evolution in terms of a humble hero going on a journey; Jerome Bruner (1990) has examined canonical narratives and their breaches; Langdon Elsbree (1982) has looked at how people 'emplot' their lives, such as 'taking a journey' and 'engaging in contest'; Hayden White (1973) has examined how classical devices such as metaphor work to create modern stories. The list goes on. Suffice is to say that experience is viewed as organised through narratives and that understanding these narratives is a way of understanding lived experience.

Narrative has also been influenced by discourse analysis, particularly Potter and Wetherell (1987). There is an increasing focus on the discursive, strategic view of language and how narratives are performed in moment-to-moment interactions. Bamberg (2006) has referred to these as 'small stories'. These look to the positioning and jostling between participants and the production of 'small story' narratives in particular contexts. Identity, here, is considered to be open to flux and change and mediated through the desires and goals of the different conversational partners. This form of narrative analysis, in its affinity to discourse analysis, swings towards suspicion.

A more recent approach in narrative is Darren Langdridge's (2007) development of 'critical narrative analysis'. Here, he uses Ricoeur as a basis for introducing a 'moment of suspicion' into the interpretation of the text. This suspicion can relate to the politics of the narrator's own point of view as well as the politics of the narratives being produced. Unlike other approaches concerned with small stories, however, Langdridge (2007) makes clear that the goal of this approach is to offer up new understandings and possibilities in the interpretation that do not supplant empathetic understanding. Ultimately, like Ricoeur, suspicion, here, is only a moment that allows for an empathetic opening up of the possibilities of the text.

As we can see, there is a bewildering array of qualitative methodologies that demand different attitudes towards the text from the interpreter. At the

Table 1.2 Attitudes and strategies in qualitative methods

Interpretative attitude and spirit	Method name	Analytic strategy	Role of author
Suspicion of what author is doing. Critical anthropology.	Discourse analysis.	Coding for function, variation, contradiction.	Author as marginal to text; text is *exposed* as produced by power.
Trust in what author is saying. Adventurous anthropology.	Grounded theory.	Line-by-line coding; generation of themes via hierarchy; constant comparison.	Author as gatekeeper to lived experience. Text is *revealed/created* as opening a strange world.
Trust in what author is saying. Adventurous anthropology.	Phenomenological analyses.	Reading of whole text for meaning; generation of themes via hierarchy.	Author as gatekeeper to lived experience. Text is *revealed/created* as opening a strange world.
Suspicion and trust. Adventurous anthropology from a critical distance.	Narrative analysis.	Coding for emplotment, rhetorical structure, coherence.	Author as marginal to text. Text is *revealed* as opening a world of possibility from the reader's perspective.

risk of simplifying this somewhat, but with the goal of easy navigation, I have compiled a summary box, shown in Table 1.2, of these different approaches.

The dialogical contribution to qualitative methods

Bakhtin's work on dialogue is very wide-ranging and is also very stimulating and interesting. For this reason, it has been appropriated by discourse analysts (e.g., Fairclough, 2003), narrative researchers (e.g., Czarniawska, 2004) and interpretive phenomenological analysis (e.g., Ní Chonchúir and McCarthy, 2007).

This incredible fluidity is in one respect a reflection of the different readings that are possible of Bakhtin's work. As we saw earlier, 'Bakhtin', for some, can also signify a 'circle' including Voloshinov and Medvedev. There are also differences within Bakhtin's writings. His earlier work has a strong emphasis on embodiment and his later work turns much more to process of language, including narrative, historical consciousness and carnival (see Hicks, 2000). These different emphases allow for many different means of appropriating his work across different qualitative frameworks.

Indeed, Bakhtin, in terms of his appropriation in qualitative methodology, is a jack of all trades but a master of none. Here, I aim to give 'dialogue' a methodology and place of its own within the qualitative paradigm. Is it deserving of such a place? There are a few crucial insights from Bakhtin's (1981, 1984 [1929], 1990, 1993) work that is uneasily grafted on to other methodologies. I will discuss these, including their methodological implications, below.

The existential insistence on a needy self. As we saw in the first section, self and other are theorised as anticipative of each other. This means that the attitudes of trust and suspicion which qualitative researchers bring to the analysis may also be attitudes that the participants bring to their own experience. They are not just subjects to be known, but also selves as knowers – who are capable of interpreting and re-interpreting what they had trusted as being suspicious, and vice versa.

Methodologically, this means that there is more than one interpretation possible of a text/data. It can have many different meanings. For example, a wink can be interpreted as friendly, flirty, and/or parodic (see Geertz, 1973). From the point of view of a dialogical analysis, however, nobody, including the actor, may know for sure what they are doing. This means that the aim of the interpretation is not to recover a singular meaning, but to make sense of the different and ambiguous ways in which a meaning may be experienced.

The difference with other forms of analysis is that rhetorical features of language are viewed as both internally addressed to self and externally addressed to others. This sounds complicated but some concrete examples may help clarify what I mean. For example, what discourse analysis refers to as a 'disclaimer', Bakhtin (1984) refers to as a 'word with a sidewards glance' and the 'word with a loophole'. In disclaiming, the author throws a sideward glance in the direction of another's judgement. They may also disclaim as a way of escaping from a definitive statement they may not be entirely committed to. What discourse analysis refers to as an 'extreme case formulation', Bakhtin (1984) would refer to as a 'sore-spot'. The exaggeration is tangled up with a fear of being wrong. These are technical terms that will be more extensively discussed in the next few chapters. For now, however, it is important to draw attention to Bakhtin's trusting assumption that the author is trying to make sense to themselves as well as to others of their experience.

Similarly, where varieties of grounded theory and phenomenology tend towards trust, Bakhtin reveals a parallel suspicious undercurrent. The quotation should not just serve coherence – even if it is 'co-created' and 'multiple'. The quotation may also indicate interpretations that speak to participant uncertainty, ambiguity, anticipation of another's judgement, dilemmas and a search for resolution – even amidst claims of certainty. Perhaps these can be drawn out by the form that the talk takes – not only in the utterance, but also in the speech genre and the syntactical structure.

The emphasis on 'truth' as 'pravda' in a dialogical approach. This kind of 'truth' does not refer to whether something can be independently verified as existing. Instead, 'pravda' refers to a person's stake or investment in a belief that others may resist and/or dialogue with (e.g., the existence of God, the value of reproduction, the virtue of suffering). Such beliefs can acquire the status of 'truth' but may still be contested. Such truths can be embodied in different lives and indeed lifestyles (e.g., a priest living according to their anticipation of judgement).

In various writings, Shotter (e.g., 1997) has drawn attention to the importance for psychology in addressing knowledge that is grounded in the concrete, the particular and everyday life. Methodologically, a focus on *pravda* allows an examination of different 'lived' truths, with different levels of personal investment, in terms of how they shape self and other. As such, a focus on *pravda* foregrounds the aesthetic dimension of discourse.

For example, in an epic way of speaking, a future 'truth' (e.g., 'we will be victorious') aims to transform the chance events of the present, and power relations that are out of an individual's control, into a character-test with a predetermined outcome ('victory will be ours with enough courage'; 'I will succeed despite money'). In a lyric (e.g., folk tales), the past can assume a Romantic truth of a golden age in contrast with an alienated subjectivity in the present. In a confession, a threshold-present moment of immense change, a break with the past and a future full of creative potential can be felt. To a perhaps greater extent than other approaches, dialogue brings an intense focus to the transformative effect of genres on experience, particularly on the experience of space and time (or 'chronotope' in Bakhtin's words).

The impact of these genres on the audience partly depends on the level of authority that is involved in the exchange. Some genres are invested with the authority of the person who is speaking or the traditions that they invoke. Indeed, to disagree with someone, depending on their investment in what they are saying, may risk causing offence. Bakhtin (1981) refers to a singular, monological insistence on reaching truth, based on personality, position or tradition as an 'authoritative' discourse. One response, on the part of the audience, may be an ironic agreement (creating an inner truth against an outer truth). In contrast, if the author juxtaposes different truths against each other (no matter how difficult or offensive it may be), the discourse becomes more 'internally persuasive' – rather than relying on authority from outside the text.

Otherness and mystery can be built into the fabric of talk. In other words, there is an emphasis not only on the actual address and response to a real other (whether person or material) but a focus on the anticipated response of the other's judgements and attitudes that reflexively interrupt and change the speech.

Methodologically, the emphasis on the anticipated response translates to an analytic focus on the boundary lines between self and other. As well as the sympathetic reading of rhetoric above, it also means that there is a focus on varieties of 'direct' and 'indirect' discourse. Direct discourse refers to the encapsulation of other's words within a reporting context – e.g., He said 'I am unhappy'. Here, the other's words are relatively untouched within the author's discourse via quotation marks. Indirect discourse refers to the paraphrasing of the other's words by the author – e.g., 'How could he say that I am unhappy?' Indirect discourse allows an active intermixing of intonations between author and hero while direct discourse tends to separate out the intonations. As Gillespie and Cornish (2009) point out in relation to direct and indirect discourse, single utterances reveal multiple perspectives.

In Bakhtin's (1984) terminology, single utterances reveal 'double-voiced' discourses where the presence of more than one voice can be detected (faintly or strongly). We will explore this in more detail as the book progresses. For now, what is important to note is that, to a greater extent than other qualitative methods, there is an emphasis on the changing boundary lines between self and other.

It may be of benefit to return to the example of the individual in pain to establish the differences to other qualitative methodologies. A dialogical approach would focus on how the 'pain' is authored or the value it is given by the participant, it would examine their anticipation of judgements of others around how they are authored as a person in pain (for example, through paying attention to their reservations in speech and the introduction of other voices through indirect discourse) and explore their dialogues with their own self around the significance of the pain. It would seek to locate these in a particular conception of time and space (chronotope), such as future redemption, past suffering, the potential of the present, the significance of others on the landscape of the pain.

In Table 1.3, I outline the contributions of the dialogical approach to qualitative methodologies as well as the differences that establishes.

Table 1.3 The place of dialogue in qualitative methods

Interpretative attitude	Form of analysis	Role of the author	Differences from other approaches	Similarities to other approaches
Trust and suspicion. Adventurous anthropology.	Coding of utterances in terms of genre, discourse, chronotope and emotional register.	Central to analysis. Vulnerable to uncertainty. Other already within self as anticipated response.	Focus on voice feeling truth. Self viewed as anticipating other's replies. Self viewed as indigent or 'needy'.	Focus on discourse, narrative and lived experience but from the self–other viewpoint.

The methodology I focus on in this book is not the only interpretation of dialogue. Other methodological interpretations have also been developed that draw on Bakhtin's work. I will briefly outline these here, partly as a dialogical exercise. That is, there is more than one way of doing a dialogical analysis and indeed possibilities for adding to and changing different methodologies.

Some other methodological readings of dialogue

Hubert Hermans (e.g., 2001a, 2001b, 2002) is well known in psychology for his theory of the 'dialogical self'. According to this theory, the self consists of a number of 'I-positions' that struggle for dominance at different times, depending on the context and the relationships with others. Methodologically, this has led to a method known as the 'Personal Position Repertoire'. This involves identifying various internal and external 'positions' that the self assumes. The participants then give these a weighting in terms of their significance. Hermans (2001b) outlines the usefulness of the approach through examples from therapy sessions.

In education, authors such as James Wertsch (1991, 1998) and more recently Eugene Matusov (2009) have been very influential in bringing Bakhtin's dialogism to a wide audience. Wertsch emphasises the social, historical and institutional 'voices' that interpenetrate discourse. He uses these 'voices' to analyse text, i.e., identify various relationships between a speaker, the historical context and their role in constituting the dialogical experience. Matusov (2009) draws our attention to the variety of such institutional but also interpersonal dialogic relations in an educational context and the possibility of designing safe learning environments as a result.

Deborah Hicks (1996, 2002) has also developed some very interesting methodological interpretations of dialogue within psychology and education. Hicks (1996) has developed 'contextual inquiry' from a reading of Bakhtin's work. This involves looking at the significance of different symbols in a cultural setting for the participants and examining their moment-to-moment shifting valuations through a detailed examination of their narratives and discourses. More recently, Hicks (2002) has shown how an impressionistic, imaginative form of ethnography, which combines the participant's experience with one's own experience, is possible on dialogical principles. Hicks' (1996, 2002) work is an excellent example of how to apply dialogical principles to the data.

Finally, John McCarthy and Peter Wright (2004) have combined Bakhtin's dialogism with John Dewey's aesthetics to do an in-depth analysis of various activities including online shopping, a pilot's experience with procedures and experiences of ambulance control. In particular, they analyse these experiences in terms of relevant themes that they drew from dialogue and aesthetics, such as 'answerability', 'the sociality of experience' and 'the emotional-volitional nature of the act'.

These methods are all interesting uses of Bakhtin's work. In different ways, they highlight the various possibilities of an imaginative engagement with his work. In this book, however, I bring dialogue in a slightly different direction. In particular, I use his work to develop analytic tools that frame discourse and narrative in terms of self as author and other as hero. This involves a re-valuing of discourse to include a sense of a conflicted author and a linkage of narrative to our emotional connection to various truths. The aim in doing this is to bring subjectivity and experience to a more central place in qualitative methods (see also Sullivan and McCarthy, 2005).

About this book

Now that I have introduced dialogue's place in the maze of qualitative methodologies, I will briefly outline the structure of the rest of this book. In varying ways, the book develops on the rough sketch, outlined in this chapter, of dialogue's potential as a qualitative methodology.

In Chapter 2, I examine how qualitative methodologies deal with subjectivity. This establishes what practices are useful and consistent with a dialogical approach and what are less useful. I develop the boundaries of a 'dialogical approach' further in Chapter 3. Here I elaborate on a dialogical approach to subjectivity with reference to narrative structures and phenomenological experience. I present the argument that an aesthetic view of discourse allows a rich exploration of subjectivity.

Although Chapters 2 and 3 use many examples, they primarily serve a theoretical function. This function is to justify and develop where a dialogical approach to qualitative analysis is coming from. If you are looking to just get stuck into the data, then Chapters 4–7 are particularly appropriate.

In Chapter 4, I outline procedures for data preparation and analysis, including transcription and coding schemes. I make a distinction between 'bureaucratic' approaches to data analysis and 'charismatic' approaches. I argue that a dialogical approach combines both of these practices.

Chapters 5–7 use different case studies to exemplify a dialogical approach in action. In Chapter 5, I give advice on how to write up an analysis, partly by embedding an analysis of artists' experience into an actual write-up. This chapter forms the basis of a standard dialogical analysis. In Chapters 6 and 7, I focus in more detail on the analysis of some particularly interesting features of the data that may arise. In Chapter 6, I give advice on how 'double-voiced' discourse can be analysed. For this chapter, I draw on the analysis of a health care organisation or 'HCO'. Chapter 7 also involves looking at the analysis of double-voiced discourse, but in this case I analyse reciprocal reconfigurations between self and other in written commentaries on subjectivity. In particular, I look at two case studies that 'write-up' the analysis of schizophrenia in different ways.

Chapter 8 moves back into theory. It is concerned with the evaluation of a dialogical analysis. The various configurations of time and space that structure evaluation practices in general are drawn out and applied to a dialogical analysis. This chapter uses many concrete examples (including critiques I got in writing earlier versions of the chapters). Finally, the discussion takes a reflective look at the limits, boundaries and future potential of the approach.

Further reading

Bakhtin, M.M. (1981) *The Dialogic Imagination: Four Essays*. Trans. C. Emerson and M. Holquist, Ed. M. Holquist. Austin, TX: University of Texas Press.

Hicks, D. (2000) Self and other in Bakhtin's early philosophical essays: Prelude to a theory of prose consciousness. *Mind, Culture and Activity*, 7(3): 227–42.

Langridge, D. and Hagger-Johnson, G. (2009) *Introduction to Research Methods and Data Analysis in Psychology* (2nd edition). London: Pearson.

McCarthy, J. and Wright, P. (2004) *Technology as Experience*. Cambridge, MA: MIT Press.

Morson, G.S. and Emerson, C. (1990) *Mikhail Bakhtin: Creation of a Prosaics*. Stanford, CA: Stanford University Press.

Roberts, J.M. (2004) Will the materialists in the Bakhtin Circle please stand up?, in J. Joseph and J.M. Roberts (eds) *Realism Discourse and Deconstruction*. London: Routledge. pp. 89–111.

Shotter, J. (1997) Dialogical realities: The ordinary, the everyday and other strange new worlds. *Journal for the Theory of Social Behaviour*, 27(2/3): 345–57.

Sullivan, P. and McCarthy, J. (2005) A dialogical account of experience-based inquiry. *Theory and Psychology*, 15(5): 621–38.

2

ANALYSING SUBJECTIVITY IN QUALITATIVE RESEARCH

In this chapter, I examine how participant subjectivity is theorised and dealt with analytically in qualitative research, particularly in varieties of discourse analysis, grounded theory and phenomenology. I undertake the examination of subjectivity by looking at various assumptions around language. This is important because the kind of subjectivity that is revealed in qualitative analysis depends on the view of language that each qualitative method holds. This sets the ground for the next chapter where, drawing on the insights of this chapter, I discuss how a dialogical approach can theorise a 'dialogical subjectivity' and develop tools to explore it. In this next chapter, I also reconnect with some aspects of narrative theory, which, due to its breadth, diversity and some overlap with dialogue, is left out of this chapter.

The basic structure of the chapter draws from Parker's (1994, 1997) classification of subjectivity in qualitative research as: blank, complex, and uncomplicated. 'Blank subjectivity' is Parker's term for methodological approaches that dismiss individual experiences as an effect of language or of rhetoric. A 'complex subjectivity' is one that does allow for individual intentions and desires but views these as enmeshed and 'tangled up' in social structures and discourses. An 'uncomplicated subjectivity' assumes that the individual's subjectivity can be discerned from examining what they say.

I look at these various types of subjectivity from a methodological point of view. 'Blank' and 'complex subjectivity' are particularly relevant to varieties of discourse analysis that assume an attitude of suspicion towards the data, while 'uncomplicated subjectivity' is relevant to forms of grounded theory and phenomenology that adopt an attitude of trust towards the data. I outline their strengths and the problems they create for the dialogical analyst, who starts off with the assumption of a sensing self.

Blank subjectivity

In this section, I examine the relevance of 'blank subjectivity' to qualitative analysis. My aim in doing this is to establish what is useful and what can be left behind in a dialogical approach to subjectivity. I examine 'blank subjectivity' by briefly surveying some key theoretical literature around language that is responsible for such an analytic assumption and associated methodological practices. I also outline how 'blank subjectivity' contains an undercurrent of a 'strategic subjectivity'. Finally, the relevance of this discussion to dialogue is outlined.

A 'blank subjectivity' is relevant to different qualitative methodologies but perhaps it is most relevant to 'fine-grained' forms of discourse analysis. While there is some overlap, discourse analysis can be broadly divided into two varieties – fine-grained or 'micro' and large-scale or 'macro' discourse analysis (Burr, 1995; Gough, 2004; Ratner, 2008). While these distinctions are useful here, they reflect tendencies in methodological approaches rather than hard divisions.

'Blank subjectivity' is most relevant to fine-grained analysis of discourse. Such analysis tends to look at the moment-to-moment of conversational exchanges and/or lines of text, tends to use a very detailed transcription of the data, and is interested in how knowledge is constructed in these moments. While there are different methodologies within this broad form, including, for example, the detailed analysis of conversations known as 'conversation analysis', they are united by their assumption of a 'blank subjectivity'. For this reason, I refer generically to 'fine-grained' discourse analysis. Differences notwithstanding, Jonathan Potter and Margaret Wetherell (e.g., 1987), Derek Edwards (1995) and Sue Wilkinson and Celia Kitzinger (e.g., 1995) are well-known theorists of fine-grained discourse analysis.

So what does a 'blank subjectivity' look like? To use the example of the previous chapter, the utterance 'I am in pain all of the time' is not viewed as reflecting an internal state in discourse analysis. The internal state is a 'blank space'. In other words, it is irrelevant whether or not the participant is, or is not, in pain all of the time. Instead, what is relevant is the function that the statement is serving in a particular context (e.g., is the statement treated sympathetically?), the identification of any relevant rhetoric structure (e.g., is it an exaggeration or an 'extreme case formulation'?) and any variation or contradiction to other statements.

There is good reason for a 'blank subjectivity' in discursive psychology. As John Shotter (1975) has put it, mainstream psychology has sought to explain phenomena either through looking inside the head or looking at outward behaviour. This narrow focus has a dualism that separates the individual from their wider social world with the result of reducing the complexity of people's action and negotiated social meanings to a few basic causal mechanisms and processes, i.e., conditioning, neural networking and personality. The great advantage of fine-grained discourse analysis is that it shows how our social worlds are constructed and, in a sense, how fluid and responsive they are.

Despite these advantages, I should note that fine-grained discourse analysts do not like being characterised as assuming a 'blank subjectivity' in their analysis. Potter and Wetherell (2005), for instance, argue that the term 'blank subjectivity' reveals nostalgia for more traditional forms of psychology, where explanations for action could be located inside the person as fixed essence rather than out in the social context of language use.

Without a theorisation of subjectivity, however, as John Cromby (e.g., 2004) argues, lived experience can be reduced to discursive effects. Listening to someone talk about music, Cromby points out, is not the same as directly experiencing music. We need to theorise subjectivity to account for such experiences. Along similar lines, but in a counter-intuitive vein, Parker (1997) argues that resistance to theorising subjectivity in discourse analysis can mean that it 'creeps' into the analysis anyway but is 'unreconstructed' and 'untheorised'.

Below, I will expand on Parker's (1997) and Cromby's (2004) critique by looking in more detail at the assumptions that underpin such fine-grained discourse analysis. In particular, I argue that fine-grained discourse analysis draws on two competing linguistic traditions. One tradition views language as a 'structural system' and leads to the 'death of the author' and a blank subjectivity. The other tradition views language as a form of strategic action and leads to a 'strategic subjectivity' creeping in to the analysis but untheorised and unreconstructed. I will outline both of these below.

Language as a structural system

As Potter and Wetherell (1987) argue, Ferdinand de Saussure is a very important figure in discourse analytic research. In particular, he is influential in 'fine-grained' discourse analysis and conversation analysis. As is well documented in this literature, Saussure (1974 [1916]) provides a structural model of linguistics. What this means is that words acquire their meaning from their place in a structure of other words and they do not acquire their meaning from the external world they refer to. In other words, there is an arbitrary relationship between the sounds and written appearance of words (signifiers) and meanings (signified) of words (the sound 'dog' could mean a table). As a consequence, what we *know* is theorised as also being arbitrary. There is not an essential relationship between the world and words (there is nothing about a table that means we have to use 'table', as indeed other languages reveal).

So, this begs the question of how do things acquire meanings and words that we do know and can use all the time. Well, one implication of this approach is that 'things' do not acquire meanings because of what they are but rather that the structure of language gives 'things' a life. So, for instance, we know a 'chair' as a 'chair' as opposed to 'firewood' or 'art' because the word 'chair' gives the 'thing' a recognised life as a chair (although this may be debated – e.g., someone may insist it is 'art'). What we are doing when we give it a life as a 'chair' is that we are placing it in a system of differences within the structure of language. We are defining it, in a particular instance, as what it is – a chair – but also we are defining what it is *not* in that instance – a table, firewood, art – although under different circumstances a chair may be used as all of those things. So, the 'signified' exists only in a system of differences and similarities to other things in the present moment.

It is the structure of the differences in languages (sign systems) that Saussure (1974) was interested in studying. In what is now a classic division, he divided the study of language into *'langue'* and *'parole'*. *'Langue'* refers to the recognised social system of classifying concepts and 'things' into a structure of differences. *'Parole'* refers to the individual usage of this sign system. Saussure's focus was on the social system of the language as opposed to the individual speaking it. This is because Saussure wanted to construct an objective science of sign systems and argued that this was only possible through looking at the levels of signification at a societal level rather than at the individual using the language.

Langue has general rules that can be studied and universal dictionary definitions. *Parole* resists generalisation and systematisation. For example, there is ongoing invention of words, words may acquire different connotations in particular relationships and people continually generate unique metaphors. As such, Saussure's emphasis is on *langue* or culturally shared and recognised words rather than individual idiosyncrasy, the present moment (synchrony) as opposed to historical change (diachrony) and structure as opposed to usage and function.

While generally agreeing with the arbitrary relationship between word and meaning, the division between *'langue'* and *'parole'* has been criticised by discourse analysts. Potter and Wetherell (1987), for instance, point out that *'langue'* is too idealised and too static for an empirical programme in social psychology. Discourse analysts study language in use in order to understand how the arbitrary link between words and meanings can be used in a psychologically meaningful way. Gunter Kress (2001) has also pointed out that there is a 'motivated' relationship between signs and signifiers. Words acquire meanings due to politics and vested interests rather than being completely arbitrary.

While these are interesting critiques of the Saussurian approach to language, his basic point that what we know depends on the conventions of society (motivated or not) has been influential in doing fine-grained discourse analysis. There is an emphasis on uncovering these conventions of society. Rules and procedures are seen as given and sanctified by institutional traditions and social convention. The participants in research are conceptualised as instantiating and adding to these rules and procedures in their conversation to construct their social world, and looking at these rules in action (e.g. 'turn-taking') is the focus of fine-grained discourse analysis.

There is also an analytic focus on the system of textual features and oppositions that occur within the text. It is these contrasts and alternatives that influence a traditional discourse analysis. Edwards (1995), for instance, has looked at a set of emotional rules and oppositions in counselling talk. The focus here is on how the speaker uses the resources of language to construct knowledge (e.g., of their own and others' emotional state).

While the Saussurian theory of knowledge (epistemology) is that knowledge depends on how the set of social meanings relate in any particular structural instance, his ontology (theory of being) is that of the 'death of the author'. Indeed, 'the death of the author' was famously coined by Barthes' (1977) in his revisionist reading of Saussure's structural linguistics. More specifically, what Barthes means by this is that if there are confusions in the text or debates around what is intended by the text (whether the text means a novel, the law, an utterance, a command, a news article, etc.), we do not ask the author what he/she intended to say. Instead, we start from the assumption that the text has multiple meanings that can be worked out and interpreted in the act of reading.

What dies, here, is the author who knows what they mean and who can provide the definitive explanation for the text. In discursive psychology, this has been translated as the irrelevance of what participants intend to say in making sense out of what they do say. Instead, the concept of intention enters into the social text to form part of the analysis and part of the system of oppositions and contrasts. For this reason, the 'subjectivity' can be viewed as 'blank'. There is only a set of textual contrasts to analyse.

What is lost, however, in this 'death of the author' (the author who already knows the system of differences that give things meaning) is the author who is seeking to find out through the text what they mean. This author is not looking to act as a point of authority over what is said, but is present within the text as an author who is struggling to find out. In this view, to say that we need to focus on the 'social' function of a text does not mean looking at the sets of interpersonal dynamics and language games within the text (a traditional discourse analysis), but means also to look at the *intrapersonal* relationship the author has with his/herself within the text. This kind of intrapersonal relationship tends to be neglected in discourse studies.

This lack of focus on the self-self relationship is partly because the Saussurian model defines the social as groups of individuals and the individual as being alone. Alternatively, one could say that social means a relationship to other people as well as *simultaneously* to the speaking/writing subject. Rather than clear boundaries existing between these, in a non-Saussurian, dialogical system, self exists as a 'boundary phenomenon' (Emerson, 1983). That is to say, words addressed to others may also be rhetorically addressed to self as alien and be open to the study in the text (e.g., as ellipses, qualifications, and indirect speech).

The interpenetration of the individual with the social brings us to a further complicating factor in my description of the 'death of the author' in discourse analysis. Despite its claims, traditional discourse analysis occasionally does implicitly assume an author in the text, albeit a manipulative, game-playing author. Subjectivity 'creeps' back into the analysis as Parker (1997) suggests. This leaves us with an 'official' line of a 'blank subjectivity' where the author, viewed as a desiring subject, dies; but the unofficial analytic practice often involves the assumption of a background, strategic author. This assumption means that the data is viewed suspiciously rather than objectively. The origins of this unofficial epistemology lie in 'speech act theory' and 'ethnomethodology'. These theories of language and social interaction are somewhat awkwardly bolted on to Saussurian linguistics. This is the subject of the next section and the next main influence on discourse – 'speech act theory' and 'ethnomethodology'.

Language as strategic action

In a seminal article, Anna Madill and Kathy Doherty (1994) argued that notwithstanding the methodological merits of discourse analysis, it implies a notion of the person as 'strategic language user'. This, they argue, arises from some key analytic planks of discourse analysis – the emphasis on the 'function' of words and the emphasis on the notions of 'stake' and 'interest'. 'Function', they argue, implies a subject motivated to carry out certain intentions. 'Stake' and 'interest' similarly assume that the participants have a vested interest or stake in how they use language.

To fully appreciate the origins of the tension between a denial of authorial intention and its implicit usage in analysis, it is important to look in a bit more detail at some of the history behind this kind of analysis.

Austin's (1962) speech act theory

Formulated by John Austin (1962), and developed by John Searle (1969), the general theory of 'speech acts' argues that words both describe and perform functions in the world. Words have a social force (an 'illocutionary' force) that varies with context. The more the words satisfy 'felicity conditions' or conventional social conditions, rules and procedures, the more force the words will have. For instance, if someone asks for the salt at dinner, this is a convention that gains particular force in that context, demanding compliance at the dinner table; although it does not determine compliance. For example, one may reply – 'the salt is pretty happy, thanks for asking'.

Potter (2001) and Potter and Wetherell (1987) outline how instrumental Austin and Searle (1969) have been for discursive psychology. In contrast to the traditional psychological view that language describes and communicates known intentions, this view of language makes it far more active. Language has effects in how we think and act in the social world. In this approach, the social context enters into the study of language, particularly through its focus on illocutionary force and felicity conditions. Deconstructing the moves, rhetoric and devices associated with 'discourse' is a main goal of discourse analysis.

While influential in conversation and discourse analysis, speech act theory has been critically, rather than wholeheartedly, appropriated by these disciplines. Potter (2001) makes clear that speech act theory has been criticised by conversation analysts for not attending sufficiently to the 'uptake' of speech acts by the listener (the perlocutionary force) and as such the interaction between participants can be under-emphasised. Similarly, Potter and Wetherell (1987) suggest that speech act theory is constrained by an idealised view of language and 'made-up' sentences. In 'real' discourse, speech acts can perform a number of functions simultaneously or a single speech act may occur over a long speech. Despite these criticisms, however, speech act theory is foundational for discourse analysis in terms of drawing attention to the usage of language (or what language achieves for participants – in the social world).

Ethnomethodology

Ethnomethodology is concerned with how people understand the rules of social life and rhetorically use these rules to account for their actions – such as evasion of responsibility, justification, claiming credit and so on. It is centrally associated with the sociologist Harold Garfinkel (1967) and links with 'speech act theory' through its emphasis on talk as action. While 'speech act theory' looks at the 'felicity conditions' that give an utterance illocutionary force, ethnomethodology looks more closely at how the felicity conditions themselves are drawn upon in the organisation of everyday social life. These include presuppositions, tacit assumptions and inferences. These are drawn upon to account for action.

For example, when people draw on a social code in language (e.g., by saying 'you shouldn't cheat on your spouse!'), ethnomethodologists are interested in what that declaration is achieving socially – it is constructing an action as wrong, constructing the speaker as a moral judge, defining a situation in an unfavourable light and so on.

Assessing blank subjectivity

So far, I have looked at a number of assumptions that underpin a 'blank subjectivity'. In order to assess this form of subjectivity from a dialogical point of view, I will enter into dialogue with a typical fine-grained discourse analysis.

Edwards (1995) looks at an extract of dialogue from a marriage counselling session with an Irish couple – Connie and Jimmie – and aims to analyse how emotion is 'constructed' in the exchange, particularly the emotion of jealousy. The transcript below is very detailed. Underlined parts indicate emphasis, while dots mark pauses. So, for instance, Connie says:

according to Jimmy I was
a: lways doin' it and .hhh y'know a:lways
aggravating him. He was a jealous person, I:
aggravated the situation. .h And he walked out that ti:me.

(1995: 331)

From extracts such as these, Edwards argues:

> Connie's discourse possesses a reflexive, rhetorically symmetrical design of blaming Jimmy while at the same time protecting her own conduct from blame.

(1995: 331)

Edwards' (1995) analysis makes sense under the assumptions of speech act theory, ethnomethodology and Saussurian linguistics. Connie is doing things with words (blaming Jimmy) rather than representing her internal experience. These words are enmeshed a quasi-Saussurian structure ('rhetorically symmetrical design'). Moreover, in a nod to Barthes, it is discourse rather than Connie herself that reveals these characteristics.

If we step back for a moment and assume that Connie does not know how to make sense of Jimmy and his action, the analysis assumes a different hue. From the fact that she and Jimmy are in therapy, I do not think it is an unreasonable assumption that they are trying to make sense of each other, with the help of a therapist, as opposed to strategically using discourse to account for a known relationship to serve their own ends best. The former is at least as plausible as the latter and therefore offers an alternative analysis based on an alternative epistemology and ontology.

We could look at the use of direct and indirect speech (not discussed in the analysis above). In particular, Jimmy's voice enters into Connie's speech through indirect discourse ('according to Jimmy...'). It is unclear as to whether she agrees with the accusation that she was 'always doing it' because the boundary between her voice and Jimmy's voice is vague. What is 'according to Jimmy' and what is according to Connie? Does Jimmy's indirect voice end at 'aggravating him' or is the 'I aggravated the situation' also 'according to Jimmy'? The transcription system is unable to tell us this. If it is the former, then there is a sudden confessional quality to Connie's direct discourse where her 'I aggravated the situation' introduces confessional tones into the accusatory – 'I was always aggravating him'. In this reading, the status of 'aggravation' swings from tones of condemnation to tones of pathos and confession – the one word becomes full of such emotional-valuation meanings and gives added poignancy to her husband walking out.

If, however, the indirect speech (or Jimmy's sudden presence in her discourse) ends at 'I aggravated the situation', but only according to Jimmy, then we can understand its presence in her speech as introducing tones of condemnation and accusation into her talk which she struggles and grapples with as evidenced by her strong reaction – 'to me it was totally ridiculous the way he goes on'. Either way, Jimmy's indirect and sudden appearance in her discourse introduces his emotional-volitional tones into her words and the discourse. It is the process of working these out emotionally in a therapy context that is the task to be achieved by Connie – perhaps on top or even apart from strategically blaming her husband.

This kind of analysis throws up some features of discourse not typically used in discourse analysis – indirect speech, emotional-volitional tone of words and speech genres – such as the confession or the accusation. It also illustrates the possibility of bringing our textual analysis back to the author – not the dead author but the seeking author. An appropriate metaphor for this kind of author could be the 'idea-hero' (Bakhtin, 1984 [1929]) as opposed to the strategic language user.

Table 2.1 The relationship of dialogue to 'blank' subjectivity

Type of subjectivity	Interpretation attitude	Form of analysis	Gap	Benefit
Blank with a strategic undercurrent.	Suspicion.	Fine-grained discourse analysis.	The sensing self is missing. The author who is seeking to understand is missing from the analysis.	Gives attention to possibilities for constructing self and the social world through discourse.

This brings us to the end of our discussion on 'blank subjectivity'. I summarise this discussion in Table 2.1. I then move on to examining how 'complex subjectivity' forms a central plank of other forms of qualitative analysis and the benefits and difficulties that this brings from a dialogical point of view.

Complex subjectivity

In this section, I focus on both 'social structures' and 'psychoanalytic discourses' as features of qualitative methods that draw on a 'complex subjectivity' as part of their analysis. Complex subjectivity is most relevant to 'large-scale' discourse analysis. There are also many different schools and methodologies within this broad framework. Ian Parker (e.g., 1997, 2010), Erica Burman (e.g., 2009), Valerie Walkerdine (e.g., 1987) and Norman Fairclough (e.g., 1992) are associated with this form of analysis, although, again, the field is very big.

So what is a 'complex subjectivity'? Parker (1997) argues that a complex subjectivity is one that does allow for individual intentions and desires but views these as enmeshed and 'tangled up' in social structures and discourses. For example, the discourse around psychoanalysis in society is drawn upon by individuals to make sense of experience – e.g., in referring to a 'big ego' or 'defence mechanisms' (Billig, 1999). Peter Branney (2008) has outlined how Parker's 'complex subjectivity' moves psychology away from the conservative conception of 'personality' towards a view of the person as an agent who draws from and adds to resources in their social context to make sense of experience.

There are two assumptions about language that are sometimes treated separately and sometimes combined in discursive approaches concerned with a 'complex subjectivity'. One is that language involves relationships of power. The other is that language involves unconscious desire. In both of these assumptions, there is a suspicious attitude adopted towards the data. The text can be analysed to expose the workings of a complex subjectivity. These assumptions and their difficulties from a dialogical point are outlined below.

Language as involving power relations

Michel Foucault (e.g., 1973) is interested in the ways that power operates – how it 'conducts conduct'. In particular, Foucault argues that power operates productively as well as 'repressively'. Even our modern sense of self, with its conscience, guilt, sexual desire and sense of autonomy, has developed, at least partly, from the emergence of 'expert knowledge' in the eighteenth and nineteenth centuries. What we know (epistemology) depends on what these experts tell us. With the emergence of 'disciplines' such as economics, psychology, psychiatry, geography and so on, there has been a widespread 'disciplining' of consciousness and fostering of our sense of subjectivity. We are (ontologically) the subjects of discipline.

Foucault is a very significant figure in discourse analysis, but like Saussure, Austin and others, his work tends to be used in conjunction with other theorists. Parker (e.g., 1992) and Valerie Walkerdine (1981) and Cathy Urwin (1984), for instance, tend to use Foucault alongside Jacques Lacan, while Norman Fairclough (1992, 2003) is influenced by Foucault alongside Michael Halliday (1994) and Bakhtin (1981).

Foucault's influence on Parker, Walkerdine and Urwin is notable through their linkage of discourse to power – embodied in institutions, history and culture and manifest in the text as being open to study. Foucault opens the door to looking at how some discourses (e.g., patriarchal, religious, psychological, medical) can operate oppressively, can reproduce dominant and subjugating power relations and position or govern the individual subject in particular ways.

Depending on how the subject is governed, they have varying rights to speak within the discourse. These rights may also involve complex and contradictory access to discourses. For example, Julian Henriques, Wendy Hollway, Cathy Urwin, Couze Venn and Valerie Walkerdine (1984) point out the contradictions of being a woman academic in terms of access to power. In identifying these dominant discourses, the discourse analyst participates, in part, in an emancipatory project. This is not to say that all discourses are ideological or that all discourses have power, but it is the specific relationships between discourse, knowledge and ideology that form the backdrop to this kind of analysis.

Foucault is also an important figure in 'Critical Discourse Analysis' or 'Textually Oriented Discourse Analysis' (e.g., Fairclough, 2003). This is also influenced by Michael Halliday's (1994) 'systemic functional linguistics' and Bakhtin's conception of dialogue (albeit in a more political than humanist reading of Bakhtin). Rather than a distinct 'method', Critical Discourse Analysis involves the identification of power struggles and ideologies through the medium of language. Fairclough (2003), for instance, looks at how features of language, including rhetoric, words, grammar and genre, are used institutionally by various groups, including the media and politicians, to create powerful discourses (such as the 'New Labour' discourse of New Capitalism) that impact in a real way on society (e.g., downsizing and restructuring). This kind of analysis is very effective for looking at how experience is shaped from outside forces but is less effective for understanding how the person reflexively understands their own experience.

Some difficulties from a dialogical point of view

The question as to whether Foucault would agree with discourse analysis has itself come under question from Derek Hook (2001). He has argued that there is an assumption behind much of discourse analysis that the text makes power relations visible when much of the time they are invisible. Parker's aspiration to expose power relations in the text are problematised by this quality of power itself – to remain hidden.

Charles Taylor's (1984) critique of Foucault presents an even more salient critique of Foucauldian power relations from a dialogical point of view. He argues that for Foucault, action involves 'purposefulness without purpose'. Taylor agrees with Foucault that not all actions are consciously willed – this is a hangover from Cartesian thinking. There are clearly some actions with consequences that are not consciously willed, such as unacknowledged actions; actions and intentions that result from economic conditions; unintended consequences where a social condition is created that runs counter to the original intention. The point for Taylor (1984), however, is that these effects need to be explained with reference to human actors. Foucault, he argues, leaves us hanging with a history that involves strategies (of power) without human projects. The mechanisms of governance are mysterious and extra-personal – ungrounded in human experience or voice.

This is perhaps the key point that a dialogical approach would take from Taylor's critique of Foucault. Subjects may not be aware of mechanisms and effects of governance but these need to be explained with reference to human projects. In a dialogical approach, a key human project, as we saw in the previous chapter, is an aesthetic one – to give form to the other while being authored by the other.

A dialogical aesthetics contrasts sharply with Foucault's (1986) later turn to the aesthetics of self-creation through the mastery of technologies. This misses the contingencies of meeting others and the indigency of our own existence.

An example here may illustrate this. Parker (1997) draws attention to the capacity of subjects to 'render themselves one to another', using technologies such as self-help books. Such analyses informed by Foucault more generally tend to focus on identifying mechanisms of governance and technologies of control. While this is important, it is far too impersonal from a dialogical point of view. If anything it is the particular appropriation of these these technologies in dialogue with others and the contact that they facilitate that can enrich an analysis. The implications of an 'aesthetic' view of discourse will be worked out in Chapter 3.

Language as unconscious desire

This brings us finally to Lacan's influence on a 'complex subjectivity' (e.g., 1977). On the surface, psychoanalysis and discourse analysis are strange bedfellows. As Burr (1995) and Gough (2004) note, there is an inherent tension between traditional psychoanalysis, with its emphasis on psychic energies as well as conscious (ego) and unconscious (id, superego) conflicts, and social constructionism which resists 'real entities' such as the id or ego. A guiding assumption of social constructionism is that language creates an arbitrary world or at best a world that reflects dominant interests. Despite this tension, there have been efforts to integrate psychoanalysis into discourse. Here, I will focus on the Lacanian integration (e.g., Walkerdine, 1987; Parker, 2010) but there is also a Kleinian strand (e.g., Hollway, 1984; Gough, 2004).

There are good reasons for attempting such integration. Most notably, as Burr (1995) and Gough (2004) point out, powerful desires and urges are not dealt with very well by more rhetorical and critical strands of discourse analysis (such as the desire to get married, have sex or control someone, or all three). Even after a person becomes aware of the power relations behind these desires, they may nonetheless feel conflicted or motivated to act against their better judgement. Psychoanalysis, with its assumption of a divided and conflicted consciousness, appears to account for this better than traditional forms of discourse analysis.

Lacan, although notoriously abstruse and difficult to understand, has presented the discourse world with a very sensuous view of language. It is one where the infant's identity becomes structured into a relationship of difference from what it is not – e.g., a girl and not a boy or vice versa, or a child and not an adult. What we know is given by language but in the process we lose knowledge of our original, primary self without boundaries – we are left only with repressed desire to regain this state.

To elaborate – language offers us a system of positions among oppositions (e.g., male, female, son, daughter) which, by inhabiting, we are also renouncing the possibilities that exist before language (a primary and limitless infant state). In this sense, language is alienating and repressive. There is a self, analogous to a living, feeling character of a story, that takes its place within the structure of language, as much as there is a self that exists outside language. There is an experienced *gap* or *lack* between these two – of what we have to give up by submitting to the system of oppositions within language (e.g., the alternative gender).

Psychologically, as Walkerdine (1987) has illustrated, this ontology gives us the tools to examine the dynamics of gendered subjectivity. Psychic conflicts (such as separation from the mother and desire for the phallus) are channelled and resolved through social discourses. In girls' comics, for instance, as Walkerdine (1987) argues, valued qualities such as victimisation and self-lessness serve to structure the girl's subjectivity in terms of becoming an object of desire for the man; qualities that may foster a sense of lack of worth, guilt and rejection. Females, then, enter language in terms of a set of significations that take up and intermingle with original and primary conflicts.

Some difficulties from a dialogical point of view

This kind of ontology is valuable in so far as it allows us a way of conceptualising desire and subjectivity as part of the dynamics of language. As Parker and others have noted, it helps to overcome the neglect of subjectivity that bedevils Foucault's work. The difficulty with it, however, is that there is an emphasis on unconscious, primary dynamics that become causal explanations for types of subjectivity. This overlooks the immediacy of the present (e.g., existential problems) and the potential of the future, within the word. Moreover, in foregrounding our *primary* immersion in the *structure* of language, the beliefs, feelings and intonations of a speaking subject attached/detached to *what* they are saying is missed. In the case of the confession, for instance, we may experience a pleasurable encounter of understanding (possible only from the standpoint of alterity) and expansion of selfhood rather than a feeling of lack or a sense of being manipulated via a dominant discourse.

In a sense, these criticisms are based on values – they boil down to a value judgement in terms of how we view the gap between self and word. As Emerson (1983) notes, in a Lacanian world, the word signifies the gap between self and other and the pain of desire. In contrast, in a Bakhtinian world, internal conflicts are socialised, are greeted by others and serve as a point of pedagogy and organisation. The stuff of the outer world is not alienating but full of promise as it is out of this material that our own subjectivity is shaped.

Combining Foucault and Lacan

There is much theoretical work done in putting Foucault and Lacan into dialogue for discursive social psychology. Parker (1992) and Henriques, Hollway, Urwin, Venn and Walkerdine (1984) provide some instances of this kind of dialogue. At a risk of generalisation, Lacan is considered as a corrective to Foucault's neglect of subjectivity, including desire, emotion and feeling. On the other hand, Foucault is considered as a corrective to Lacan's universalising assumptions of a 'symbolic order' that cuts across time and culture. Instead, a 'discursive order' is considered to position the subject in various ways, reflecting different power dynamics across time. It is an order that interacts with and develops original primary conflicts (such as the gap between self and other).

To help to bring some of this theory to light, I will briefly discuss some of Walkerdine's (1981, 1989) analysis of a nursery school exchange between two boys (Terry and Sean) and their teacher (Miss Baxter). This is a particularly interesting and seminal analysis, often reproduced – e.g., in Burr (1995). In the extract that follows, the boys turn the traditional power structure upside-down, after being reprimanded by their teacher for being disruptive (they called a girl a 'cunt' and messed up the lego construction of another child):

Terry: Get out of it Miss Baxter
Sean: Get out of it Miss Baxter Paxter
Terry: Get out of it Miss Baxter the knickers paxter knickers, bum.
Sean: Knickers, shit, bum
Miss B: Sean, that's enough, you're being silly
Sean: Miss Baxter, knickers, show your knickers
Terry: Miss Baxter, show off your bum (they giggle)
Miss B: I think you're being very silly

Part of Walkerdine's analysis

The boys' resistance to her can be understood as an assertion of their differences from her as the powerless object of sexist discourse. Although they are not physically grown men, they can take the position of men through language and in so doing gain power, which has material effects. Their power is gained by refusing to be constituted as the powerless objects in *her* discourse and recasting her as the powerless object in *theirs* – 'woman-as-sex-object'. Of course, she is still a teacher, but it is important that she has ceased to *signify* as one: she has become the powerless object of male sexual oppression. The boys' resistance takes the form of a seizure of power in discourse, despite their institutional positions.

(1989: 66)

Walkerdine does not explicitly link Foucault or Lacan to this analysis. However, one can read Walkerdine's analysis through this lens – as indeed much of her work involves a meditation on these theorists. I read Foucault's influence above through the emphasis on a sexist discourse that serves to govern, oppress and subjectify. In turn, the boys are considered to *resist* institutional power through the employment of this discourse. Power, governance and resistance in discourse produce subjectivity.

I read Lacan's influence in the idea of a 'seizure of power' by the boys detailed above. In Lacan's writings, the phallus is considered as gendered symbolic power (rather than biological possession). In this sense, both men and women struggle for the phallus. The boys' 'seizure of power' runs against Foucault's emphasis on power as extra-personal. In the extract above, the teacher is considered to lose her 'professional' power through the boys' employment of a sexist discourse. They exploit the gap within the contradictions of her position as a professional woman. Walkerdine points out that a 'professional woman' may feel contradictions between experience and role. The boys, on the other hand, are considered to overcome their institutional control through this seizure of power. The idea of a 'seizure of power' resonates with the idea of seizing the phallus as part of a gender identity struggle.

Assessing complex subjectivity

Walkerdine's analysis helps us to assess 'complex subjectivity'. It reveals many political and psychological dimensions of the discourse. Desiring, feeling subjects are explicitly brought into the analysis and made sense of with reference to their surrounding culture. There is something quite creative about the contact between the person and cultural resources. The person is not made but actively shapes their world and in turn is shaped by their world.

However, there are some gaps in this analysis, from a dialogical perspective. First, the lived experience of both the boys and the teacher is underplayed. We are told that the boys gain power through articulating this sexist discourse but the speech is spontaneous and unreflective in so far as they are of nursery age. The atmosphere, for these boys, is one of ribaldry and fun as is evidenced by their giggling (not mentioned in Walkerdine's analysis). They are, after all, in a playful context with the toys.

Elsewhere we are told that the teacher viewed the outburst as harmless and was unperturbed by it. This is then interpreted by Walkerdine as the teacher actively colluding in her own oppression. While this may be so, the teacher's voice, embodying her own truth, lacks any real presence in the analysis.

Finally, there is much that operates unconsciously and outside the awareness of the participants in Walkerdine's analysis. What this misses is consciousness. A similar neglect of consciousness is evident in other forms of 'complex subjectivity'. It is unclear sometimes just how aware the participants are of the impact of the discourses they are using, their attitude towards these discourses and their capacity to mix, in odd ways, different kinds of discourses. For example, the children above mix laughter with a sexual discourse.

This reading of Walkerdine's analysis points towards the need for a qualitative analysis that will do justice to lived experience. This is important when the analyst is concerned with understanding the spontaneous moves between self, other and social context. It is also important when we are trying to get a grip on the emotions, feelings and thoughts of the participants. Finally, we need a discourse analysis that will help us to understand the interaction between authority and the carnivalesque as it takes place spontaneously and in consciousness.

The particular interpretation of 'complex subjectivity' I have given here is summarised in Table 2.2.

Table 2.2   The relationship of dialogue to 'complex' subjectivity

Type of subjectivity	Interpretation attitude	Form of analysis	Gap	Benefit
Complex.	Suspicious.	Various combinations of psychoanalysis and Foucauldian power with discourse.	The linkage of power to projects and desires is missing. Assumption that power can be revealed in the text.	The person is fluid rather than fixed. Subjectivity is at heart of analysis and linked to discourse.

Uncomplicated subjectivity

This brings us finally to 'uncomplicated subjectivity'. My discussion of this kind of subjectivity will be far shorter than the other forms of subjectivity that come up in qualitative analysis. This is because it is fairly uncomplicated. It is relevant to any methodology or methodological practice where the self is considered to deposit meanings in the text that can be recovered by the analyst. This is 'uncomplicated' by power relations, rhetorical moves, interactional patterns in the data collection and the strategic elements of gaining advantage through positioning self and others in different ways.

In particular, Parker (1997) relates an 'uncomplicated subjectivity' to methodologies such as classic grounded theory. Elsewhere, Parker (2005) has also argued that students should be alert to the dangers of 'interpretive phenomenological analysis'. In both these approaches, the effort to carefully code for the content of the participants' experience assumes that language gives an uncomplicated access route to the content of their experience (e.g., 'what is it like to be depressed?' – Giorgi, 2009). Instead, Parker (1997) argues that subjective experiences should be analysed in terms of the complex subjectivity discussed in the previous section.

Where, then, does this view of language come from? That the self can be essentially a large object sitting inside language, ready to be discovered? While there are many different influences, here I will briefly discuss the seminal role of Husserl in these approaches.

Language as a transparent medium

Husserl is a significant figure in various forms of phenomenological analysis (e.g., Smith, 1996; Giorgi, 2009). A key idea of Husserl's that captures the imagination of phenomenological approaches is the concept of *Epochè* or 'bracketing'. This involves suspending our judgement and ideas around an 'object' in perception. While sounding slightly mysterious, it means something like lingering over an object in order to appreciate its complexity and the role of consciousness in constituting it.

In methodological terms, what this means is that the analyst should be able to experience the text objectively, bracketing their own prejudices, past knowledge and political concerns, in order to appreciate just how different and complex it is. This does not mean forgetting about past knowledge of similar texts, but rather preventing such past knowledge from distorting the new object or text. It involves a heightening awareness of the present.

In analytic terms, this involves a duty on the part of the analyst to linger over the experiences articulated in the text. Indeed, most qualitative analysis involves an intense familiarisation with the data set. This can be viewed as a form of lingering – of looking at words and lines in counter-intuitive ways as well as in conventional ways; trying to remain open to what the text could be saying.

The difference with other qualitative approaches, however, is that the text is viewed as revealing a 'life-world'. This 'life-world' is the everyday world of peoples' experiences (waking up, relaxing, drinking tea), apart from everyday abstractions, such as business, entertainment and academia (these are all derivations). People are able to describe their experiences of the life-world, outside theoretical abstraction, and careful attention to their descriptions (e.g., of depression) can give an 'opening' into this world for the analyst.

'Bracketing' and the 'life-world' have been appropriated in various ways by qualitative psychology. Most obviously it has been appropriated by phenomenological analyses such as Jonathan Smith, Paul Flowers and Michael Larkin (2009) and Amadeus Giorgi (2009). While there are many differences between these approaches, some of which are outlined in Chapter 1, they both share the uncomplicated view of subjectivity outlined by Parker (1997). In particular, lived experience, e.g., of depression, is problematised only in terms of its articulation. In other words, the experience is there already and the task for the participant is to express the experience and the task for the analyst is to understand this expression. This is done through careful coding, questioning, examination of linguistic features such as metaphor and the iterative building up of themes. The experience is deconstructed and then reconstructed psychologically but is essentially unchanged.

In a 'complex subjectivity', in contrast, the experience does not rest inside the person waiting for a good articulation. The articulation of the experience, itself, is seen to constitute it. For example, if one uses psychoanalytic terminology to make sense of depression (e.g., 'my inner child is hurting'), the significance of the experience is shaped by the person's contact with a cultural resource for its articulation.

Grounded theory: reverse engineering through language

Husserl's influence is also clear from the focus in grounded theory methodology to start with the data itself. This is a form of 'bracketing' or 'Epochè'. This is particularly true of classic forms of grounded theory. Barney Glaser and Anselm Strauss (1967) argued that qualitative research should work a theory up from the ground of lived experience. This is done through the generation of codes of every line. These are grouped in concepts. These concepts then can be used to generate themes, from which a theory, explaining the experience, can be generated. The emerging ideas are 'constantly compared' to the data and different pieces of data are compared with each other. Sometimes, the researcher also goes back into the field to collect more data to compare with the analysis of existing data.

It is 'reverse engineering' because often a theory is used to make sense of the data (in dialogical approaches, the theory of dialogue is used to make sense of the data). Here, instead, it is the ground of experience that subsequent theory relies upon.

As we saw in the previous chapter, there are different strands of grounded theory, like almost every other methodology. Strauss (1987) and Strauss and

Corbin (1990) have moved grounded theory towards an acknowledgement of the co-construction between the researcher and the participants. Kathy Charmaz (2006) has also developed this 'constructionist' line of grounded theory. The style of the analyst, particularly in the write-up, can also shape the experience (see also Madill, Jordan and Shirley, 2000).

Despite these differences, what combines them is 'uncomplicated subjectivity' that the method reveals. Hence the ground of experience, consciousness and the activity of the participants is a central plank of these strands of grounded theory and the text is the gateway into this experience. Like phenomenology, there is a tendency to code for content at the neglect of form, including the discourses that the participants draw upon in articulating experience. There is an assumption that the participants already know their own experience although the researcher may interact with this experience in their analysis. This is a trusting attitude but one which does not do justice to the complex intermixing of rhetoric, discourse and power with subjectivity.

Benefits and difficulties of an 'uncomplicated subjectivity'

There are many benefits of this 'uncomplicated subjectivity' and the view of language that it assumes. First, in contrast to other forms of 'subjectivity', there is an emphasis on consciousness. In the forms of 'blank' and 'complex subjectivity' outlined so far, the analytic strategy tends to be a little ambivalent around consciousness or how aware the participants are of what they are doing with words. In contrast, in this form of phenomenological analysis, the participants' consciousness is given centre stage. This is an important methodological insight. It gives the capacity for participants to be aware and to be active in the creation of their own experiences.

On the other hand, however, as Parker (1997) points out, such participants are 'already given' and this comes through in coding for content. From a dialogical point of view, it is possible to be 'conscious' and not 'already given'. This is because the focus is on 'voice', understood as point of view, rather than the 'individual' with experiences. We appropriate the voices of others, have conflicted voices of our own and an address can be directed at someone 'outside' the self as well as the anticipated judgements of others. Methodologically, this means that language is much more important than these methods assume, although consciousness and awareness can still be a feature of the analysis.

In Table 2.3, I outline the main points of the preceding discussion.

Table 2.3   The relationship of dialogue to 'uncomplicated' subjectivity

Type of subjectivity	Interpretation attitude	Form of analysis	Gap	Benefit
Uncomplicated.	Trust.	Grounded theory. Phenomenological analysis.	Lack of attention to discursive processes. Assumption that the 'self' is fully known and available.	Focus on consciousness and lived experience.

------ **Discussion: towards a complex, conscious subjectivity** ------

All three forms of subjectivity discussed here have something to offer a dia-logical analysis. In fine-grained discourse analysis, there is an emphasis on the moment-to-moment fluidity of the social context, the linkage of words to action and the capacity of language to construct the world in different ways.

In 'complex subjectivity', there is more of a recognition of the thinking, feeling, and desiring subject than in fine-grained discourse analysis. It is the contact that the person makes with broader cultural forms that tends to inform the analytic practice. The aim of this kind of analysis is to expose mechanisms of governance of subjectivity – whether this is through the capacity of psychoanalytic discourses to give shape to experience or the capacity of individuals to master systems of governance in their everyday encounters. From a dialogical point of view, this shows that subjectivity is an open text, but also involves an embodied subject actively engaged in appropriating systems of governance.

In 'uncomplicated subjectivity', there is a focus on consciousness and lived experience. While the particular way that this consciousness is theo-rised is problematic, there is something very valuable about a methodology that trusts the efforts of the participants to articulate their lived experience and seeks to reveal the 'life-world' of this experience.

In the next chapter, I seek to bring these broad advantages to bear on a 'dialogical' subjectivity. In sum, such a theorisation would involve placing the conscious, feeling subject at the centre of the analysis, but would view such a consciousness as open, fluid and responsive to the words of others. In terms of analysis, this will involve an examination of the ways in which participants seek to make sense out of experience. Language is central to this and we will examine how language can be analysed to reveal a sensing self addressing and anticipating other voices. In such an analysis, intonation, viewed as the sound that value makes, takes centre stage.

Following Parker's (1997) description of a 'complex subjectivity', such an analysis would also examine how participants appropriate cultural resources. Crucially, however, in line with Taylor's (1984) critique of Foucault, my aim is to show how this appropriation relates to human projects. In particular, we will examine how cultural resources can relate to an aesthetic project of giving shape to other subjectivities. To do this, I will also bring in some insights from 'narrative analysis'.

Further reading

Branney, P. (2008) Subjectivity, not personality: Combining discourse analysis and psychoanalysis. *Social and Personality Psychology Compass*, 2(2): 574–90.

Charmaz, K. (2006) *Constructing Grounded Theory: A Practical Guide through Qualitative Analysis*. London: Sage.

Gough, B. (2004) Psychoanalysis as a resource for understanding emotional ruptures in the text: The case of defensive masculinities. *The British Journal of Social Psychology*, 43: 245–67.

Madill, A. and Doherty, K. (1994) 'So you did what you wanted then': Discourse analysis, personal agency and psychotherapy. *Journal of Community and Applied Social Psychology*, 2: 261–73.

Parker, I. (1994) Reflexive research and the grounding of analysis: Social psychology and the psy-complex. *Journal of Community and Applied Social Psychology*, 4(4): 234–9.

Parker, I. (1997) Discourse analysis and psycho-analysis. *British Journal of Social Psychology*, 36: 479–95.

Potter, J. and Wetherell, M. (2005) Postscript to Chinese Edition of 'Discourse and Social Psychology: Beyond Attitudes and Behaviour'. Available at: www.staff.lboro. ac.uk/~ssjap/JP%20Articles/Potter%20Wetherell%20new%20DASP%20post-script%202005.pdf.

Smith, J.A., Flowers, P. and Larkin, M. (2009) *Interpretive Phenomenological Analysis: Theory, Method and Research*. London: Sage.

3

USING DIALOGUE TO EXPLORE
SUBJECTIVITY

In this chapter, I argue that a dialogical approach allows the qualitative analyst to explore a complex and conscious subjectivity. As we saw in the previous chapter, subjectivity, viewed dialogically, is social, relating to self as well as to others. This kind of subjectivity is also complex in so far as it emerges and draws from a network of history, tradition and power. Most importantly, subjectivity from a dialogical point of view is conscious. It anticipates ideas and judgements of others.

What we did not discuss in the previous chapter, however, were the methodological tools that would allow this exploration. To tackle this, I discuss how 'discourse' can be used as a broad methodological tool for a dialogical approach to qualitative analysis. In contrast to the views of 'discourse' outlined in the previous chapter, here I interpret 'discourse' aesthetically. That is, I look at its potential to shape selves and look at how selves can respond, in different ways, to this shaping. As part of this interpretation, I also draw on the narrative concept of 'genre'. This chapter provides the foundation for Chapter 4 where I outline how an aesthetic view of discourse can be of help in data preparation and analysis.

Discourse viewed aesthetically

The variety of methodologies associated with doing discourse analysis has meant that 'discourse' has come to mean 'language in action' (Gee, 2005). For Bakhtin, language in action involves the expression of an embodied subjectivity. The quotation below puts this rather well:

> Logical and semantically referential relationships, in order to become dialogic, must be embodied, that is, they must enter another sphere of existence: they

must become *discourse*, that is, an utterance, and receive an *author*, that is a creator of the given utterance whose position it expresses.

(Bakhtin, 1984 [1929]: 84)

Bakhtin's dialogue with Saussure is clear in this quotation. Relationships between signs can also become embodied as words in the act of speaking. They are embodied in an author who expresses a position or a point of view, and who will be emotionally invested in this point of view. Discourse, in this view, consists of a multiplicity of speaking voices that express and respond to value judgements in their articulation of a point of view.

'Voice', here, is a very interesting concept. On one level, in expressing a point of view, it gives a particular intonation to an issue, a person, a thing (e.g., condemnation, absolution, regret, indifference and so on). Intonation is 'the sound that value makes' (Clark and Holquist, 1984: 10). Such intonation gives discourse a textured feeling of heaviness and lightness and also colour as discourses become lived experiences. For example, questions such as 'the meaning of beauty' or 'the relativity of morals' can be logically and analytically deconstructed but these questions 'enter another sphere of existence' or come alive when they gain the emotional texture or intonation of different voices – e.g., passionate defences or soul-searching questions.

'Voice' is also an ambiguous construct – at times more appropriate for others than for self. That is, while we discern the intonation of other voices, it is not always clear just what our own 'voice' is. Occasionally, we may surprise ourselves by the otherness of our own discourse (for instance, passionately defending a position one would normally feel indifferent towards), while at other times we may feel that what we say is the most authentic reflection of who we are. Moreover, in some dialogues we sound and feel quite different than in other dialogues.

'Outside-in' and 'inside-out' discourses

With the admission of 'voices' and intonation into discourse, an aesthetic quality to discourse becomes apparent. In particular, there is the author's (or self's) voice in a discourse and there is the hero's (the other's) voice. There are different kinds of power relations between the author and the hero. Some discourses are dominated by a singular authorial voice with its intonation pervading the discourse and shaping the 'hero' (e.g., even the physical world can gain the quality of 'beauty' in our response to it). Here, the 'hero' is shaped by the author, has no agency to disagree with the author or to introduce their own intonation and point of view into the discourse. Such a discourse moves the hero from the outside world, with all of their complexity, into the centre of the author's discourse, where they are saturated with the author's intonation. For this reason, such a discourse can be referred to as 'outside-in'.

This is not the only kind of aesthetic discourse available for study, however. More particularly an 'inside-out' discourse refers to the movement of the hero's voice, from within the author's intonation, to retaining their own independent intonation. Such a discourse is both internally dialogical and externally dialogical and as a consequence is what Bakhtin (1984) refers to as 'double-voiced'. The form-shaping activity of authorship gains a response from the hero within the same discourse that may agree with, challenge or subvert the author's intentions. In such a discourse, more than one truth is possible. For example, in parody, the voice of the parodied other can still retain its own intonation and truth although the author tries to appropriate it for their own uses.

At the heart of this aesthetic account of discourses is a principle of non-identity. That is, that the self is not identical with itself but relates to itself as well as relating to others. Our 'authorial' discourse – that which is felt as uniquely our own – may admit (willingly or unwillingly) a 'hero' or another, inside it and gives it a voice – even if a silent voice – and wrestle with its internal presence while simultaneously addressing an outside other.

Hopefully this will become clearer when I discuss some examples in more detail later. Suffice is to say for now that a dialogical approach involves looking at the difficulties that selves experience in negotiating the 'outer–inner' boundary or deciding 'what is my voice here' – difficulties that are detectable through the analysis of discourse.

My method in outlining these 'outside-inside' distinctions is to look at some features of different discourses as they come to light in concrete examples. In the next sub-section, I outline the importance of genre to understanding the aesthetic dimension of discourse.

The relationship of genre to discourse

Genres have a pivotal relationship to discourse. A genre can be broadly understood as a loose set of stylistic conventions. Ricoeur (1973) argues that discourses are organised by genre. The organisation of discourse by genre means that its interpretation can vary tremendously. A discourse on sex, for example, can be interpreted quite differently depending on whether a sexual or a medical genre (for example) is used. The intonation of the speaking voice may significantly shape our interpretation of which genre the discourse belongs to. Equally, however, the genre gives clues to the emotional intonation of the discourse (a medical genre tends to strive towards neutrality and detachment for instance). This is relevant to our aesthetic view of discourse because 'outside-in' and 'inside-out' discourses are associated with different kinds of genre.

Bakhtin (1984) points out that epic, tragedy and lyric tend to organise 'outside-in' types of discourse, while irony, parody and the novel, tend to organise 'inside-out' types of discourse. 'Outside-in' discourses are more 'monological' in so far as they privilege a singular truth. Even a loving discourse championing the wondrousness of the other can be slightly on the monological, lyrical side. As David Lodge (1990) argues, however, there are many examples of these genres that can be creatively used in a very dialogical sense. Only the data itself can show the particular meaning of a genre in a specific situation.

The more 'dialogical' genres are more anti-authoritative and irreverent than the monological genres. There is potentially more equality between voices in these genres – such as in irony, parody, carnival, argument, confession, and the novel in general. There is conflict and interaction and movement between different genres as they are drawn upon by the author.

Genres are particularly interesting in their capacity to organise the time–space dimension of subjectivity. Bakhtin argued that different social genres (each with their own social memory, values and traditions) offer different sets of potential to experience and give value to time and space. He referred to the mix of time, space and value as the 'chronotope' and argued that different genres have identifiable chronotopes. For example, in epic genres, the future is certain, as long as the characters pass a test of virtue. The changes that the hero undergoes in time are fixed, stage-like and formulaic. Often, the hero has a static personality. In novelistic genres, the future is more open, as the characters are more vulnerable to internal crisis and feel the potential of different possible truths. Their personalities can change through contact with time.

The chronotope, embodied in different speech genres, has the potential to transform phenomenological experience. The form of language we are surrounded with and employ opens up a world through which we can *see* time, space and value, and in doing so, help structure our experience of the world. Genres, as Morson and Emerson (1990) point out, are a tool of perception. We can perceive an epic struggle with the University, for instance, or ironically detach ourselves from it. With the expression of this attitude, we also invest a genre with our own intonation and may also combine it with a variety of other genres. In this sense, genres, in their articulation, also respond to their contact with authors and heroes, and do change over time.

Indeed, from a methodological point of view, it is worth noting that genres can sometimes be very difficult to identify, partly because of their capacity to change and transform through usage. Fairclough (2003) makes the point that any single text is likely to include a combination of different genres. Some genres, such as research papers, tend to be very well defined, to the point of ritualisation, while others, such as advertisements for academic posts, are much more variable. Some genres have established names and terminologies, while others do not have established names and may refer more to different social contexts – e.g., in a professional context a 'professional' genre, with formal address, may be evident but also draw in other genres, such as an argument.

In recognition of this variability, Bakhtin (1986) drew a very broad distinction between 'primary', 'simple' genres (such as those of greeting people, asking for a drink, returning a compliment), and more complicated, complex 'secondary genres'. These secondary genres tend to include more written forms of communication, such as drama, novels, commentary and cultural communication. Secondary genres can absorb primary genres, incorporate different elements of each other and evolve over time and through different usages.

In this chapter, I use relatively straightforward genres to interpret discourses as they relate to selves authoring selves. In an actual data set, this may be more difficult due to the variegated quality of genres. For this reason, I suggest examining the data for the variety of 'voices' it includes, as well as doing research into a particular genre that may be relevant. If it is a fairly monological discourse and singular, then it may be an 'outside-in' discourse with an associated genre such as epic or lyric; if it is double-voiced, then it may be an 'inside-out' discourse with one of those associated genres such as parody or irony.

A summary of the relationship between genre, discourse, chronotope and voice is presented in Table 3.1.

In the next section, I use some concrete examples to outline the differences between 'outside-in' and 'inside-out' discourses in more detail.

Table 3.1 The relationship between genre, discourse, chronotope and voice

Discourse	Genre exemplifications	Chronotope	Voice
Outside-in.	Epic, lyric, tragedy.	Distance between author and hero, self and other. Hero as static and/or undergoes fixed changes in time.	Singular and controlling of hero.
Inside-out.	Parody, irony, novel.	Closeness between author and hero. Time as full of potential and uncertainty.	Multiple and less in control of hero.

Epic and 'outside-in' discourse

In this section, I outline in more detail what an 'outside-in' discourse is and the effect it can have on lived experience. I do this by analysing one example – in this case of an epic form of speech. My intention here is to demonstrate the methodological efficacy of the concept.

In the epic, time and space are abstract in so far as they make little contact with the individual. Instead, the heroes travel great distances over many years but do not age and their personalities and feelings are statically the same. In the classic Greek Romance, for instance, the plot is built around the adventures the hero encounters in his search for a lover taken away from him or somehow separated from him. All of these adventures, however, do not age the hero nor does his love change from the moment of meeting to the moment of reuniting. There is no significant contact between the hero and time or space in these narratives. It is a static world.

In this kind of genre, action is public and controlled by great forces – such as the will of the gods. There are no 'private doubts', characteristic of the novel, but emotion is dramatically and publicly expressed. That is, the outer world reflects the interior. It also assumes a shared destiny that will be fulfilled, regardless of adversity and the 'spontaneity of the inconclusive present' (Bakhtin, 1981: 35). Instead, what matters is that the participants pass a test of character such as a test of their virtuosity. While such genres may have been used in antiquity, they are still used today to bring the other (or the hero) from the outside world into the centre of an authorial discourse, and potentially transform subjectivity in doing so.

To illustrate the qualities of the epic and the 'outside-in' discourse in more detail, it is worth taking a look at an example. The example below is taken from a speech that George W. Bush gave about the war in Iraq, to military graduates, in November 2005. In it, we can detect a strong epic resonance or echo. While there are many other discursive features of the text, it is this resonance that I will focus on here.

Victory in Iraq will demand the continued determination and resolve of the American people. It will also demand the strength and personal courage of the men and women who wear our nation's uniform. And as the future officers of the United States Navy and Marine Corps, you're preparing to join this fight. You do so at a time when there is a vigorous debate about the war in Iraq. I know that for our men and women in uniform, this debate can be unsettling – when you're risking your life to accomplish a mission, the last thing you want to hear is that mission being questioned in our nation's capital. I want you to know that while there may be a lot of heated rhetoric in Washington, D.C., one thing is not in dispute: The American people stand behind you.

(www.whitehouse.gov/news/releases/2005/05/20050527.html, 2005, as cited and also discussed in Sullivan, 2008)

This is just one example of many where an epic genre is used to author epic subjectivities. It works on a number of levels. It is delivered by a powerful figure of symbolic authority – the President of the USA. The intonation is overtly one of admiration, respect and encouragement – 'the strength and personal courage' of the cadets for the danger and sacrifice that they are being asked to make in 'joining the fight'. Through this value, they are constructed as courageous heroes who the whole American people stand behind. Through this overt intonation, Bush also authors himself as the carrier of an authoritative discourse.

Of course, this tone may well be covertly insincere and manipulative. Moreover, as Goffman (1981) points out, there is a difference between an 'animator' of a discourse and an 'author'. Bush may simply be the 'animator' of a pre-written speech rather than the 'author'. The point, from a dialogical point of view, however, is that this intonation exists in a responsive relationship with his audience. That is, the actual response of the audience (both there and now here) will author Bush as a manipulator or an inspiration, a puppet and/or an author. What we are drawing attention to is the mere potential of Bush's epic style from the overt intonation of the speech.

In terms of the content of the speech, the final result – victory in Iraq – is constructed as guaranteed, providing that there is evidence of 'continued determination and resolve of the American people' and 'strength and personal courage' of the audience he is addressing, the cadets who will go to Iraq to fight. This kind of speech has the potential to create epic heroes of the audience (and indeed it assumes epic heroes are already fighting), who must remain completely focused on achieving a righteous goal, the achievement of which is certain if they show that they have the necessary qualities. As such, rather than be encouraged to engage intelligently with debate, such heroes would only be 'unsettled' by it, much as they would be 'unsettled' by the unexpected appearance of an enemy.

The epic style is also very powerful for organising subjectivity along the lines of a test of virtuosity, the result of which can only validate the transcendent truth that is at stake (rather than critique it or challenge it). The test presented to the cadets is to ignore the debate and to show strength and personal courage. In common with all epic tales, the result of this test of character (rather than intelligent debate, manpower, strategy, terrain, etc.) determines whether the battle will be won or lost. In brief, this example illustrates the potential of an outside-in discourse, in an epic genre, to organise and give shape to the subjectivity of the audience. It is only a potential, however, and the cadets may ironically distance themselves from it or even parody it.

So far, we have looked at the 'outside-in' discourse and discussed the role of authority and intonation. Generally, much of discourse analysis focuses on the effect of rhetoric on the audience. In this sense, it tends to focus mainly on the 'outside-in' type of discourse, where authority and power can be carefully discerned, although the role of genre and authorial intonation in organising subjectivity tends to be underplayed. Bakhtin is careful to point out, however, that there is also an 'inside-out' element to some discourses – where the other is given an actual voice, from within the authorial discourse. This allows the other not merely to be shaped but also to answer back and respond to the author from within the same discourse (e.g., a parody of another or even a self-parody). In the next section, we will look at the variety of discourses that have this quality.

Parody and 'inside-out' discourse

In this section, I outline how 'parody' is one example of 'inside-out' discourse. There are gradations of equality between the authorial voice and the voice of the other in an 'inside-out' discourse. In parody, the hero's voice is relatively powerless within the authorial intonation but their original intonation can be heard echoing through. Here, I discuss the weak presence of the other's voice within an authorial discourse through focusing on parody while in the subsequent section I outline how the other's voice can more directly challenge and subvert the authorial voice.

Bakhtin (1984) describes how parody permits two voices. There is the authorial voice and the voice that it overtly ridicules. It does this by changing the intention and intonation of another's discourse to suit its own ends – ends that are different from the original text. For example, the parody may expose the other as ridiculous through humour and exaggeration. This is especially important if the other's discourse is invested with social authority – e.g., a religious text, or even a canonical style of music.

In the example of Bush's speech, although the epic delivery has the potential to bestow an authoritative value upon the cadets, its tautological logic, its formulaic structure and clichéd phrases leave it very vulnerable to parody. Indeed, as we often see, the media, simply by putting music to Bush, can create a parody of him and his speeches. Equally, a cadet may be very capable of parodying the speech by perhaps speaking of the desire of 'American Industry' as opposed to the 'American People to 'stand behind' them. For Bakhtin (1984: 127), parody is 'organically alien' to serious genres such as epic. It is also irreverent and anti-authoritative.

The anti-authoritative dimension to parody is very important because 'outside-in' discourses tend to have a surplus of vision over the self and seek to authoritatively give shape to the 'hero' or subject of their discourse. Bush, above, is one example, but even more prosaically, everyday judgements of value (absolution, condemnation and so on), depending on our relationship to the addressee, can be quite authoritative. One way of 're-accentuating' (giving it a new value) this discourse, from the addressee's/hero's point of view, is to parody it. It is given a new intonation and a new form from within our thinking, feeling response to it. Despite this, however, the original intonation may still be felt resonating through the discourse. Generally, parody does not aim to destroy another's discourse but to give it a new context and, in doing this, reveal another dimension of it (e.g., a humorous, ridiculous dimension).

To more fully draw attention to the meaning of parody, I will give an example from some data taken from a focus group. This study is explicated in more detail in Chapter 6 and published as Sullivan and McCarthy (2008). For now, what is worth noting is that the focus group is undertaken with managers of a large health care organisation. The managers appear ambivalent around how they are viewed by others inside and outside the organisation (e.g., the media). In the example below, they parodically draw on the discourse they think is used to represent them:

> Management: all these people going around wearing white coats are necessarily good and they're trying to deliver the best to the patient in the bed but this crowd in the back office are you know, they're dark and and they're not helping them

In the example above, we can see that the parody contains the syntactic, semantic and intonational structure of a discourse that critiques the role of management. Syntactically, propositions about the virtue of doctors and nurses are declared in a polemical vein – 'they're trying to deliver the best to the patient in the bed'. Semantically, central ideas, such as the powerful controlling the system from behind closed doors, have a lively presence. There is an intonation of denigration of management – 'this crowd in the back office'. In many ways, the voice of critique and vilification is unmistakably present through these devices.

However, this voice of critique and its central truths are rendered very passive and powerless by the authorial intonation of ridicule. The assertions are made to look ridiculous through exaggeration and contrasts. White is contrasted with darkness. All of the people wearing white coats are good without any exception. Management are dark and unhelpful without any exception. The bold assertions around delivering care are mixed in with a philosophical absurdity that they are 'necessarily good'. Amidst the formal professional expressions such as 'deliver the best to the patient', there are more colloquial, informal expressions such as 'this crowd in the back office'.

More broadly, this parody can be viewed as involving an 'inside-out' dimension in so far as the voice of critique takes a social form from within management's authorial discourse. The serious 'point' of this voice of critique is that doctors and nurses have more direct contact with patients than the management do and they are more directly responsible for the delivery of care. This point is overwhelmed and 'subservient', however, to the authorial voice and its associated tone of ridicule. Those who critique management exaggerate the virtue of doctors and nurses and exaggerate the management's vice. Within this parodic discourse, then, although there is a clear inequality between management's authorial voice and the voice of critique, it is a discourse that is marked by the presence of more than one singular 'form-shaping' truth. This contrasts with the singular truth of the epic discourse in the previous example.

In terms of subjectivity, we can see that the authorial discourse anticipates and is aware of the voice of critics. In this sense, it is conscious as well as social. It authors others through giving them a ridiculous presence. It is also complex in so far as it draws upon a well-known cultural resource (parody) to make its point. As we will see in more detail in Chapter 6, other groups within the organisation also make use of parody in authoring 'management' as 'other'.

Parody is not the only sense in which the other's voice can be powerless but still heard from within the authorial discourse. In 'stylisation', the other's voice echoes through in a relationship of agreement to the author, such as, for example, my bending of Bakhtin's voice, with all of its competing interpretations, to suit my intentions here. Equally, in the speech of Bush above, some elements of stylisation also creep into his epic style when he invokes the voice of the American People in a relationship of agreement.

So far, we have looked at a strong authorial voice and the relatively powerless intonation of an other within this discourse. In the next section, I will outline some examples of how the 'hero' or 'other' can more directly challenge and subvert the author's discourse.

'Outside-in' and 'inside-out' struggles

In this section, I discuss a 'struggle' between 'outside-in' and 'inside-out' discourses. Such a struggle occurs when we feel uncertain as to what our own 'voice' is amidst the authoritative voices of others. We anticipate what these other voices say, internally wrestle with their judgements and values, and try to give our own shape to an issue as authors. As this struggle goes on, our intoned response to the other may be divided, contradictory and complex. Bakhtin (1984) describes a number of varieties of struggles under the term 'active double-voiced discourse'.

Such a discourse is active and 'double-voiced' because the voice of the other is considered to come into the shaping discourse of the author, almost against the author's will. These types of discourse go above both stylisation and parody in so far as the other's voice has a more equal presence – rather than being dominated by the author's intentions. That is, more than one 'authoritative' truth is detectable within the discourse. Here we will briefly discuss: 'the word with a sidewards glance' and hidden dialogue.

The word with a sidewards glance

The key aspect of this kind of discourse is the active presence of other voices *wedging* their way into the author's voice from outside. The author's more or less certain ideas are disturbed by the anticipated disagreement of another. While both parody and stylisation work inside the authorial discourse as containing voices subordinate to the authorial voice, the word with a sidewards glance, as part of an internal polemic with self, invades from outside the authorial discourse and reflexively reworks it.

Such speech is most marked by a 'certain halting quality to the speech, and its interruption by reservations' (Bakhtin, 1984: 205). Reservations and hesitations anticipate the disagreements and judgements of the other. These words may intrude into discourse through a sense of shame or fear that these judgements are true but yet contain a 'muffled challenge' to them (1984: 205). In Bakhtin's (1984) description, the other has the potential to 'penetrate' self-consciousness, at various levels, structuring both what is said and how it is said.

This kind of analysis, which assumes a struggle between 'I-for-self' and 'I-for-other' is described very well by Billig (1987), although in somewhat different language. He describes these features of discourse in terms of 'dis-claimers', 'logos and anti-logos' and the 'internal critic'. Drawing on classical rhetorical theory, Billig describes a disclaimer as a subset of the argumentative device *prolepsis*. In this device, possible counter-arguments to an attitude or a position are anticipated. In the disclaimer, a common ground is also sought with the audience. A proposition or an argument for one side of an issue is the 'logos' and the arguments against or for the other side of an issue is the 'anti-logos'. When we argue with others, as well as with ourselves, we are embroiled with both sides of an issue – the logos and the anti-logos.

Sometimes, when arguing against an other, we may anticipate their objections as a means of identifying or establishing common ground with the other/audience. We may also utter an objection to our own 'logos' in the face of agreement by the audience – in order to open up the issue under exploration. In the face of open disagreement, there may be little need to identify with their position as they embody the 'anti-logos', apart from the odd identification, via a disclaimer, of the opponent's disagreements.

Perhaps most interestingly, for our purposes, Billig (1987) describes the holder of the 'anti-logos' as the 'internal critic'. The 'internal critic' is that aspect of ourselves that questions and doubts our attitudes and experiences. Drawing from G.H. Mead and William James, Billig makes the point that the self can be divided against itself as it takes the perspective of another. Much of our thinking depends on the capacity to argue with ourselves the merits and demerits of contradictory positions. Depending on the rhetorical context, the 'internal critic' may be given more or less force to voice an objection, i.e., via disclaimers and reservations. Moreover, this does not necessarily mean hypocrisy (although it can do), but rather reflects the power of the logos and anti-logos within the individual.

A good example of a disclaimer is offered by Billig (1987). He describes a letter written to the newspaper *The Sunday Times* where a socialist author, a critic of capitalism, complains about monopolies in the book trade that he thinks have harmed the sales of his own book. The letter ends:

> In the long run, the only hope is to dismantle these monopolies and reintroduce market forces. An argument which might sound strange coming from a socialist.

> (Letter, *The Sunday Times*, July 29, 1984, cited in Billig, 1987: 246)

Billig (1987) points out that in the letter above this author moves from generally attacking market forces to defending them. The disclaimer here is the acknowledgement, and implicit agreement with a judging other, that it may sound 'strange' to make this point considering his general socialist anti-capitalism. For Billig, the author is placed in a rhetorical context where the internal critic, holder of the 'anti-logos' is given room to speak and indeed to come clean that what they are saying contradicts other theoretical arguments.

Unlike other discourse analysts, Billig is very comfortable with the idea of the author seeking to understand their own discourse. They are taken as thinking through the contradictory issues with contradictory feelings. So, bearing in mind Billig's analysis of the disclaimer, why should we use the expression 'the word with a sidewards glance'?

While an 'internal critic' suggests a thinking division or weighing-up between the logic of two persuasive positions, the 'sidewards glance' refers more to the emotional response and consequent intonation of the discourse. With the 'word with a sidewards glance', it is possible to add another layer of meaning to Billig's interesting analysis of the disclaimer, which again is the intonation that the disclaimer introduces. That is, the disclaimer is a very interesting discursive device that these dialogical concepts can further enrich.

In the example above, for instance, there is an initial tone of self-confidence where the author argues that 'the only hope' is to dismantle the monopolies. This is then qualified by an anticipated condemnatory objection from the other. That is, the other could object that it is hypocritical or euphemistically 'strange' to make those particular arguments considering the author is a socialist. This condemnation is overlain with an ironic response on the part of the author in the guise of an admission that it 'might sound strange' coming from a socialist. This creates a form of dramatic irony (where the audience knows more than the character), but here the writer takes the perspective of the audience. Within this dramatic irony there is also defiance that the virtues, or indeed the logos, of the argument are still relatively strong as it disclaims these arguments of hypocrisy.

On another level, the ironic admission and defiance can be viewed as an effort to parody the authoritative objections of an unknown other. That is, the objection is made to look humorous rather than serious. However, in contrast to a parody, the objection has an active rather than passive presence within the discourse of the author, leading to a 'double-voiced' discourse, with opposing intonations of condemnation and justification and an author torn between these. In this sense, the logos and anti-logos come wrapped, in a dialogical view, in tones of condemnation, absolution, ironic defiance and so on.

So the disclaimer, read as the 'sidewards glance' is one example of active, double-voiced discourse. As the intensity of the active 'double-voicedness' increases, Bakhtin (1984) introduces us to further discursive features. I will describe some of these below.

Hidden dialogue

Like 'the word with a sidewards glance', what Bakhtin refers to as 'hidden dialogue' refers to a discourse that on the surface appears straightforwardly referential, e.g., denial of wrongdoing, but continually clashes with the anticipations of alternative judgements and evaluations. Another way of putting this is to say that the authorial discourse is full of sideward glances and anticipations of different viewpoints. It is directed at: (1) the other as the author would want the other to understand him/her – this is also what Bakhtin (1986) refers to as the 'superaddressee' or an ideal, understanding other; (2) how the other might actually understand him/her; and, leading from this second viewpoint, (3) how the author would respond to this actual understanding of the other (Morson and Emerson, 1990). These three positions create many interruptions, protests and confusions in the authorial discourse.

Burkitt (2008) has recently looked at double-voiced discourse and makes the point that the author is unable to fully articulate some of these orientations (e.g., how the ideal other would perceive the self). Nonetheless such others are responsible for the structure of the speech – e.g., by introducing a reservation. Other voices, such as the ideal other, can be more fully articulated and are more responsible for the actual content of what is said (e.g., open disagreement with the actual other). These different positions or orientations are foregrounded at different times with different levels of emphasis and articulation (e.g., an authoritative other that structures our discourse as a hidden addressee (stylized or otherwise) may become an explicit 'hero' to discuss with the 'ideal' other in a confessional context).

In the example that follows, I will outline the crucial role of intonation and re-accentuation in moving and shifting between these three different orientations and the struggle with identifying subjectivity with a singular authoritative tone. I will do this by first outlining a short excerpt from Dostoevsky's novel 'Poor Folk'. I will then follow this with part of Bakhtin's (1984) analysis. Dostoevsky's novel takes the epistolary form of letters between Makar Devushkin and Varvara Dobroselova, who both live in terrible poverty across from each other. Devushkin occupies a lowly clerical position as a copying clerk. Although it is taken from fiction, and in this sense violates an important discourse analytic maxim to use real-life talk, it nevertheless sheds light on discursive processes and in this sense acquires some validity (see also Chapter 6 for further empirical examples of hidden dialogue).

DOSTOEVSKY'S 'POOR FOLK'

My crust of bread is my own; it is true that it is a plain crust of bread, at times a dry one; but there it is, earned by my toil and put to lawful and irreproachable use. Why, what can one do? I know very well of course, that I don't do much by copying; but all the same I am proud of working and earning my bread in the sweat of my brow. Why, what if I am a copying clerk, after all? What harm is there in copying, after all? 'He's a copying clerk', they say, but what is there discreditable in that?

(Cited in Bakhtin, 1984: 207)

Part of Bakhtin's analysis

The embedding of words and especially of accents from the other's rejoinder in Makar Devushkin's speech is even more marked and obvious in the second of the quoted passages. The words containing the other's polemically exaggerated accent are even enclosed here in quotation marks: 'He's a copying clerk...' In the preceding lines, the word 'copy' is repeated three times. In each of these three instances the other's potential accent is present in the word 'copy', but it is suppressed by Devushkin's own accent; however, it constantly becomes stronger, until it finally breaks through and assumes the form of the other's direct speech. We are presented here, therefore, with gradations of gradual intensification in the other's accent:

'I [then follows a reservation – M.B.] Why, what if I am a _copying_ clerk, after all? What harm is there in _copying_, after all? 'He's a _COPYING_ clerk!'...' We have indicated with italics and underscoring the other's accent and its gradual intensification, which finally dominates utterly the line of discourse enclosed in quotation marks. But even in these final words, obviously belonging to the other, Devushkin's own voice is present too, for he polemically exaggerates the other's accent. As the other person's accent intensifies, so does Devushkin's counter-accent.

(Bakhtin, 1984: 209)

We can see in the above analysis the emphasis Bakhtin places on 'accent' or 'intonation' in terms of identifying the words of the other and the words of the self – or indeed how different accents can compete within the very same words. Later on in his analysis, Bakhtin takes Devushkin's letter and re-writes the presence of the other right into it to expose the 'hidden dialogue' and the direct 'accent' of the other. So, for example, when Devushkin asserts 'I'm not a burden to anyone. I've got my own piece of bread', Bakhtin turns this into a response to 'The Other' who says 'One must know how to earn a lot of money. One shouldn't be a burden to anyone. But you are a burden to others' (Bakhtin, 1984: 210). In the penultimate chapter, I will try to answer some of the objections around validity that this kind of analysis immediately raises but I will put it to one side for now.

We can also see in this analysis the different variety of others that are taken to structure the content and form of what is said. The 'ideal' other here would agree with Devushkin's own assessment that he is an honest, noble worker; the dreaded, actual other may well be less sympathetic and more accusatory, saying something along the lines of 'but you are a burden to others', as Bakhtin points out, and of course Devushkin polemically exaggerates this accusation in his response to the anticipated judgement. There is also the addressee of the letter – Varvara, who is the unknown other in her possible response and whose understanding he is constantly trying to anticipate but also trying to shape via a self-confident, somewhat monological 'outside-in' discourse.

The active presence of the other is too strong to allow this confident monologue. Indeed, there is an important struggle with authority in this kind of dialogue. The dreaded words of the other overwhelm Devushkin's efforts at self-sufficient, confident discourse. The mocking accent comes into his discourse from outside via a direct quotation ('"he's a copying clerk", they say') and subsequently reworks the whole structure of this discourse from within – having an equal presence to Devushkin's own voice. As Morson and Emerson (1990) point out, in his polemical exaggeration, Devushkin is trying to gain some personal authority over the dreaded words of the other – in this case, the words 'copying clerk'.

These are just some of the features of the 'hidden dialogue'. I will briefly enumerate some further refinements below, although for a more exhaustive understanding, it is advisable to turn to either Morson and Emerson (1990) or Bakhtin (1984).

Some other features of the 'hidden dialogue'

If we were to take Varvara out of the letter above as an addressee, one would be left with a diary where the main addressee is oneself. Bakhtin (1984) refers to such dialogues as 'microdialogues', which could also include forms such as a soliloquy, fantasy dialogues, replayed dialogues and diary keeping. Recently, Rom Harré, Fathali M. Moghaddam, Tracey Pilkerton Cairnie, Daniel Rothbart and Steven R. Sabat (2009) have argued that more attention needs to be paid to these kinds of 'self-self' dialogues as a form of 'private discourse', in the discursive literature.

For Bakhtin, 'microdialogue' refers to our capacity to 'recreate' the voices of other participants in our own minds as part of an 'inner' conversation with ourselves (sometimes while engaged in a parallel outer conversation with others). One of the examples that Bakhtin (1984) gives of microdialogue is Raskolnikov (the central character of Dostoevsky's novel *Crime and Punishment*) reading a letter informing him of his sister's engagement and 'angrily debating its sentiments and intonations with himself' (Emerson, 1997: 139).

Characteristic of the hidden dialogue and the microdialogue are 'sore-spots', 'loopholes' and 'the penetrative word'. 'Sore-spots' refer to sensitive parts of consciousness, where consciousness does not wish to look but is yet aware of as a possibility. Hence, when reading student feedback on my lectures, I may be outraged at a suggestion that I am a dull lecturer. Although I may complain vociferously about this, using what discourse analysts more generally refer to as 'extreme case formulations' (Potter and Wetherell, 1987), the strength of my vehemence is tangled up with the anticipation that the other may be right and that I am indeed a dull lecturer.

In a 'penetrative word', an outer other may recognise my unsaid anxieties and fears from my agonised expression and vehemence, and confidently reassure me that I have nothing to worry about – and in this way interrupt my own internal dialogue. Nevertheless, however, I may react with terrible fury because this other has touched my 'sore-spot'. Then again, I may not be such an ungrateful so and so and genuinely take comfort in the words. Either way, the other has the potential to recognise and interfere with the 'unsaid' in dialogue.

Indeed, this primacy on the presence of the 'unsaid' and 'repressed' as being detectable within discourse and therefore open to dialogical response is a feature of 'hidden dialogue' more generally. Some commentators have explicated this feature of discourse in some detail but have referred to it as the 'dialogic unconscious' (e.g., Shotter and Billig, 1998; Billig, 1999; Burkitt, 2010). In different ways, these theorists draw attention to the active silencing of some voices and openness of others – as in, for example, when we say yes to an invitation but our face betrays dismay.

To wrap up this section, I will briefly mention 'the word with a loophole' in a hidden dialogue. The 'word with a loophole' is one that, like the sidewards glance, is speech that on the surface appears to be an ultimate judgement but retains the possibility of being a penultimate judgement. It refers to the potential rather than the actual self. For example, a confession that expects disagreement ('I am a miser with money, I suppose') is one example of a 'word with a loophole'. The author thinks in two different directions at once – genuinely confessing to being a miser to the actual other, but hoping for disagreement from the ideal other (superaddressee). It is only a supposition, after all – perhaps there is room for undermining it. In contrast to the 'sidewards glance', which is based on fear of the other's negative judgements, the 'loophole' is based on hope of an unlimited self and a potential future redemption – again perhaps from the 'penetrative word' of the other.

These are some of the discursive registers of the self–other, self–self relationship or outer–inner relationships. The self does not simply express or project their identity into the discourse in a speech act, but the very fabric of the other enters into the discourse of the self and into consciousness

Table 3.2 Rhetorical features of discourse interpreted dialogically

Rhetorical feature	Relationship to other	Otherwise known as
Hidden dialogue.	The other's voice is continually anticipated.	Reservations and hesitations.
Micro dialogue.	An internal dialogue with self, re-creating other's points of view.	Private discourse.
Penetrative word.	Capacity of other to reassure us when we are torn between different judgements.	Interruption.
Word with a sidewards glance.	Fearful of other's judgement.	Disclaimer.
Word with a loophole.	Escape from a definitive statement. Hope of vindication.	Disclaimer.
Sore-spots.	Strong reaction to other's words.	Extreme-case formulation.
Stylisation.	Agreement with other's words.	Stylisation.
Parody.	Disagreement with other's words.	Parody.

'intra-atomically' (Bakhtin, 1984: 211). This is conceived by Bakhtin as a potentially intense emotional struggle with others words and judgements as they are 'willed to order'.

It is the wrestle with the authoritative words of others and the search for a confident, clear response that most defines this kind of 'active double-voiced' discourse. In this sense, making the words of others one's own is also a process of figuring out where 'outside' lies and where 'inside' lies for our own subjectivity. In Table 3.2, I summarise the various rhetorical features of dialogical interactions discussed so far.

The novel and the shaping of subjectivity

These kinds of struggles between voice and subjectivity are championed by Bakhtin as moving towards the more novelistic end of genres. 'Novel' here means an anti-authoritative, even anti-genre genre (Morson and Emerson, 1990). By this, I mean the novel foregrounds the diversity of truths and the mix of voices that make contact with the self. The novel also absorbs and takes on the singularity of other genres (such as the epic, the lyric and the tragic) as they are given a response within the novel. Of course some novels are better at doing this than others, and for this reason Holquist (2002) refers to 'novelness' as a general tendency.

In terms of subjectivity, the other is given a very significant place in the novel. They make contact and challenge the self as an equal that deserves a response. The other can work to expand the self – by listening to its truth and revising taken-for-granted assumptions. Of course, there is a way to go between casting a sidewards glance at the other and expanding the self. However, once the truths of other are given a response, even if they are ultimately rejected, then they begin the work of making one's own view or voice 'internally persuasive' or thought through/felt through as opposed to inherited from the dogmatic discourse of others. Removing the distance of authority allows this move to an internally-persuasive discourse.

In many ways, Bakhtin's theory of novelistic perception, where the other is always worth listening to (unless they are very repetitive and/or dogmatic), reflects his earlier work on the ethics of the interpersonal encounter, but widens it out. Hicks (2000) has made this point very well. He has widened out the 'other' to include the diversity of social voices that imbue discourse but contain the potential for creating a more heterogeneous and, indeed, more unstable self. The comfort of rooting oneself in solid, unquestionable values may be uprooted by the ambivalence of multiple sides to an issue or other.

The contrast with the epic genre here is an easy one to make. Indeed, one would be forgiven for thinking that the singularity of the epic resides in an earlier, more primitive history of consciousness and the more enlightened individual is the more novelistic. However, as Holquist (2002) argues, in Bakhtin's dialogism epic and novel exist more as possibilities and tensions – between the singular (or centripetal) and multiple (centrifugal). In everyday life, reflected in everyday discourse, these possibilities are always available. It is not that we have left the epic behind us.

However, these possibilities have the potential to structure subjectivity in different ways. We saw earlier that the epic relies on a teleological assumption that the future will be realised by the intrinsic character traits of the heroes. As such, the public and private boundary is erased. Nor is the ambivalence of parody present. In terms of the chronotope of the novel, in contrast, it is the present moment that takes centre stage. More particularly, the novel is characterised by 'threshold' moments and 'threshold' dialogues. These are dialogues with intense potential to speak to the uncertain openness of the future (as opposed to the sanctified tradition of the idyll or the certain future of the epic). The possibility of ambivalence and double-voicedness arises. In this sense, the novel brings to light the crisis of self-awareness without the certainty of any resolution – except perhaps the temptation of the regular and the routine.

In summary and moving on

In this chapter, I have looked at a dialogical approach to discourse. We can see that intonation and re-accentuation, as expressive of subjectivity, take pride of place in this kind of analysis. Moreover, genre, as a collective, historical tendency in discourse, is seen to admit to different kinds of accents and creates potential to shape subjectivity in different ways. In shaping subjectivity in different ways, discourses have been interpreted as aesthetic.

In making use of the 'genre' concept to elaborate discourse, I have employed one concept in a broad narrative approach to qualitative data. Narrative analysis shares many similarities with a dialogical approach in assuming a complex and agentive subject. However, narrative analysis alone is inadequate for understanding the rhetorical features of double-voiced discourse, such as the 'sidewards glance' and 'hidden dialogue'. These allow us to foreground the self–self relationship as well as the self–other relationship. They also allow us to examine the aesthetic capacity of discourse to author selves and for selves to ambivalently experience the intrusion of other voices into this authorship.

This focus on voice explicitly brings an emphasis on emotion, feeling and subjectivity to discourse analysis. At the same time, however, it does not assume that emotions and experience are lying in the content of the text, waiting to be uncovered through a thematic analysis alone. Instead, our subjectivity is taken as bound up in social relations and dynamically responsive to different sets of social/discursive relations. These are seen to fill the utterance with a complex set of different voices and accents.

Understanding these discursive devices demands both an attitude of trust and of suspicion towards the text. We can trust that George W. Bush articulates a discourse that seeks to author others as epic heroes, but we can be suspicious of the kind of subjectivity that this produces – one where character alone is enough to overcome great odds. Similarly, we can be suspicious of the 'word with a loophole' but trust that it reflects an authorial ambivalence around the other's judgements.

Finally, I should note that viewing discourses through an aesthetic, dialogic lens has many potential flaws from a traditional discourse analysis point of view. I will get into these flaws, such as its view of power relations and its optimistic view of conscious awareness, in the discussion chapter (Chapter 9). For now, however, it is worth noting that there is a reason Bakhtin drew so heavily on literature to make his points about discourse. This is because dialogue is an approach that is particularly suited to understanding lived experience, authorship and subjectivity. The implications of this for data preparation and analysis will be drawn out in the next chapter.

Further reading

Billig, M. (1987) *Arguing and Thinking: A Rhetorical Approach to Social Psychology.* Cambridge: Cambridge University Press.

Billig, M. (1999) *Freudian Repression: Conversation Creating the Unconscious.* Cambridge: Cambridge University Press

Burkitt, I. (2008) *Social Selves: Theories of Self and Society* (2nd edition). London: Sage.

Burkitt, I. (2010) Dialogues with self and others: Communication, miscommunication, and the dialogical unconscious. *Theory and Psychology,* 20(3): 305–21.

Ricoeur, P. (1981) *Hermeneutics and the Human Sciences: Essays on Language, Action and Interpretation.* Ed. and trans. J.B. Thompson. Cambridge: Cambridge University Press.

Shotter, J. and Billig, M. (1998) A Bakhtinian psychology: From out of the heads of individuals and into the dialogues between them, in M. Bell and M. Gardiner (eds) *Bakhtin and the Human Sciences: No Last Words.* London: Sage. pp. 13–30.

Sullivan, P. (2008) Our emotional connection to truth: Moving beyond a functional view of language in discourse analysis. *Journal for the Theory of Social Behaviour,* 38(2): 193–207.

4

DATA PREPARATION AND ANALYSIS

In this chapter, I give some guidelines on data preparation and analysis. I do this within a broader discussion of the value of guidelines in qualitative research. So, I first of all outline how qualitative research in general involves a dynamic engagement with the text along both 'bureaucratic' (guideline-following) and 'charismatic' (stylistic) lines. I then examine in more detail how 'bureaucracy' and 'charisma' are principles relevant to a dialogical approach to qualitative analysis. The examination of bureaucracy will involve outlining how the data can be prepared, including principles of transcription and the selection of units of analysis. It will also involve examining how the data can be analysed and the coding scheme that can be employed. The examination of charisma will involve outlining how the analyst(s) bring their own style into the analysis.

'Bureaucracy' and 'charisma' are terms borrowed from Max Weber (1947). He uses these terms to refer to the kinds of authority that permeate different organisations. Here, I apply these terms to qualitative analysis in order to illustrate how the authority of analysis resides both in the bureaucratic procedures that are followed and the charismatic style of the analyst. As we will see, both 'bureaucracy' and 'charisma' offer the researcher different and complementary possibilities for analysing the data set.

──────── **Bureaucracy and charisma in qualitative research** ────────

This section explains a bureaucratic and charismatic approach to qualitative data analysis, adapted from Weber (1947), for our purposes here. In bureaucracy, there are the following features: (1) authority lies in rules and procedures; (2) these can be verified; (3) it is systematic/exhaustive; and (4) value resides in the impersonal. In the case of data analysis, this means that there is a procedure to be followed, this can be left as an 'audit-trail', the procedure systematically processes all of the data and the findings can be corroborated or at least given independent value on the basis of the procedures followed.

I should note, however, that Weber argued that such 'ideal' types are rarely found in reality. These are the values that underpin a bureaucracy but they may not always be realised. In qualitative analysis, for instance, the following may 'corrupt' the ideal sense of the bureaucracy: (1) ungrounded but provocative interpretations; (2) mixing the data with theory in an unpredictable way; (3) mixing the analysis with personal musings and reminiscence; and (4) using aesthetically pleasing language to give weight to an interpretation. This latter tendency is particular salient in many key authors in the social sciences, including Freud, Goffman and Weber. Their style is non-systematic, unpredictable and often dependent on the personality of the analyst for its claims.

These characteristics, which disrupt the bureaucratic approach, involve a charismatic element coming into the analysis. According to Weber (1947), a charismatic style of organisation gets its authority from the personality of the leader, who is often seen to have magical or exceptional properties. This kind of leadership is often revolutionary but may subsequently become bureaucratic, as in the case of Christ and the Christian Church. In research, the authority of the leader arises from the writing style of the analyst.

The example below illustrates this charisma. Goffman (1981) discusses Richard Nixon's treatment of a female journalist – when he asked her to change from wearing pants to a skirt, to keep her husband happy, and the audience laughed:

Example of a charismatic analysis

> I surmise that although his audience may have laughed loudly, they may have seen his gesture as forced, wooden and artificial; separating him from them by a behavioural veil of design and self-consciousness. All of that would have to be understood to gain any close sense of what Nixon was projecting, of his alignment to those present, of his footing, and I believe structural linguistics provides us with the cues and markers through which such footings become manifest, helping us to find our way to a structural basis for analyzing them.

(1981: 157)

Here, although Goffman recommends structural linguistics, his own style of interpreting the interaction is characteristically charismatic. He surmises the audience's reaction although he is not aware of what it is; he uses lovely metaphorical adjectives and tautology – 'forced, wooden and artificial' – as well as vivid images – 'behavioural veil of design'. His unique writing style enters into his interpretations and he relates these to the other theory that he has read. An audit trail is difficult here.

I am using the 'bureaucratic' and 'charismatic' distinction not to signify that one is better than the other, but rather to highlight these as different tendencies in qualitative research. These tendencies are apparent in every stage of the research. Even a transcription of the data defies total bureaucracy. Instead, the analyst needs to make choices around what symbols to use and how relevant they are (Gee, 2005). Nonetheless, there is a transcription scheme available, to help make it as bureaucratic and systematic as possible.

When it comes to the analysis of data itself, often there are guidelines as to what to follow to make the analysis systematic and impersonal. In the appropriation of these guidelines however, the personal style and charisma of the researcher(s) makes a significant difference. Madill, Jordan and Shirley (2000), for example, have demonstrated that the personal style of the analyst plays a significant part in the analysis of grounded theory. In their study, two different analysts followed the general procedures of grounded theory in the analysis of the same data set. It emerged that one analyst had a 'serialist' style, following the process step by step – generating themes from clusters of lower level categories. The other analyst was a 'holist' learner, generating higher-order categories before moving on to examine lower-level divisions within these categories. These two styles were quite complementary, leading to a rich analysis. Their personal styles and the guidelines worked well in the analysis of the data.

In Table 4.1, I list more generally the bureaucratic and charismatic elements of various schools of qualitative analysis. The aim of doing this is to show how both bureaucracy and charisma are important elements of qualitative research, in general. I do not elaborate on Table 4.1 as it would take us back into other qualitative methodologies, an introduction to which can be found in Chapter 1. The bureaucratic and charismatic features of qualitative methods listed in Table 4.1 are not exhaustive. It is only an indicative list.

Now that I have outlined the dynamic interplay between bureaucracy and charisma in the analytic engagement with the text, in the next section I will examine how 'bureaucracy' and 'charisma' can underpin a dialogical approach to qualitative analysis. For ease of organisation, I will discuss methods of data preparation and analysis as 'bureaucratic'. I discuss impersonal procedures that can be followed in doing an analysis. I also discuss 'charisma', particularly as part of a write-up, but in much less detail, as there are no real guidelines in a charismatic approach. As we will see, however, some charismatic elements (e.g., making choices) come into bureaucratic procedures and some bureaucracy can come into the write-up through following guidelines. In this way, a good analysis should depend on its authority from both bureaucracy and charisma.

Table 4.1 Bureaucratic and charismatic elements in qualitative research

Qualitative method	Bureaucratic elements	Charismatic elements
Grounded theory.	Line-by-line coding, constant comparison, triangulation, iterative processes.	Memo-taking, quotation selection, choosing labels for codes, categories and themes, writing up the analysis. Analytic style. Stating the key 'take-home message' of the study.
Fine-grained discourse analysis.	Detailed transcription. Identification of interpretative repertoires, rhetorical features, turn-taking functions.	Choosing what data to leave out and put into analysis. Organising the write-up. Linking the analysis to other studies and theory. Rhetorically protecting the study from potential criticism.
Critical, large-scale discourse analysis.	Identification of power dynamics, technologies of control and the production of subjectivity. Examination of discourse, linguistic features and positioning.	Highly theoretical and meditative. Efforts to link research to real-world relevance. Imaginative play with symbolic significance of discourses.
Narrative analysis.	Identification of plot types, narratives and genres. Identification of metaphors and tropes. Examination of the context of production.	Deciding what narratives are significant. Linking narratives to lived experience. Relating the stories to theory. Deciding what data to include and what to leave out in the final analysis.
Phenomenological analysis.	Identification of themes, meaning-units, the lived world of experience.	Deciding the labels for codes, and for themes. Analytic style. Linking to other theory and deciding a 'take home message'.

Bureaucracy in a dialogical approach

In this section, I outline the bureaucratic procedures that can be involved with a dialogical approach. This is further broken down into two sub-headings – data preparation and data analysis. In 'data preparation', I discuss how the data can be selected and transcribed in a dialogical approach. In 'data analysis', I discuss how the data can be coded. In both these cases, I use concrete examples from empirical research to highlight the procedures involved. It is also important to note, however, that the judgement as to whether or not these exact procedures should be followed does depend on the charisma, aims and goals of the researcher.

Data preparation

Qualitative data includes interviews, focus groups, diaries, images and video. Researchers are often faced with a daunting data set after engaging in a qualitative project. How, then, should one prepare a systematic analysis under a dialogical framework? In what follows, I will offer some thoughts on transcription, using a concrete example. I will also describe how Anna Madill and I prepared our data for a dialogical analysis in a recent collaboration (Madill and Sullivan, 2010).

How should the data be transcribed?

In this sub-section, I briefly introduce transcription notation and outline some of the dilemmas that are associated with transcription. I use a concrete example to illustrate some of these issues.

There are some disputes in the literature (e.g., O'Connell and Kowall, 1995) as to which transcription symbols should be used, and how to denote the features of talk that go beyond words, such as the prosodic (including intonation and stress), paralinguistic (e.g., whether the words are said in a joking manner) and the extra linguistic (e.g., gestures). Part of the problem is that these symbols are interpretations rather than reflective of objective reality. Eliot Mishler (1991), for instance, has shown how the same extract can be transcribed in different ways reflecting different purposes. Moreover, what these sounds signify (e.g., does emphasis signify sarcasm or enthusiasm) is also a matter of interpretation and judgement.

The dialogical approach has been inspired by the literary analysis of Bakhtin. As such, it is worth briefly speculating on what he would advise in terms of including these extra-discursive markers when transcribing interviews and focus group data. As we saw in previous chapters, for Bakhtin (1981), the genre, the use of direct and indirect speech and types of discourse are the key markers of emotional intonation. As well as this he relies on the narrator/author to give the extra-discursive detail in a character's speech. We saw that in his own analysis, he re-writes written speech with capitals to denote emphasis even though it is missing in the text that he takes.

There is also some degree of ambivalence in Bakhtin's writings when it comes to the potential of audible speech to reflect the emotional register. He argues that verbal speech can sometimes distort the emotional register of the voice:

loud and living intonation excessively monologizes discourse and cannot do justice to the other person's voice present in it.

(Bakhtin, 1984 [1929]: 198)

I am not sure why Bakhtin believes this to be the case exactly as it is a rather cryptic comment. It is a charismatic claim without any evidence. Perhaps he makes the claim because, when spoken out loud, our own inner doubts may be steamrolled away by the 'position' we assume in relation to the other – e.g., a position of righteousness. Possibly an emphasis on oral speech brings too much attention to the self–other dialogue at the expense of the self–self dialogue. As Billig (1987) points out, the absence of an outer critic can sometimes allow the 'inner-critic' to be foregrounded.

Either way, I disagree up to a point with Bakhtin's reading of verbal versus written speech. For the purposes of examining subjectivity and emotion, some discursive markers may be useful guides to the emotional register. In particular, I use the following aspects of the well-known Jefferson system, named after Gail Jefferson who developed it (see Atkinson and Heritage, 1984, for a more complete description):

[ ]	Square brackets mark the start and end of overlapping speech.
((swallow))	Additional comments from the transcriber in double parentheses, e.g., about features of context or delivery.
CAPITALS	Capitals mark speech that is emphatic.
( )	Empty parentheses signify inaudible talk.
_	Underlined words signify stress in tone.

I hasten to point out that there are many other symbols in the Jefferson system, such as markers that give in-breaths and out-breaths and markers that time pauses. However, I prefer not to use these as I find that they detract away from the readability of a transcript and foreground attention on the sounds of the words, for the reader, at the expense of what is being said and the format used to say them – e.g., genre, direct and indirect speech and types of discourse. As Gee (2005) point out, the validity of an analysis does not depend on how much detail is in the transcript, but rather on how the transcript works together with the other features of the analysis and the goals of the study.

Even for the conventions outlined above, I prefer to use them only minimally. In this sense, the transcription system here is what one may call 'broad' or less detailed as opposed to 'narrow' or very detailed. When transcribing, judgements need to be made around the context of the discursive marker. For instance, emphasis in speech may be important in some contexts but, as I exemplify in a moment, in other contexts it may not be relevant to the argument being made or the features of the talk that are foregrounded.

Transcriptions build on each other as the significance of what is being said comes into focus. Initially, interviews, for instance, may be transcribed without extra-discursive features. Langdridge and Hagger-Johnson (2009) refer to this lack as 'simple transcription'. For many researchers, this can be done by a typist.

From reading this transcript (further familiarisation), the researcher may focus on some key areas of the interviews/focus groups and particularly important interactions. These can be given further transcription attention. Although this iterative process may build further detail into the text, in a dialogical approach, the judgement on whether or not to use them (e.g., mark emphasis) depends on how relevant they are to the emotional register of what is being said.

An example may help clarify some of these issues around transcription (the same example will be used later to illustrate data analysis). The transcribed data below is taken from an artist instructing students on how to make glass. It is reported in McCarthy, Sullivan and Wright (2006) and Sullivan, Smith and Matusov (2009). The artist's real name is Donna but the students' names (Jane and Zoe) are pseudonyms. The transcription presents a number of interesting features which may help clarify the level of appropriate transcription in a dialogical approach:

Transcription example

Jane: can I use this ruler
Donna: sure honey, how you doing
Zoe: grand
Donna: OKAY ((said in funny/joking voice))
Zoe: are we able to do uhm, like, I have rods upstairs and uhmm, will I just bring them down and we'll leave them together and stuff and ( )
Donna: sure they'll be gorgeous, yeah, wiRED up [on a panel
Zoe: just wired]
Donna: you know like some of those pictures you have, they'd be simple, bring down anything like that that you LOVE
Zoe: o.k.
Donna: because if you love it you know, it will all happen and come together then in the piece, you know
Zoe: o.k., so you don't, so it doesn't have to be like, well I will do this ( ) as well anyway
Donna: so like the little journey around America

Here, Donna's emphasis on 'love' is capitalised because her emphatic speech also reflects the value she places on this concept. In her diaries and interviews she also talks about love and art. Putting it in capitals brings out her investment in the word, in the broader context of her life. On the other hand, perhaps it was a mistake to put wiRED in caps because it does not add much to the analysis. I could have used another Jefferson convention of underlining the word to signify a rise in tone, but it was difficult to discern whether it was a rise in tone or an emphasis. Indeed, it is hard to know why she put stress on this word in any case.

There are some other notations that are included that are worth mentioning. Putting contextual information in brackets – e.g., (said in a funny/joking voice) – helps us to understand not only the kind of atmosphere that Donna is feeling and/or trying to create, but also that Donna places value on this joking atmosphere. On the other hand, perhaps I should have directly used notation to try to follow the sounds of the voice rather than giving the contextual information of it being said in a joking voice. I definitely read it as a joking voice but there was no laughter in the voice. Finally, I marked the overlap using square brackets which could also indicate that there is some interruption between the speakers, but in the overall context of the extract it is difficult to interpret what this signifies. As such, maybe I ought not to have marked the overlap.

It should also be clear that in this particular case, only some transcription conventions were used. I see this as both a weakness and strength. It is a weakness because there may well be very important signs around the talk that would aid my interpretation of what Donna is doing. By not transcribing these, I am ignoring data. On the other hand, as Gee (2005) points out, even the most detailed transcription systems also miss data. Perhaps more importantly, however, I want to do an analysis that will direct the reader towards the most significant details of what is being said for the argument that I am making. There is a risk in transcribing other details that the reader will consider these as very significant, because they are present in the transcription, when in the overall context of understanding the emotional register, these may be insignificant details. This is a judgement call that the researcher needs to make – and as such militates against the bureaucratic dimension of a transcription convention.

Despite my preference for the bare minimum in terms of transcription convention, it is clear from discourse and conversation analysis that detailed transcription systems are very effective in drawing attention to what initially appears insignificant and giving it significance in subsequent interpretation. However, as we saw in Chapter 2, this kind of discourse analysis often has quite different aims from a dialogical analysis – particularly in terms of foregrounding the game-playing subject and/or understanding the rules that structure talk.

Key moments

Most approaches to qualitative data involve an initial familiarisation with the entire data set. However, reduction is necessary for an interpretation and analysis to take place. In thematic-led approaches, this tends to be done by systematically coding all of the data from the bottom-up and then putting these in hierarchical categories. Hierarchy is a key part of a bureaucratic approach in general.

However, another approach that I favour, is to focus on the 'key moments' or 'key extracts' from the data set to achieve a reduction this way. The use of 'key moments' emerged out of a recent collaboration with Anna Madill (Madill and Sullivan, 2010). 'Key moments' are an 'utterance' of significance. An utterance is a significant unit of meaning, different from the sentence or the line and is defined by its readiness for a reply/reaction. As a unit of meaning, it can be of variable length.

The Donna example above, for instance, is a 'key moment' in so far as it captures a significant aspect of her interaction with Zoe and Jane (it shows the emphasis she places on love, her informal, chatty style with the students and Zoe's questions). Later in the chapter, I do an analysis of this 'key moment' along with an analysis of an interview done with another artist. This other interview extract is also a key moment but longer than Donna's example. Again, however, it captures a significant aspect of what the experience of making art involves for her, over a number of conversational turns.

Originally, Anna Madill and I decided to use 'key moments' as part of managing a large data set of transcribed interviews with eleven different medical students (each interviewed at least twice) taking a year out to do psychology. We were interested in their experiences of doing medicine. After going through the entire data set, we reduced all of the interviews to forty 'key moments'. This involved an iterative process. We first selected a wide variety of different extracts. These were a mix of what we found interesting and what seemed most relevant to the research question. In the second stage, the more peripheral of these were excluded on the basis of relevance and we were left with forty 'key moments'.

It is possible to decide on criteria for selecting parts of the data as 'key moments'. These criteria may differ across studies, but to give a sense of the kinds of criteria that are possible, I will outline some general criteria that Madill and I decided on in the study of intercalating medical students.

In terms of content, what counted as a key moment, in this particular study, included the following: (1) an anecdote around a difficult or interesting teaching or medical situation; (2) Managing interpersonal relations in order to secure medical knowledge, such as taking patient histories and taking blood; (3) their expectations as to what the branches of medicine would involve – e.g., psychiatry offers different possibilities for dealing with people from surgery; and (4) their reflection on their relationships to other staff and students in the hospital.

In terms of form, a key moment was given a boundary by a move in the interview to relating: (1) an anecdote relating to self or someone else who had a personal impact; (2) a significant belief or expectation around medicine; and (3) a reflection on their own identity and practice in medicine. These often overlapped – e.g., an anecdote was intertwined with a personal reflection. Generally speaking, these moves were prompted by an interviewer question, but occasionally the interviewees spontaneously moved the interview in this direction.

Because these 'key moments' are given their boundaries by the content and form, they are of unequal length. Some are a few hundred words long, while others are up to a thousand words long. Finding the precise place where the 'key moment' begins was sometimes easy to identify as the participants moved into and out of an anecdote/belief/reflection to something quite different. Sometimes, however, the interview meandered in different directions and here the key moment had fuzzy boundaries. In these cases, the key moment begins and ends at what we considered to be the outer periphery of the personal significance that the interviewees attached to the moment.

Moreover, while we tried to find at least one 'key moment' in each interview, some participants had far more reflections, anecdotes and experiences to relate than others and across different interviews as well. This means that some participants are more represented than others in the list of 'key moments', although each participant has at least one key moment and most have more. We gave each 'key moment' a label to help identify what its referent was – e.g., 'facial injuries', 'psychiatry', 'dressing up'.

While these key moments were extremely useful in our study, there are no definite rules in a dialogical approach. For some research questions it may be better to package the data into relevant 'key moments'; for others, it may be better to count everything as relevant but still divide the data set into 'key moments' or utterances; for others still, it may be better to dispense with key moments and put separate parts of the text together under 'themes' and then analyse these along dialogical lines.

Sound bites

Regardless of whether one uses 'key moments' or not, it will not be possible to use all of the data in the final report or the article. This can create some difficulties. For example, the participants may use a particular expression or put things in an unusual way that one wants to bring into the analysis.

However, this interesting nugget or 'sound bite' may not be in one of the quotations you selected – generally because within a longer quotation it may lose its impact. Often, in qualitative data, this difficulty is overcome informally by saying: 'Elsewhere, this participant also said...'.

I suggest formalising this habit in qualitative analysis. In other words, while going through the data set and the 'key moments', it is possible to take a separate note of all the particular expressions or 'sound bites' that seem to articulate an experience in an interesting way. Below, I list some 'sound bites' I wrote down in my analysis of a 'mental health' team who participated in a focus group discussing their place in the organisation. The details of this study are published as Sullivan and McCarthy (2008) and explicated further in Chapter 6. For now, these are just examples of the kinds of sound bites that can be written down:

> We haven't had enough change.
>
> Often you have people making plans who have no concept of the impact on the ground of what they are talking about, they have no clue whatsoever.
>
> The prospectus report was all put together without a single conversation with anyone in the health board anywhere. If that's not detached I don't know what is.
>
> And yet at the same time big areas seemed to be unclear and grey. And still are unclear and grey and may be getting greyer, do you know what I mean.
>
> I would say a lot of it is the bureaucratic system. Em, the protect your back system, the don't make a mistake, because again nobody will take responsibility.

These sound bites are useful because they can be explicitly brought into an analysis of a broader data set to substantiate it. We will see in Chapter 6 how 'sound bites' can be presented in a table. In Chapter 6, we will examine how 'sound bites' from different areas can be used to create a dialogue among participants and points of view that would not otherwise be in direct dialogue.

Data analysis

Much of data preparation also involves data analysis in so far as one is continually making interpretations around what to transcribe, what to focus on, what arguments to make and what to leave out.

In the bureaucratic side of the analysis, however, there are a number of further steps that are possible. One can identify: (1) the genre and the type of discourse; (2) the affect or the emotion; (3) the time–space that is being used (more technically – 'the chronotope'); and (4) The context of where it is happening or what is being said. As I discussed in Chapter 2, these are all significant aspects of the data.

This way of organising the data emerged through the same collaboration with Madill (Madill and Sullivan, 2010) and it is worth reading this study for some further detail. Here, I analyse the interaction between the artist, Donna, and her students (data also presented on p. 70 as an example of transcribing data). This assumes that this interaction is a 'key moment'.

In Table 4.2, Donna's interactions with Jane and Zoe are organised according to the genre and discourse, the emotional register, the time–space elaboration of this and the context.

Table 4.2   An analysis of a key moment in the case of the artist, Donna

Participant(s)	Key moment	Genres and discourse	Emotional register (of learning/truth)	Time–space elaboration	Context
Donna, Jane, Zoe	1	Epic elements (love of piece leads to ultimate success). Expert–Novice genre Lyric praise (sure, they'll be gorgeous). Outside-in discourse (the piece given a central place in discourse as beautiful; Jane authored as 'honey') Hesitations and uncertainty for Zoe. Stop start. Possibly anticipating Donna's views.	Love (Donna). Praise (Donna). Encouragement and exhortation (Donna). Reassurance (Donna). Humour (Donna). Uncertainty (Zoe).	Future certainty linked to internal psychology (if you love it, it will all happen and come together). Moment-to-moment potential of conversational interaction.	Donna instructing Jane and Zoe on making glass. Key moment: Love of the piece.

As we can see, Table 4.2 shows one method of coding the data. It involves outlining various aspects of the talk, such as the genre, discourse and chronotope (or time–space). It is also possible to include short quotations, alongside a label, to remind oneself of what exactly one was referring to with a coding label – e.g., 'Jane authored as "honey"'. Although not done here, if there are other key moments that are also similar to the kind of genre and discourse evident in this particular extract, the reference to these can also be included under 'extract' – e.g., (Key moment 12, 49).

Below, I give another example of this kind of initial data analysis in order to illustrate the variety of contexts in which the coding scheme can be used and the variety of ways in which the genres and chronotope can be employed. While the data above is taken from a study of a glass-making workshop, the data below is taken from an interview with an artist, Christine (pseudonym) who discusses her experience of different levels of consciousness in making art. I then present the analysis of this in terms of the coding scheme above.

Extract from interview with Christine

C: Christine;

R: Researcher

R: o.k.

C: I suppose its like medit.., meditating, you're, you, you let go of that, of the surface

R: yeah

C: right, the surface world, that the

R: yeah

C: that the noise is from the radio, the [people

R: yeah]

C: walking outside the, you know when I'm picking up now

R: yeah

C: you, you sort of sink into a different conscious level where you are just making, you are just doing it and your hand is reaching out for blue because it knows blue is the right thing to do or and its like driv..., you know its like all those unconscious levels where you're just submerged and you're not thinking uhm 'why yellow'?

R: yeah

C: you, you don't, because if if you actually want pull yourself away from that

R: all right

C: Level of consciousness well I think, well, I mean, I mean suddenly as you come out of it then, when you feel, you know like you might look at your watch or something, something jolts you like, you say 'ohh, I must pack up'

R: yeah

C: you suddenly have realised that you have made something or started HALF of this might have been completed and that all those decisions were quite sort of (short pause) there was a flow going that you can't really explain

R: yeah
C: but, there there, its not there because of uhm, its not there in a, on a TOTal intuitive level, its there on a, a, a sort of uhm EDUCated intuitive level

This 'key moment' is coded like the previous one, in Table 4.3, according to genre, discourse, emotional register, chronotope and context. It allows for different codes, however. You may also note that this particular 'key moment' has fuzzy boundaries and is a little longer than the extract of Donna teaching art.

The analysis in Table 4.3 gives a starting point for coding Christine's 'key moment'. Some of these codes may appear vague. Other descriptions may also be possible. For example, one may have included 'exposition' or 'confession' in the coding of genre. Hopefully, this shows that although there are guidelines, like other qualitative approaches, the actual choice of codes can reflect the personal style of the analyst(s) and what their particular interests are. In Chapter 8, I outline how, bearing this charisma in mind, it is still possible to evaluate a dialogical approach.

Table 4.3   An analysis of a key moment in the case of the artist, Christine

Participant (s)	Key moment	Genres and discourse	Emotional register (of learning/truth)	Time–space elaboration	Context
Christine and Researcher	13	Romantic genre – absorption and intuition, non-cognitive. Adventure (suddenly in different zone). Character tests – 'pull self away', 'letting go'. Indirect discourse – you say 'oh I have to pack up'; 'why yellow'. Outside-in elements – giving shape to the experience of making art. Inside-out elements – anticipating words of generalised others: 'you're not thinking – why yellow'.	Daring of letting go. Jolting out of a state. Intuitive absorption. Feeling a flow. Feelings beyond words.	Hierarchy of consciousness (thinking and intuition). Hierarchy of world (surface world and deep world). The self can travel through levels. Let go of surface. 'Sudden' movement between levels.	Explanation of process of making art.

So far, in this section, we have looked at the value and importance of a bureaucratic-led approach to data analysis in dialogue. In summary, it allows one to be systematic with the data set. What this means is that the authority for the interpretation does not depend on the magical properties of the individual making the interpretation, but instead depends on the procedures that were employed in arriving at the interpretation.

At the same time, however, in qualitative research, following procedures rigorously is still not enough to guarantee a good analysis. As we saw already, many individual judgements are possible. Choices around what codes to use can be an exercise in creativity in some cases. There are also a variety of charismatic styles that are possible in the appropriation of procedures. This has not been demonstrated here as the codes I used are my own, but Madill, Jordan and Shirley (2000) do give an excellent example of different styles in following procedures in qualitative analysis.

The charismatic side of dialogical research

In this section, I outline how a 'charismatic' side of data analysis is relevant to a dialogical approach. I do this through using an example of Bakhtin's (1984) analysis of data.

In a dialogical approach, the strengths of both bureaucracy and charisma should intertwine. Bureaucratic procedures and the charismatic engagement with the data may wax and wane as the analysis proceeds. This is particularly so in the write-up. In the write-up, perhaps a vivid image may be useful here, a theoretical reflection there, a pointed comment somewhere else. The point, here, is that writing an analysis involves taking ownership of it through one's own style. In this way, the authority of the interpretation depends on more than just the capacity of the analyst to rigorously follow procedures. Rigour is important but it is not the only quality that is necessary in a qualitative analysis. Authority also lies in the charismatic capacity of the individual to actualise procedures.

One final example may suffice to illustrate this charismatic-led interpretation, but one that intertwines with some generic and traceable bureaucratic steps. It is taken again from Bakhtin's analysis of Devushkin in Dostoevsky's novel 'Poor Folk'. We examined some of this analysis in the previous chapter. Here, however, Bakhtin does not add capitals to denote what he considers to be the internal amplification of a sound-value in 'copying', but rather he takes Devushkin's speech and re-writes it as a dialogue between him and an anonymous 'other':

Example of a re-written dialogue

THE OTHER:	One must know how to earn a lot of money. One shouldn't be a burden to anyone. But you are a burden to others.
MAKAR DEVUSHKIN:	I'm not a burden to anyone. I've got my own piece of bread.
THE OTHER:	But what a piece of bread it is! Today it's there, and tomorrow it's gone. And it's probably dry one, at that!
MAKAR DEVUSHKIN:	It is true it is a plain crust of bread, at times a dry one, but there it is, earned by my toil and put to lawful and irreproachable use.

(Bakhtin, 1984: 210)

Bakhtin, here, re-writes a monologue as if it were a dialogue. He invents the interrogatives of THE OTHER and thereby puts a context to Devushkin's polemical certainty. In this context, far from being certain, Devushkin is fighting his own doubts, embodied in the mocking voice of a generalised other. Bakhtin (1984) is unable to prove this charismatic claim as he makes up the interrogatives of THE OTHER, but it certainly allows a provocative interpretation. Bakhtin (1984) brings to life the dialogical quality of speech through this charismatic analysis.

In Chapter 6, I use a similar technique with the 'sound bites'. I put various sound bites, which embody particular viewpoints, in dialogue with each other. This can help to shed light on how the different participants in an organisation anticipate each other's judgements and attempt to answer these back.

There is more to this kind of analysis, however, than just a charismatic writing style alone. In the example above, for instance, Bakhtin also illustrates, and elsewhere comments on, the emotional register (Devushkin's defiant despair), the genre (a confession), the struggle between self and other (a hidden dialogue) and the time–space (a threshold moment). These are all generic, even impersonal features, central to his analysis and emerge from the data set that he seeks to describe.

His analysis is charismatically led but underpinned by sound bureaucratic requirements. He uses quotations to back up his claims, he deals with alternative interpretations of his 'data' and he compares it to other data sets (other Dostoevsky novels). As such, somebody else may reveal these features of discourse as well but perhaps not do it in such a dramatic or charismatic way. Consistent with Bakhtin's (1984) own theory, the ideas are given life and take on colour in their unique embodiment in the speaking personality.

Discussion

I am suggesting that a dialogical analysis can be used both in a bureaucratic way – leaving an audit trail – but with charismatic elements nonetheless – e.g., choosing extracts that reflect personal interest; judging what transcription symbols to use; judging how the audience will react to particular directions in the analysis; judging how to present the argument and how the data fits in with this.

In my own research, I sometimes endeavour to write bureaucratically and sometimes charismatically, depending on the audience. Needless to say, the approach needs to meet the expected requirements of the audience. In the case of journals, some expect a lot of quotations and an exhaustive analysis, while others are more concerned with the theoretical issues at stake and a few exemplars may suffice here.

Nonetheless, there is a lot of scope for the researcher to combine these approaches and use them flexibly. There is a lot of strength in dynamically moving between bureaucratically-led and charismatically-led approaches. Perhaps in the earlier stages, a bureaucratic-led approach may dominate, while later, in writing-up, a charismatic-led approach may dominate or even intertwine with the bureaucratic approach.

In the next chapter, I will bring further attention to the interplay between the 'bureaucratic' and 'charismatic' approaches. I do this by giving some general guidelines on how to write up a dialogical analysis. These guidelines are exemplified through an analysis of three artists making art.

Further reading

Charmaz, K. (2006) *Constructing Grounded Theory: A Practical Guide through Qualitative Analysis*. London: Sage.

Madill, A., Jordan, A. and Shirley, C. (2000) Objectivity and reliability in qualitative analysis: Realist, contextualist and radical constructionist epistemologies. *British Journal of Psychology*, 91(1): 1–20.

Madill, A. and Sullivan, P. (2010) Medical training as adventure-wonder and adventure-ordeal: A dialogical analysis of affect-laden pedagogy. *Social Science and Medicine*, 71(12): 2195–203.

O'Connell, D. and Kowall, S. (1995) Basic principles of transcription, in J.A. Smith, R. Harré and L. van Langenhove (eds) *Rethinking Methods in Psychology*. London: Sage. pp. 93–104.

Weber, M. (1947) *The Theory of Social and Economic Organization*. Trans. A.M. Henderson and T. Parsons. Glencoe, IL: The Free Press.

5

WRITING UP AN ANALYSIS

In this chapter, I discuss some of the ways in which a dialogical analysis can be written up and presented. I outline some of the strategies available to help organise the write-up, such as gaining an overview of the analysis, organising the analysis by genre, doing background reading and putting various voices into dialogue with each other. I also look at different tools of presentation, including 'summary tables', 'sound-bites' and 'quotations'. In varying ways, moving from reported speech in summary tables, to fragments of voices through 'sound-bites' to presenting full-blown quotations, these methods allow the introduction of participant voices into the analysis. Dialoguing with these different voices, in the write-up, is also an important feature of the analysis.

I exemplify these guidelines through presenting an analysis of six interviews done with three artists (each interviewed twice) about their experiences of making art as well as a diary from one of the artists. This data has been reported elsewhere (see McCarthy, Sullivan and Wright, 2006; Sullivan and McCarthy, 2007), but the analysis here is a new one. My intention is to use this embedded write-up as an opportunity to reflect on the methods used and decision-making involved in a write-up.

With regard to the interviews, the artists' names are Ina (pseudonym), Kevin (pseudonym) and Donna (real name). Christine (pseudonym), of the previous chapter, participated in the same study but is not included. Instead, I focus on these three artists here as I wish to reflect upon the writing-up process as well, and reporting the results of four artists would limit the space available for such reflection. Ina's interviews mainly concern an installation piece of art – an installation is a temporary art show. Here, she presented objects she found on the street. Kevin's interviews are about his experiences of printing art, using steel and copper plates. Donna's interviews and diary are about her experiences of making glass art pieces.

As this book is explicitly concerned with the analysis of all kinds of qualitative data, it does not deal with various interview techniques and methods. Some good sources on this side of qualitative methods include Steinar Kvale (1996), Tom Wengraf (2001) and Nigel King and Christine Horrocks (2009).

There is a danger with writing this kind of chapter of prescribing a cookbook type formula for 'writing-up'. This is not the intention of this chapter. A dialogical approach embodies creative charisma and bureaucracy as we saw in the previous chapter. For this reason, I urge the reader to approach the following sets of writing-up suggestions, simply as suggestions. As we will see in subsequent chapters, there are many different ways of writing up an analysis.

Gaining an overview of the analysis

In this section, I discuss the importance of gaining an overview of the analysis. This depends, in part, on the question that has been posed to the data. I will briefly discuss this. I will then discuss how an overview of the data can be presented.

Choosing a question

Different analyses of the same data are possible in qualitative research. Gaining an overview of the analysis depends on having a good understanding of the research question. Understanding the question is crucial not only for choosing the key moments, as discussed in the previous chapter, but also in terms of shaping an overview of the analysis. As the study progresses, the questions may evolve and change, in dialogue with the analysis. More generally, this is known as the 'hermeneutic circle'. What this means is that the questions change in response to the data and what comes out in the data changes as the questions change. For this reason, very often it is only when you begin to understand the question(s) that you begin to gain an overview of the analysis.

In the case of the artists' study, for instance, I started out with the broad question: (Q) is there anything we can learn about the self from how some artists describe the process of making art? Of course, other practitioners may also teach us something about the self. I chose to study artists partly because it is an area I find personally interesting. I enjoy art. It is also because so much of a dialogical approach is a meditation around the act of creation – of others and of self, that it seems appropriate to take a professional group whose lives are wrapped in the project of creating, and gain a sense of their unique point of view (or intonation) on what it means to create.

There was a lot of data generated from the study. They were each interviewed twice, lasting an hour and a half, and one artist also gave me her diaries to examine. As we saw in the previous chapter, one way of reducing the data is to select 'key moments' according to the question. So, I subsequently started to analyse the 'key moments' for each participant under the following headings: 'genre' and 'discourse', 'emotional register', 'time–space elaboration of genre' and 'context'. A key moment was defined both by form (e.g., an anecdote, a belief, a reflection, a genre) and content (the particular anecdote, the process of making art, the relationship with the wider art world).

As the tables progressed, the key areas of concern for the participants became clearer, as did the major genres. This allowed me to disqualify key moments that appeared on the periphery of the major areas I wished to pursue.

Presenting a summary

While I selected and analysed the 'key moments' according to the broad question above, there was still far too much text to include in the write-up, and I was unsure what the overview was or what the specific questions would be. This is a common problem in qualitative research more generally. For this reason, presenting a general summary of the initial analysis can be useful. It can act as a starting point for further dialogue with the data. It is possible to use the same headings as the key moments, but by participant.

In Table 5.1, I present a summary that gives both the reader and the analyst a general overview of the analysis of artists making art. This summary table, while interesting, only introduces us to the early stages of an actual analysis. In so far as it misses the subtlety, nuances and contradictions within the analysis, it is a little coarse. Added to this, the reader is deprived of access to the data so it is also a little rude from a qualitative point of view. On the other hand, it serves the function of allowing the reader to feel an entire data within the write-up and to begin to gain an overview of what the results are like.

This summary of the analysis also helps to clarify how exactly one should continue with the write-up by foregrounding what is particularly significant in the analysis of the data. In Table 5.1, the 'romantic' and the 'professional' genre seemed particularly useful in serving as a spring-board to discussing the data. They are sufficiently broad to allow variety and contradiction into artists' accounts of the life of objects, process and self – a key concern of the genre. They also very pragmatically foreground the arrangement of time–space, emotion and lived experience within the discourse.

With the broadness, however, comes vagueness and some vacuity. As we saw in Chapter 4, genres are difficult to pin down. They mix with each

Table 5.1 Overview of analysis

Participant	Genres and discourses	Emotional register	Time-space elaboration	Context
Donna	Lyric. Magic Realism. Professionalism. Romanticism. Outside-in discourse with some double-voicing.	Love, passion, tenderness.	Threshold moments. Absorption in space. Potential of present.	Glass-making. Family, friends.
Ina	Romanticism. Magic Realism. Professionalism. Outside-in discourse with some double-voicing.	Admiration, re-valuation of objects.	Reflection, creating new space, re-valuing, accessing the roots of creativity.	Installation, art world, giving meaning.
Kevin	Lyric. Romance. Adventure-wonder. Travel. Professionalism. Outside-in discourse with some double-voicing.	Passion. Bodily pleasure.	Bodily intensity of time, space. Financial pressure.	Printing the material. Gallery.

other, speak to content but also forms of language, they evolve and change. For this reason, it is important to try to specify as much as possible some of the major genres, serving as a point of organisation for what the analysis actually means. This involves doing some background reading.

Writing about a major genre

In this section, I move on to one possibility for organising the analysis in the write-up. This is to write about a major genre. Identifying a major genre is possible from the overview of the analysis. To write about it will involve doing some background reading on the genre, presenting an analysis of 'sound bites' and presenting an analysis of relevant quotations. In the following section, we will examine how this analysis can be contextualised through comparing and contrasting it to an alternative genre.

Doing background reading

Perhaps the first, most important thing to do, when writing up the analysis, is to creatively mix theory with data. The outline of theory is often presented in a 'literature review' at the beginning of the paper, but it can also continue to dialogue with the data within the analysis. This creative mixing allows meaning to emerge as a joint creation between the theory and data.

In the context of Table 5.1, one of the major genres is the 'Romantic genre'. Doing some background reading on this helps give some contours to the Romantic genre. This then helps to make sense of the data.

So, what is Romanticism? Isaiah Berlin (1999 [1965]) argues that Romanticism can be viewed, with some exceptions, as a general movement towards a celebration of the inner life of the person – and particularly of passion, emotion, mystery and commitment to ideals. What is significant in Romanticism is the act of commitment, the investment of passion and emotion in activity, the tragic incompatibility of different morals and the fundamental obscurity of the self in nature. In these respects, at least, Berlin points out, it differs from, and is a reaction to, the Enlightenment. This was a movement in European history that was generally concerned with the compatibility of morals with each other, the order behind nature and the principles that govern human nature.

Philosophy, literature and art all contain traces of the Romantic Movement. In philosophy, Kant, who was so influential in the Enlightenment, also had a significant influence on the Romantic Movement (among many others too numerous to mention). This is because he champions, as a self-evident proposition, the concept of the 'will'. We are at our freest, he argues, when we impose our will upon nature, our commitment to certain morals and ideals that can transcend impulses (e.g., sexual or appetitive). Nature, here, becomes somewhat plastic and open to being shaped by the personality.

In visual art, some artists gave increasing prominence to the brushstroke and the free handling of paint (e.g., Turner, de Goya, Delacroix) as much as they did to representing the objects classically and faithfully. Rather than effacing him/herself behind classical ideals with a uniform standard, the personality of the artist, interpreted as their life force, came into the process of creating and featured in the judgement of the art work.

What's important to understand here is that the Romantic genre, in broad terms, calls attention to character, to inner life and to action. We can only gain knowledge of the mysteries of life by participation, and even then we ought not to destroy the mystery by a classification system. Indeed, the Romantic Movement tends to stand against the Enlightenment idea of knowledge gained from disinterested, contemplative reason. One knows love, for instance, by loving.

This kind of theoretical background involves library-based research. It is important in order to give a contextual framework for the data that will be subsequently organised around it. The theory needs to enter into dialogue with the data. In the next section, I will introduce a method of presenting this data which I call a 'table of sound-bites'.

Using a 'table of sound bites' as a presentation tool

While the theoretical background may give some indication as to what the 'genre' means, it is also important to see how this is evident in the data. One way of doing this is to cut across different participants using 'sound bites'. A sound bite, as we saw in Chapter 4, is a fragment of text taken from the participants and kept in diary format by the researcher. In Table 5.2, I have included a few 'sound bites' from the three artists, where they make clear that inner-depths are considered very important to the work. What is significant is the emphasis placed on 'intuition' and 'mystery', while 'intellect' is more problematically felt as getting in the way.

Much of Table 5.2 speaks for itself. 'Intuition', the visceral, the mystery of the self and of the work and the active participation in a project of creation are all celebrated as important values. Qualities such as passion, inner-depth and commitment to creation 'out of necessity' are all given a high value. Such qualities are explicitly contrasted to the 'intellectual', which acts as a blocking force that misses the point of creation.

The difficulty, needless to say, with this kind of table is that it decontextualises where the talk is coming from. These sound bites are cherry-picked. This is generally a bad research practice. In the context of this kind of analysis, however, the sound bites are intended only to help introduce the range of participant voices as they speak, in varying ways, using a common genre. In this sense, they are used as a tool to introduce more intertextuality into the text.

In the next sub-section, I will examine how these sound bites, which help give us a taste of the voices of the participants, can also help contextualise

Table 5.2 'Sound bites' of the Romantic genre

Donna	Ina	Kevin
• I would be quite kind of an intuitive kind of person. • The way I take in the world is I kind of feel it. • I do what I do which is my kind of passion. • I've been you know kind of driven to just make it for myself.	• This interests me without thinking. • Again there's no issue, it's not intellectual, it's the opposite of intellectual. • I'm drawn to doing it because I need to do it. • These people are creating out of necessity.	• Keep it intuitive but sensibilities in that. • Stop you being precious. • I have to keep this out of my head and just work with this. • (I love) getting a metal sheet, putting it in nitric acid and beating the fuck out of it.

and introduce more full-blown quotations, within the write-up. Here, I will take one quotation from each of the artists to illustrate how the quotation operates as a central plank to the write-up. The quotations, a bit like the sound bites, are selected broadly in terms of the original question. In this case, I choose quotations in terms of how they deepen our understanding of the Romantic genre through drawing attention to the creation of a life of objects, personality and art. As discussed in Chapter 3, genres organise perception but are also embodied and intoned in particular experiences. Quotations are particularly useful for showing this. Each of the quotations below has been picked from a 'key moment' as offering particularly interesting features of discourse and experience to discuss, from the point of view of the question.

Using quotations – the discourse analysis

Quotations or 'data extracts' and their analysis form a major part of any qualitative write-up. Choosing which quotation to use in the write-up is difficult. As I mentioned earlier, a good idea is to choose extracts that will raise particularly interesting issues, nuances and additions to the emerging picture of what the data is like, from the sound bites and summary. As the redrafting of the write-up takes place, you may need to reduce the number of these, including your analysis of them. Indeed, in this very chapter, many extracts from artists were taken out from the original draft in order to keep a manageable word count.

What is particularly important to point out is that because the quotation is entering into your write-up as a piece of discourse to be analysed, it will need even more analysis, thought, reflection and feedback than the analysis of the key moments that was done at early stages of the research. In this sense, 'write-up' is something of a misnomer as writing up also involves analysis.

Moving back to the art study, the following quotation serves as a good introductory quotation to the artists' voices and is something that further quotations can work well against in terms of the issues that are raised. There are also a number of illustrations of how the Romantic genre is appropriated. So, in it, Kevin talks about why he prefers steel to copper plates when he does his print-making.

Kevin: Extract 1

K: Kevin; R: Researcher
K: I like the steel anyway, the steel has a different character than the copper, copper is very smooth, this is a copper plate, its smooth, it polishes, nice clean contours

R: yeah
K: steel is DIRTY
R: right
K: it's grittier, there's more impurities in it
R: and is that why you prefer it
K: yeah and its CHEAPER
R: yeah, and it's cheaper?
K: and it's cheaper
R: yeah
K: I prefer it because it gives, its rough, it stops you being precious with it
R: yeah
K: if you get too precious and delicate you'll never do a thing
R: yeah
K: tight and and you know, you're only just kind of, go with it, you know

In general, in this quotation, we are looking out for: time–space (chronotope), emotional intonation, sub-genres, how it relates to the summary and the other artists, direct and indirect speech with the goal of how they relate to subjectivity. Wherever possible, it is important to evidence claims by reminding the reader of what you are referring to. This is possible by using line numbers. However, I prefer to put the relevant part of the quotation in brackets next to the claim to aid coherence or else to use the odd quoted word from the quotation in the narrative. Occasionally, it is also possible to work other 'sound bites' elsewhere in the data, not in the extract, but that reinforce or add colour to the extract. This needs to be clearly signposted.

Above, for instance, Kevin explains with some degree of certainty why he enjoys working with steel (I prefer it because it gives, its rough). This is an expository discourse, where he directly explains why the qualities of steel are good. It is, in this sense, an 'outside-in' discourse; one where Kevin gives shape to the world of print-making by a lyric admiration of the material. It is a lyric in so far as the words seem poetic. Steel is 'dirty', 'grittier', with 'impurities' and 'rough' and 'cheaper'. He says 'dirty' and 'cheaper' with a degree of emphasis and in the context of enjoying working with the plate. His intonation of these words gives them a positive value.

Experientially, these qualities allow Kevin to interact with his art in an uninhibited way. This uninhibited interaction or flow where one can 'go with it' resonates a lot with the Romantic genre. It is a non-thinking, intuitive space that allows him to freely give shape to nature. Worry and copper act as an inhibitor to this flow. You can become 'delicate'. Along these lines, there is also an element of magic realism as steel moves out of its passive state as raw material and acquires some agency. It acts against the impulses of his personality – 'it stops you being precious with it'. Instead of being precious, it allows him to 'go with it' without worry of destroying it. This enjoyment of shaping the material is also expressed poetically elsewhere in the interviews. He talks of 'sticking it down', 'push plate to the limit', 'throw in the acid. Have the acid eat as much as you want'. 'Strike it with a hammer, bang, get a dent in it'. 'Scrape it with a nail'. 'Accidents galore'. 'Squashes it in'. 'Slap-dash to begin with'. 'Beating the fuck out of it'.

This romantic language evocatively instantiates the world of print-making. It is a world of active participation in a process. In this language, there are alternative time–spaces created. One of 'going with it', where his participation in the act of creation becomes absorbing. Mihaly Csikszentmihalyi (1990) has referred to 'optimal flow' for artists – one where time passes quickly as they become invested in activity. The other time–space is characterised by worry, thinking, being precious and delicate. In this time and space, nothing could get done to completion – 'you'll never do a thing'. It is a space of inhibition and a time with a hopeless future. In the interview extract, Kevin paints these time–spaces very vividly and explains how the raw material facilitates entry into either.

So far, I have argued that the Romantic genre is a key genre for the artists in terms of their experience. We saw with Kevin's appropriation of the genre that it gains a very particular value or intonation. It led to a poetic admiration of steel as a material with the potential to bring him into a space-time of 'flow'. It also had the pragmatic bonus of being cheap.

We can see that the discourse analysis of an extract enables the introduction of a participant voice as the participant makes a significant genre their own. It is important, however, to also put quotations into dialogue with other participants, as well as theory, to help gain a further sense of the differences between participants and the meaning of the genre.

Dialoguing with other participants through quotation

The bulk of the write-up, in a dialogical approach, involves a direct engagement with different voices. So far, for instance, we got a taste of a few sound bites and one more elaborate quotation. It is important from here to gain a sense of how the 'Romantic genre', which is organising the write-up so far, can be elaborated. In doing this, we are not only seeking to spot features of discourse, but also to understand how the kind of Romantic subjectivity discussed so far can look and feel different as it is intoned by other participants. This will help us to gain a more interesting picture of what the experience is like and thereby address the question.

In the next extract, I will look at how Ina draws on a Romantic genre and in doing so paints a picture of art as a task of making the invisible, visible. The reason I have picked this quotation is because the outer and inner space between self and world is strongly emphasised, yet there is no conventional raw material that Ina works with, such as steel or copper. Instead, she makes a visual decision whether or not to pick up an item of 'rubbish' from the ground and put it on display.

Ina: Extract 2

Ina: I Do this because I am very draw<u>n</u> to doing it and I, I'm drawn to doing it because I need to do it, because its its like, the thing is, psychology, it's very <u>d</u>ifficult, you're talking about an invisible world which you use in a viSual capacity to try and think, make things visible, to, to place them out in front of you and to see them rather than to uhm, experience them internally, completely, so my, my work is very much based on a process, a journey, ahh exploration and uhm, I'm drawn toward, now I don't know what the end is, but all I know really is that I need to go this direction and I'm I'm very much uhm working on the basis of uhm, 'I don't know why I'm doing this', but that it feels right and that, and that is really, I reaLLy need To to have that focus, I really need to know 'is this settling o.k'; 'are my motivations o.k.' and then I know that the expression is honest annd my, my work is very much based on that, ahh bringing ahh things back down <u>t</u>o an honest level, trying to <u>s</u>trip them down as much as possible and <u>exposing</u> I suppose, what's invisible, making visible what is invisible uhmmm

Like the previous quotation, in this we are also looking for the link between the Romantic genre and subjectivity, but also in terms of how it relates to Kevin's extract. In comparison to Kevin's quotation, Ina's has a deeper, more moral dimension. It involves bringing the objects 'back down to an honest level'. She strips them down and exposes them as part of her project of revealing them. This involves a reciprocal interrogation of self. She questions her own motivations. She says she works on the basis of 'I don't know why I'm doing this' but she questions 'is this settling ok', 'are my motivations ok'. Elsewhere, she gives an example of the wrong motivation – picking up an object because others may like it, rather than herself liking it.

There is more quoted speech than in Kevin's extract. Through this quoted speech ('is this settling ok'), she introduces a double questioning voice and gives a sense of the dilemma that is involved in questioning the self as part of the activity. This double questioning voice creates the possibility of a divided, double-voiced self. One voice is intuitive, feeling and mysterious, while the other is questioning, very conscious and introduces the possibility that maybe motivations and feelings can be misleading. This second voice is reported, here, indirectly, and in this sense it is a form of double-voiced discourse. This questioning voice is ultimately subservient to a profound truth – of inner feeling and mysterious necessity being the basis of the work. I argued in Chapter 3 that an 'outside-in' discourse is one characterised by a singular, profound truth that gives shape to experience. Here, the historical romantic commitment to passion and intuition is a profound, 'outside-in' discourse that Ina does not simply repeat but aspires to and dialogues with.

There is clearly something very profound about Ina's project. She makes objects powerful, she makes them appear. It does seem very difficult and indeed she spends hours in any one site trying to discern if an object quali- fies as stimulating her artistic interests enough. It is an ambiguous space that she traverses between the visible and the invisible. It is a journey and an exploration and in this sense it is also an adventure. In this adventure space, time is also uncertain. She does not know where she will end up in her journey or how it will turn out. This resonates with Kevin's point of 'going with it'. The art work is a process that is continually changing. The only, somewhat epic certainty is that if her inner motivations are true, then she can believe in the value of the objects she creates. The value of the 'vis- ible' outer world reflects the sincerity of her invisible, inner motivations.

Ina's acknowledgement of the more questioning, intellectual voice, the one that searches for her own motivation, is integrated into a more general Romantic discourse about creating from necessity and on the basis of feeling.

We can see how a further quotation can add depth and complexity to our understanding of subjectivity. In particular, it is one that speaks much more to a division within self and between others than Kevin's extracts allude to. In this way, we get a sense of how a genre 'sounds differently' in the lived experience of different participants. In the next section, I will show how another artist, 'Donna', adds a further 'tone' to this sound.

Analysing a diary extract

This brings me to the final extract in this section. So far, we have looked at the Romantic genre as an outside-in discourse that gives shape to and instantiates time, space and subjectivity in different ways. Mystery is at the heart of the process. The inner life is invested and made tangible, for these artists, in outer forms and the process itself is transformative of their experience of time and space. In the final extract, taken from an entry in Donna's diary, I will discuss how a simple, short entry speaks volumes about the feeling and emotion involved in the dialogue between artist and their work. This extract also has the advantage of being relatively short and therefore takes up less space while being more than a sound bite:

Donna: Extract 3

Diary. 18–1–98
This piece is taking so long. Does it not want to be made!
Lay lines on lines and soften them to bed, give them care and give them love and gently touch with a magic wand. This machine can touch and care and mark in such a beautiful way. Water cut and wash.

This is a short extract from one of Donna's diaries. The first line is a short, terse note to self. I read the exclamation at the end of 'does it not want to be made' as an affectionate exclamation. The piece is anthropomorphised into having its own will which can resist hers and stubbornly not want to be made. The analogy I see here is the affection a friend can have for the stubborn refusal of another friend to do something, even though you think it may be in their best interest.

The second paragraph bursts into a lyric, poetic praise of the lines (in glass) and the machine. It is full magic realism. The lines that appear on the glass can be touched 'with a magic wand'. They are also touched by feeling and emotions of love and care. The machine comes in and plays a part and she admires the beauty of the lines.

Time and space also gain a magical quality in this note. The piece can resist its own teleology – its final state as a piece. In this space the machine can come to life and dwell over the particularity of the line by touching and caring and marking 'in a beautiful way'. Her own emotions can also bring the lines to life in this magic time–space. She gives it her ingredients of love and care.

This, while a diary entry, is also a song of praise. In this sense, it is an 'outside-in', loving and romantic discourse that makes visible the beauty of line. Moreover, this is not written for the benefit of another; it is marked as a note to herself. This makes it quite a different context from Kevin's and Ina's extracts, and it is perhaps unsurprising that the sheer joy, wonder and magic of making art for its own sake is shown. There is a singular, wonderful truth to it.

In terms of the write-up, this example nicely illustrates how different data collection methods can come into the analysis and add interesting difference to our understanding of a particular genre, against the voices of others. Diaries are particularly useful because they speak directly of the relationship between self and self.

Summarising the argument

In the analysis, it is important to regularly summarise the argument and to signpost to the reader where the argument should go. In this case, so far, I have outlined the various ways in which the Romantic genre is expressed by the different artists. They give us a sense of creating ideas, objects and time–space, and of experiencing the mystery of deep processes in doing so. By including the quotations, we get a sense of their unique voices, intoned with their particular truths. In Table 5.3, I have summarised some of the main points from these quotations, although this is not necessarily reflective of all their data.

At this point, after gaining some sense of what a major genres sounds like in lived experience, it is important to look at the experience of making art from the perspective of another genre – to help gain a sense of the variety and complexity of the experience. More traditionally, doing this is a form of 'deviant case analysis'. 'Deviant case analysis' is an important method in discourse analysis that acts as a form of validation (Potter and Wetherell, 1987) by looking at variance within the data and trying to account for it. In a dialogical approach, however, the term 'deviant' is a little problematic. This is because the focus is on the intrinsic difference between voices. For this reason, it is important to look for quite different or even opposing genres, at a large scale, in terms of how they add to an emerging interpretation of the experience. In the section below, I describe this as 'dialogue with another genre'.

Dialogue with another genre

In this section, I analyse a contrasting genre with the aim of deepening the analysis done so far. This is achieved using background reading, sound bites and quotations. In terms of content, I look at how the relationship between

Table 5.3 Summary of the Romantic genre

Donna	Ina	Kevin
Magic and lyric admiration. Time and space as transformative. Outside-in, singular truth.	Mystery and vocation. Making the invisible visible. Epic space of inner motivation and outer authenticity. Divided, second voice.	Ode to steel. Swept along in space – involvement of personality. Outside-in, singular truth.

the inner life and outer world of making a piece rests up against a wider 'outer' world of business and professionalism. This, in turn, indicates a Professional genre that is quite different from the Romantic genre and they work well to contextualise each other.

If the Romantic genre can be characterised as one where the means of the activity are also the ends of the activity, then the Professional genre is one where there are specific means to specific ends. The 'business side of things', the role of exhibiting, professional versus naïve artists, the role of the public were all recurrent features of the 'key moments'. These all seemed very 'real world' issues in contrast to the romance, mystery and mysticism of making.

Background reading

Perhaps the most seminal academic work here is Howard Becker's (1984) description of the professional art world. He describes the 'art world' as a loosely connected set of conventional relationships between galleries, artists, art training colleges, patterns of distributions, standards of taste and the State. In this world, there exists a hierarchy between 'the greats', the competent professionals, the mavericks and the naïve artists. Naïve artists are those who do what resembles art but are unconnected to any history or convention. The Art World, under Becker's description, acts as a powerful force in producing types of work and determining the value of this work. He highlights the role of the social world in producing the artists' creative work.

What Becker (1984) does not highlight and what I am interested in exploring here is how particular artists talk about and experience this conventional, professional art world as a contrast to the Romantic way of experiencing it. I do this by referring to a loose 'Professional genre' as a way artists have of speaking about this 'real world'.

Table of sound bites

In Table 5.4, we are given a taste of just how the 'Professional genre' contrasts with the inner experience characteristic of the Romantic genre. In thia table I have included 'sound bites' of the artists speaking in various ways about their professional life as it relates to exhibiting in galleries, making money, other non-professional painters and the reactions of the public. It is also important to point out that this half of the write-up is following the same pattern as the initial half. Sound bites are followed by quotations.

Table 5.4 'Sound bites' from the Professional genre

Kevin	Donna	Ina
• the way they [the gallery] work out their percentage like, two eighty and I get one twenty and I'm doing all the fucking work. • its very lah de dah here now, you know.	• His [husband's work] makes money, mine doesn't HAVE to make money but the thing that is important to me is (pause one sec) I LOVE my job. • maybe I'm not hugely ambitious I don't know.	• I destroyed the love of painting by trying to stick to the rules, trying to live up to the past greats. • I <u>n</u>eed that ex<u>tra</u> angle, you know…somebody to come down and look at it Professionally.

Further quotations

In what follows, I present three further quotations where each artist articulates a different kind of discourse and genre from their previous quotations. I am including all three for the sake of completeness. The introduction of a different quotation by the same participant is a means of putting these two quotations into dialogue with each other as well as with the other participants.

In the following extract, for instance, Kevin complains that he does all the work and the gallery take a hefty commission. The Romantic experience we saw earlier co-exists with a more professional, business experience as well. Similar to previous quotations, in this one we are also looking to see the points of connection between subjectivity and language through the details of time–space, speech type and genre.

Kevin: Extract 4

K: like, I'm still, my work from X sell for two eighty, the way they work out their percentage like, two eighty and I get one twenty and I'm doing all the fucking work

R: yeah and they're

K: whereas I, you know I'm kinda, I'm not even, I'm not even happy at that price, its, with the percent and all that, its the only way I can make a sale of it

R: right

K: you know, uhm, I mean I, I got, I sold a load of work last month which is great but I'm not kind of, I'm spending all of that, a lot of that on frames

R: Jesus

K: it sort of like pays, but even if it pays, if it pays for itself, I start to develop in a few years where it can pay for me to uhh

R: yeah

K: you know, do trips and travel and that, but Jesus
R: yeah
K: you know if I wanted money, I would have been doing accountancy or something.

The Professional genre is one that refers to the hard facts of financial exchange – one of profit, loss and exploitation. Here, this genre is uniquely combined with Kevin's sense of injustice, giving an intonation of annoyance, perhaps even outrage. We build on each other's sense of shock about the injustice (I react by exclaiming 'Jesus' which Kevin subsequently repeats). He speaks of this world as an unfair, unjust world. One where he does 'all the fucking work' and yet the gallery seem to take half of what it sells for. What is more, most of the money he does earn ends up going back on the frames. This is a passive 'double-voiced' discourse characterised by two truths – the way the art world is and the way it ought to be.

In terms of time and space, it is a world quite different from the magical, cathartic 'flow' of 'beating the fuck' out of the steel. Instead of imposing himself upon the material, he is being imposed upon by the weight of the art world, with its conventions. While he is not happy with the price, the only way he can sell it is at this cheap price. He is trapped by the outside pressures of this space. He does not work to make money, however, and we can sense a nod towards a Romantic genre in this assertion. Accountancy would be better for making money. He rails against this but is relatively powerless.

It is also a space that is quite different from the mundane space of making art. In Table 5.4, I have referred to a moment where he calls a gallery opening very 'lah de dah' – to signify posh and different from the ordinary world. The gallery space is not only one where business people take up to half the value of the work, it is also a hierarchical space, where money brings a certain posh social class.

Time, here, involves a dual aspect. On the one hand, there is the repetitiveness of this art world – one where the profit goes back into purchasing of the frames. The previous month seems to be a 'peak' here as he sold a lot of work, so perhaps this circular repetition of making to re-invest involves peak and trough moments. We also get a sense of a linear time. This is a bit more uncertain, however. Possibly in the future, he may have developed the work to a point where it can pay for him to go travelling – to make more art.

Overall, the Professional genre of selling, buying, re-investing and exploiting suggests a time and space of hard realism in Kevin's case. It is difficult to work against. It is quite different from the magic realism we saw earlier and suggests that this magical realism does not come easily. Ultimately its products are brought into the 'real world' of the art world and out of this negotiation, the time and space for creativity and the pleasure of making may be that bit easier or that bit harder to achieve.

While for Kevin the Professional genre is given an intonation of injustice and a sense of outside, powerful pressures that are difficult to struggle against, in Donna's case, the professional genre acquires a softer intonation. Part of this is clear from Table 5.4, but in the extract below we can examine it in a little more detail. Like the first half, this is done with the aim of showing the different sounds of a genre, and the ideas it contains, as it is intoned by the speaking subject.

Donna: Extract 5

D: well, I think, you know, I went to college in my early thirties annd, you know, meanwhile my husband is very successful in business

R: hmm

D: so where we are at this stage now, is I do what I do, which is my kind of passion and he does what he does

R: right

D: his makes money, mine doesn't HAVE to make money but the thing that is important to me is (short pause) I LOVE my job

R: yeah

D: and I want just to work full time at what I'm doing

R: yes

D: and I do but I don't have a problem of EARNING with it so you know I think I'm quite a SNAIL in life in my own way you know

R: right

D: (clears throat) and maybe I'm not hugely ambitious I don't know

R: yeah

D: but kinda my bottom line is I want to work and I want to keep making and generally, I mean, especially the glass area in Ireland, there's not so many people doing it

R: yeah

D: and it seems to be relatively easy to get it exhibited

In the extract above, Donna also enters into the business side of the art world. However, in this extract, the world is less pressurised than it is for Kevin. This is because her husband's job makes money and that takes the pressure off her to make money. She is not 'hugely ambitious' but, as we see in Table 5.4 above, 'aware' of her CV, in a mild way. Elsewhere she also says that there is a sense in which exhibiting her work helps to 'validate' her 'job'.

Donna's appropriation of the Professional genre involves strong echoes of the more poetic and romantic – as we already saw in her earlier extract – giving her discourse a sense of active double-voicedness. Indeed, depending on how you read it, one could say that the professional voice comes through in the structure of the discourse but the overall sentiment is romantic. So, she speaks of having a 'bottom line' but the bottom line relates to her desire to keep making. She speaks of her 'job' but she does not have the 'problem of earning'; she speaks of 'working full time' but it is driven by her passion and love rather than by money.

In terms of time, the career trajectory, normally structured by teleology and entelechy in a Professional genre (climbing the ladder, driven by ultimate success) is mixed in with being a 'snail in life' and not being 'hugely ambitious' and being 'mild'. She leaves open the possibility that perhaps she is ambitious ('I don't know'), which echoes the mystery of self-understanding common to the Romantic genre but runs against the assumption of ambition common to a Professional genre.

In terms of space, the particular world of glass making seems to be a less crowded space than other areas of art. Donna says it is 'relatively easy' to get exhibited because there are not many doing glass. Of course, this may be modesty on her part, but it adds to the impression of an outer world that is spacious and allows her to exhibit. Through exhibiting, her job is 'validated' by the response of others, but this is payment by kind – by means of reaction to the work, rather than financial payment *per se*.

Overall, one can see from this extract that the world of art making is not immune to the world of money and finance and that this world impinges on art making by creating 'pressure'. Kevin feels this pressure as a weight, while Donna feels the lack of financial pressure as a relief. Both Kevin and Donna appropriate this professional world in ways that suggest the ongoing interaction of a genre with the life history and experience of the individual artist.

The third artist described here, Ina, also appropriates the Professional genre, but gives a different understanding of her relationship to it through her reflexive questioning of art history.

Ina: Extract 6

R: would there be any artists in particular that would influence your work?

I: this is something that used to uhm <u>disturb</u> me a lot because I'm <u>not</u>, I, I I'm not uhm passionate abou<u>t</u> art or artists or art history, I'm not. MY uhm, my, I don't draw my passion from looking at other work, I mean I'm not, in the sense that I'm very conne<u>c</u>ted I'm, my, my influence really is on a different level, and I went through doing a, a whole diploma in art history in order to fi<u>n</u>d out like, you know

R: your niche

I: you know, where is it, you know

R: yeah

I: trying to find out why I was not passionate about it, why I was not
      relating to this sort of thing that you had to be passionate about if you
      were an artist and uhm really on a level, what interested ME more were
      I suppose the art of the uhmm insane, art from a LEVel I suppose, either
      that was completely naked, that was completely honest that was com-
      pletely without an agenda that had no ahh motivation, either you
      know, I don't know, it was not connected with the visual, I look on the
      visual art profession as being you know, I I dislike the profession, I
      DISlike ( ) I dislike the structure or, or the movement of these

Here, with Ina, we get a sense of intense conflict between the Professional
and the Romantic. The Professional genre – of hierarchy, training, career
and history – is present but is intoned by a Romantic concern with passion.
The Professional genre does have an active presence in the extract despite
the internal movement away from it in the discourse. It touches on 'active
double-voiced discourse' in that we have two truths actively juxtaposed. It
disturbed Ina a lot that she did not have passion for the greats and for the
art world. She went on a journey, doing a diploma in art history to try to
understand this more. She now regrets it. She dislikes the profession. The
hierarchy of art is referred to but as something that she dislikes. Instead, she
admires compulsive art, insane art, obsessive art and art from people who
have not been exposed to the structures and history of the professional
world. At the same time, however, she also refers to the idea of professional
artists coming around to this idea of 'art brute' being real. There is an effort
to connect 'art brute' back to the professional art world.

   While the movement, in this extract, is one of return and of honesty, the
space is characterised by a lack of external pressure. Such pressure comes
from the art world pushing things, such as appreciation of artists. At the
same time, however, this authentic, genuine art, is not entirely free or playful, as it is in Donna's and Kevin's case. Instead it is a space marked by
internal pressure or inner necessity, need and impulse to communicate. It is
also a very clear space that the viewer can directly see the visual.

   In this extract, then, we get quite a different sense of the Professional
genre. The movement and structure and hierarchy are all there, as they are
with Kevin and Donna, yet they exist as a source of confusion, of dislike and
as a path towards error. The extract is framed by a contrasting Romantic
concern with passion, impulse, necessity and the roots of creativity.

Table 5.5   Outline summary of the Professional genre

Participant	Genres and discourses	Emotional register	Time-space elaboration	Context
Kevin	Professional Business – profit and loss. Passive double-voiced discourse.	Irritation at art world.	Hard realism. Career movement. Pressurised space.	Galleries.
Donna	Professional. Poetic language. Active double-voiced discourse.	Love of job, enthusiasm for making.	Lack of financial pressure to perform. Internal freedom.	Her financial situation.
Ina	Professional. Active double-voiced discourse.	Alienation and connection.	Internal pressure. Back to roots.	Art history.

Summary of the Professional genre

As part of the process of signposting the argument and looking at differences between major genres, it is a clarifying exercise to sum up the analysis. My interpretation of various appropriations of the Professional genre in describing the professional art world are briefly summarised in Table 5.5.

Discussion

In this chapter, I have demonstrated one of the ways in which a write-up of a dialogical method can be organised. Part of this project was bureaucratic. It involved systematically going through all of the data and identifying the 'key moments' or utterances that could conceivably throw light on the particular question I had in mind. This was an iterative process – starting broad and narrowing down. These were then analysed in terms of their genre, their emotional register, their time–space dimensions and the context of the utterance. From here, I was able to collate a summary table that identified the major genres that were used in the articulation of experience.

The genres, however, were not studied in the abstract. Instead, it is also important to understand the intonation and the emotional colouring of the discourse. When we look at Donna's magic realism or Kevin's intense, embodied interaction with the material, we see how their art work reflects a whole way of life. This has not only found its expression in a genre, but has also given that genre a unique colouring – as for example with Donna's unique appropriation of the professional, business discourse or Ina's romantic opposition to it.

One particularly interesting feature of this kind of analysis is that through the emotional intonation, one also gains a sense of the presence of different truths. This links to the emphasis on 'outside-in' discourse and 'double-voiced discourse'. In some of the extracts, a singular 'truth' was very present, while in others, alternative truths were also given a presence. For example, Kevin, in his irritation at the gallery world, shaped it as an unjust space. On the other hand, we also got a feel for more active double-voiced discourse; for example, when Ina spoke of the impact of romantic, non-educated 'art brute' on the professional art world.

An effort was made to connect genres to an academic literature – to move away from the particular artist to general history. It is important to gain a sense of the movement of a genre in history and some of the literature it connects to. This integration of theory acts to further deepen our understanding of the genre. The movement between theory, the question and the reading of the extracts is a more charismatic than bureaucratic exercise. There are many ways of doing such an analysis and many alternative extracts and alternative questions could have been answered. At the same time, I tried to summarise the various interpretations using tables.

While there are some clear advantages to a dialogical approach to discourse (highlighting the intonation, the genre, the chronotope), this demonstration has also shown up some of the limitations. We can see that quotations are selected on the basis of how they help the coherence of the argument. While every effort is made to substantiate the quotation with other bits and pieces of the data, it is not easy for the reader to establish how representative it is. It is difficult to meditate in detail on how much theory to use or indeed how many participants and extracts. This is a difficulty with qualitative approaches in general that depend on interpreting a text. An explicit methods section in the write-up is one place to address these issues.

This chapter has looked at artists and their creation of inner and outer worlds of meaning, through the use of 'sound bites', 'summary tables' and 'quotations'. The next chapter will concentrate on the use of another feature of this kind of analysis, relevant to the write-up as well. This is the dialogue with anticipated but absent others within a dialogue. I will illustrate this through reference to qualitative data from a large health care organisation. This data was generated using focus groups. This should provide an interesting contrast to the one-to-one interview that formed the bulk of the analysis here. The analysis, in particular, lends itself to other tools, such as the 'created dialogue' that may also be relevant to the write-up.

Further reading

Hicks, D. (2002) *Reading Lives: Working Class Children and Literacy Learning.* New York: Teachers' College Press.

McCarthy, J., Sullivan, P. and Wright, P. (2006) Culture, personal experience and agency. *British Journal of Social Psychology*, 45(2): 421–39.

Sullivan, P. and McCarthy, J. (2007) The relationship between self and activity in the context of artists making art. *Mind, Culture and Activity*, 14(4): 235–52.

Sullivan, P. and McCarthy, J. (2009) An experiential account of the psychology of Art. *Psychology of Aesthetics, Creativity, and the Arts*, 3(3): 181–7.

6

DOUBLE-VOICED DISCOURSE AND
FOCUS GROUP DATA

The aim of this chapter is to demonstrate how double-voiced discourse can be used to analyse focus group data. As we saw in Chapter 3, in double-voiced discourse, there is more than one addressee in an utterance. For example, someone can address an interviewer but also address an absent other at the same time. Different focus groups within an organisation can be very anticipative and responsive to each other. Methodologically, this allows the analyst to put these anticipated responses into direct dialogue. It also allows the analyst to examine how anticipated others help participants to make sense out of their place in the organisation.

I highlight how it is possible to bring various absent others in double-voiced discourse together via a 'created dialogue'. This is a new tool of analysis introduced in this chapter. In a created dialogue, the anticipated other can be put in direct contact with the actual other. This allows an actual dialogue to take place, on paper, where the groups are no longer anticipating but directly responding to each other. I also show how this tool can be embedded within a standard write-up, answering a particular research question, and elaborated and strengthened through the use of quotations and summary tables.

To help make the analysis more concrete, I am reporting on focus groups conducted with different sections of a large healthcare organisation (HCO) as it faced a large-scale restructuring (see Sullivan and McCarthy, 2008, for more detail on the study). These focus groups included a 'corporate management' team a 'mental health' team and a 'disability services' team. The groups are in dialogue with other groups (e.g., through irony and parody), with each other (e.g., through building a consensus) and with the interviewer. While the data in the previous chapter also had much 'double-voiced' discourse, the data here particularly lends itself to a discussion of the 'dialogue within dialogue' in the analysis or the multiple addressees within utterances.

The data were transcribed using a typist. The original audio data were destroyed before I listened to the recording (as I became involved in the project a few years later) and the transcription that is available does not record emphasis in speech and various other markers outlined in Chapter 4. This leads to the added difficulty of not knowing who exactly is speaking in the group at any given time. This can still be worked out to some extent by the references group members make to each other's talk, but in some sections of the data it is still unclear who is speaking. Nonetheless, the data are very rich in terms of speech genres and double-voiced discourse.

In the analysis of this data, I settled on the general question: how do members of the organisation experience their identity amidst organisational change? The original commissioned research and the data that are generated from it revolves around these issues. I read over the focus groups a number of times and subsequently selected 'key moments' and interesting 'sound bites'. In the corporate team, I selected twelve 'key moments'; in the 'disability services', I selected twenty three; and in the 'mental health focus group' I selected eighteen 'key moments'. I then looked at each of these moments in terms of the type of discourse and genre, the emotional register, the time–space dimensions and the context that the extract was referring to.

I present the analysis according to two broad genres: (1) a folk psychology genre; and (2) a carnival genre. With regard to the first genre, the moderator asked each group why the staff, in general, comes into work. What is their motivation? In the process of answering this, the members ascribe a number of different motivations to other groups as well describing their own motivations. Common-sense ideas around the inner psychological qualities that lie behind what people do are known as 'folk psychology' – literally, the psychology that the folk use to make sense of each other (Bruner, 1990). These common-sense ideas may be distilled versions of formal psychology, philosophy and other disciplines. For example, the disability team suggest that the corporate team are motivated to add to the existing layers of bureaucracy in order to justify their own existence (in a mix of existentialism and game theory).

In carnival, as with irony and parody, the official world of experience is not rejected. Instead, carnival has a more ambivalent relationship with the official world. It decrowns it, exposes it to ridicule and laughter, but also may act to regenerate and refresh the official world. In this context, the official world does not have to weigh heavily on participants but can be experienced as intertwined with an unofficial, carnival space. This intertwining may offer an authentic space of how their job actually appears on a day-to-day level.

A folk psychology genre

In this section, I examine the relevance of the 'created dialogue' to the analysis of a major genre – in this case, the 'folk psychology' genre. I also show how this can be complemented through the use of quotation. While the created dialogue shows how anticipated others can be put into contact, the quotations highlight the role of the absent other in structuring the discourse.

The analysis of the data showed that the 'disability' team and the 'mental health' team regularly ascribe different motivations for why the 'corporate team' (or management team) do the job in the particular way that they do. In assessing the motivations for the corporate team, they make psychological judgements – looking for internal explanations for outer decisions. The corporate team, in turn, anticipate and rebut these motivations (although they do not hear them). They also guess at the motivations for why people within the organisation do their job the particular way they do. For example, they suggest that people are motivated out of a vocational commitment. These motivations, are, in turn, anticipated and rebutted by the 'disability' and 'mental health' team. As such, there is a dialogue with, on one side, the 'disability' and 'mental health' team, and on the other side, the 'corporate team' (although all of the focus groups were done separately). It is possible to present this dialogue with the different teams as if they did hear each other's folk psychology, as part of the analysis.

Introducing the 'created dialogue'

The sound bites discussed in Chapters 4 and 5 provide the starting point for the created dialogue. Sound bites are decontextualised and cherry-picked but nonetheless they allow the introduction of many participant voices into the analysis. These sound bites are written down as part of the familiarisation with the data. The created dialogue involves taking sound bites from different contexts and placing them together in the one context. This new context is defined by a common subject of conversation. This is possible when the interviews or focus groups ask generally similar questions to different participants.

In terms of a write-up, what this means is that we can potentially start the analysis of the 'folk psychology' genre with a created dialogue. In the dialogue below, CT stands for 'corporate team', DT for 'disability team' and MHT for 'mental health team'. I have also added some text to make it more coherent as a conversation. My additions are marked in bold. The rest of the text is taken from the three separate focus groups. This is illustrated below:

A created dialogue around motivation

Mark, CT: I mean I think there is a vocational aspect to our people

Mary, DT: you know this word vocation comes up and I think that the fact that we do actually care about our clients is greatly abused by management on a regular basis because they under fund us, they give us insufficient resources, they don't listen to what we say, they fail to communicate with us.

Joan, DT: I mean it's lovely for health board managers if you are considered to be caring.

Michael, CT: that sort of hints that well we haven't changed at all and I think that the organisation and its management have moved significantly from the traditional public service civil servant bureaucratic type to a far more business-like approach

DT: **(which really means)** in order to keep their job and in order to get kudos and whatever they just want to get to B you know they forget about how to get there

Patrick, CT: well I don't think the people out there fully realise or understand the actual diversity that we're coping with

MHT: **(you have a point)** talking to a colleague in other health boards they would be quite envious of the services we have, the type of team work we have, the decision-making process

CT: you have to have somebody to blame in the system. Okay, so so you blame the managerial class.

MHT: **(but)** often you have people making plans who have no concept of the impact on the ground of what they are talking about, they have no clue whatsoever

CT: **(we do try, its that staff)** don't want to get involved because: A they're too busy making money sorry seeing patients and dealing with lists and that's the right answer for that; and second of all, if they get involved then by implication they become part of the problem rather than keeping distant from it.

DT: **(I beg to differ)** it's a very authoritative style of management, there's no consultation going on for the most part

CT: you know the problem is they never say to you outright so you can actually have a really good row with them, it's always by insinuation

This created dialogue had to be redrafted a number of times to make it as coherent as possible with minimum added markers. A number of sound bites were removed and others inserted. As explained in more detail in Chapter 8, the guiding principle behind evaluating the content of the created dialogue is to read over it and see if the perspective of each group makes sense so that even if one did not agree with a view, one could still understand it. It was also important to give as equal space as possible to each different team.

The analytic value of the created dialogue

In terms of what this tool does, we can see that it gives some flavour of the ways in which the members ascribe motivations to each other, contest these motivations, disagree, agree and generally work out the meaning of taken-for-granted assumptions such as 'vocation', 'bureaucracy' and 'decision-making'. It directly presents data but it is more than 'raw data'. It is a form of analysis that allows the reader to understand the anticipations that different groups have to each other.

For example, the 'corporate team' reply to the accusation that they do not know what they are doing by saying that they exist to soak up blame in the system and that other teams do not want to 'become part of the problem' by making decisions. Members of the 'mental health team' and the 'disability team' argue back against this view by saying that they are not consulted enough ('there's no consultation going on'). The folk psychology appears ambivalent in places – sometimes seeing the value in the activity and motivation of others and other times dismissing or resisting this.

This ambivalence is particularly clear at the beginning of the extract where the corporate team ostensibly compliment the vocational commitment of the staff in the organisation. Mary and Joan in the disability team anticipate and resist the corporate team's folk psychology. While this could be viewed as a compliment, Mary answers back with her own folk psychology of what motivates the corporate team to make this linkage to 'vocation'. 'Vocation' is a tool of control and abuse. It is a way for management to give insufficient resources and to underfund services. Joan elaborates with an ironic judgement that it is 'lovely' for managers if you are considered to be caring.

This ambivalence is more generally reflected in the tone of the discourse, particularly in the irony and the joking slips, which produces a two-sided view of the members – e.g., 'they're too busy making money sorry seeing patients'. Here the official view of doctors being concerned with patient care is mixed in with a more unofficial view, slipping in as a pretend Freudian slip that they are too busy making money. Similarly, 'it's lovely for health board managers if you are considered to be caring' suggests that health board managers both cynically take advantage of being considered 'caring', but by doing so give themselves a 'lovely' existence. This kind of joking and insinuation is also mixed in with more direct complaints and compliments. Interestingly, the habit of speaking through insinuation is picked up by a member of the corporate team as being unhelpful – although, as we can see here, the CT also make insinuations.

The ambivalent tone and the changing, contested motivations ascribed to different groups (e.g., management motivated only to keep their jobs or to create an organisation the envy of others) give this created dialogue a sense of a 'polyphony' of voices – one where they have equal status. Perhaps more importantly, it is also one where they feel each other's judgements, answer back and work through the ideas they contain. The outer polyphony constructed here, reflects an inner, psychologically complex and ambivalent 'inner' polyphony, where the addressee is hidden but is nonetheless significant in shaping the discourse of the participants. Bringing this out may be useful in a final report for the participants to read but is much more difficult to achieve in real life.

A direct confrontation and discussion between the groups, in reality, may be very difficult because of a felt power imbalance. Indeed, insinuation may be the safest way to express discontent. The result of this, however, if we are to take a trusting attitude to the corporate team talk, is that they also are the ones who can feel victimised and without power – 'the whipping boys' (as they say elsewhere), the necessary part of the system that functions as a focus for blame more than anything else.

We can see here that the 'created dialogue' works by taking the absent addressees in an utterance and giving them a space to directly answer back to accusations, allusions and insinuations as well as to add their view to general issues that concern them.

The absent other in double-voiced quotations

In the 'created dialogue', the anticipated voices and viewpoints of different teams enter into direct dialogue with each other. However, there is also a possibility of analysing the dialogue with an anticipated other through looking at the role of inserted quotations, from this absent other, into speech. An inserted quotation is a form of 'direct speech' – e.g., He said that 'x'. This helps contextualise how the intense addressivity of the created dialogue above is also evident within an original quotation. In a write-up, the 'created dialogue' is only one analytic tool that, due to its imaginary quality, probably ought to be contextualised by more traditional data methods.

In this particular context, it helps further to understand the motivations that teams ascribe to each other.

In the extract below, a member of the 'disability team' discusses what she would like to see happening with the management structure and their style of encouragement. As part of her explanation, she brings the various voices of management into her discourse.

Extract 1: A discussion around motivation

Ann: Rather than 'oops we have to cutback, let's review your post now, we'll see, oh we're going to cut back these, we're going to cut out a few hours out of this with no understanding' so it comes back to listening to people who can justify 'this works', it's not just 'this is the way we want to do it', 'this actually works, this has a positive impact' and what you want is, you want to satisfy clients

This extract is a nice illustration of the various dialogues between self and the actual, anticipated and ideal other, outlined in Chapter 3. The extract begins with Ann bringing a manager's voice into her discourse, in a parodic way, humorously exaggerating the perceived ignorance of the management – 'oops, we have to cut back ... we're going to cut a few hours out of this with no understanding'. In doing so, management is presented as an unpredictable, ignorant force of destruction, but also as a clown-like figure, merrily admitting that they act 'with no understanding'. While normally the manager may say 'we have to cut back' in a tone of gravitas, in the extract above, this is prefaced by the word 'oops' – again turning this serious situation into a clownish act.

This anticipated manager is then contrasted with an ideal manager (super-addressee) who is not directly given a voice but who would listen to the people and justify change on the basis of listening to people who know what they are talking about (who can justify 'this works'). The 'this works' evokes a plaintive voice within this discourse – 'this actually works, this has a positive impact'. Such practitioners are faced with an actual management who employ a monological, authoritative discourse, 'this is the way we want to do it', without listening to the obvious point that the aim of the organisation is 'to satisfy clients'. These various dialogues in Ann's discourse suggest a lively 'micro-dialogue' taking place. A micro-dialogue, as we saw in Chapter 3, recreates and dialogues with the voices of others – ideal management, actual management, other team members.

In this micro-dialogue, management are given a significant voice. However, the voice is overwhelmed with the intonations of the author which not only serves to decrown management of their authority, but also works to portray the management as acting randomly to instigate change. This parody is also addressed to the moderator and the rest of the members of the focus group. In this sense, there is both an external dialogue with others physically present and an internal dialogue, within the discourse, with management.

Summarising the analysis

From the created dialogue and the quotation above, we are beginning to get a picture of what the analysis looks like as well as getting a taste of the intense interaction the groups have with each other. In a summary table, removing the voices, we get another look at what the groups think of each other, more than how they express this. Table 6.1 is organised in terms of the motivations the groups ascribe to each other as well as to themselves.

I have inserted Table 6.1 as a means of demonstrating how absent others structure the discourse of the participants. That is, how they are concerned and intensely dialogue with each other's assumed motivations. We can understand this by looking both at how the sound bites can make contact with each other and by analysing relevant quotations. There is not an uncomplicatedly 'good' and 'bad' picture that emerges from the organisational structure. Instead, there is an ambivalent mix of back-hand compliments, laughter, overt and parodic criticism that permeates the talk.

Table 6.1 Motivation of the different groups

Motivation	Corporate team	Disability team	Mental health team
Others' motivations	Members on the 'ground' motivated by:	Management motivated to:	Management motivated to:
	• a vocational commitment. • a professional commitment. • money. • a sense of 'ownership'. Motivated to: • make management the 'whipping boys'.	• justify their own existence. • make uninformed decisions. • manipulate the word 'vocation'. • make the most out of resources.	• produce unimportant statistics. • introduce senseless bureaucracy and massive waste. • create a system to be proud of.
Self-motivation	Management motivated to: • safeguard the best of a local tradition. • improve the service. • make the service accountable to auditors.	Members motivated by: • caring. • professional interest.	Members motivated by: • money (joke). • team support.

So far, the created dialogue and double-voiced quotations have shown the active dialogical relationship groups have with each other – particularly in terms of their efforts to understand the actions and motivations of each other (their folk psychology). We have seen that parody and argument feature heavily through direct quotation of others. This goes some way towards answering the question: how do members of the organisation experience their identity amidst organisational change?

A carnival genre in double-voiced discourse

In this section, I examine a 'carnival' genre in double-voiced discourse. Carnival is best thought of as a tool that opens up the possibility for engaging with the different sides of a concept, idea or person; sides that are normally shut away from us. Bakhtin (1984 [1929]) makes the point that the fear of violating social convention makes it difficult to engage frankly with the rules and practices of a hierarchy, but in a carnival situation, where authority and power are reconfigured in a different way, then we can sense and feel the unofficial side of the hierarchy of power.

The carnival engagement with both the official and the unofficial world is perhaps most relevant to the experience of time and space. Space is important in terms of how the members understand the hierarchical structure of the organisation. In the previous extract, for example, we saw an official hierarchy with managers and an unofficial hierarchy where the managers are not professionals but clowns. Parody is particularly interesting here. Similarly, as we will see in a moment, change is presented as both meaningless (change with no impact) and meaningful (initiatives that do have an impact).

To explore carnival, I will draw again on the 'created dialogue' and 'double-voiced quotations'. My aim in doing this is both to show the utility of the 'created dialogue' and the ways in which, in combination with quotations, it can help in the dialogical analysis of qualitative data.

The created dialogue below helps us to imagine how the various members of the organisation work out the meaning of time and space in relationship with each other.

A created dialogue around different sides to the organisation

DT: there are a lot of people who are very creative at the very top layer of management and there are a lot of hardworking people on the ground and a lot of wasters in between

CT: (actually) there is a very clear hierarchy and a very clear line down to the actual production of a good or whatever.

MHT: **(but that)** feels like power and control in a very kind of scary way you know. It is like far removed from the client.

CT: there are about seventy thousand people go through the casualty ... there's an enormous amount of work being done very very successfully

MHT: all I am just saying the amount of bureaucratic, the bureaucracy is swamping us and a lot of it is unnecessary

DT: the reason the health board is there is to help the people who have disabilities or problems or whatever. It is not to have all these fancy meetings or in-training whatever

CT: we're subject to audit, control auditor general before that local government auditors, we've never had any scandals on the audit side

MHT: a paper trail is important **(alright)**

DT: **(but still)** one manager will say 'no, it not mine here' and another manager will say 'no' and you know its just going on, its toing and froing which slows things down and delays things

CT: I think if we didn't exist, they'd have to invent us anyway, you know so it keeps the doctors happy making their millions out of the public system, it keeps the nursing staff sweet, it keeps everybody else cosy in their world

DT: **(except that)** Most people the higher up you go don't know what it is to walk into somebody's home where the child is sitting in a wheelchair

CT: **(not so, let me give you an example)** we have on the acute side made enormous strides in deinstitutionalising mental health services ... without almost any support from our professionals

Like the previous created dialogue, this too underwent a number of different revisions. It involved placing various sound bites together in terms of a common subject – the structure of the organisation. Some guiding assumptions included giving the different groups as equal a space as possible and re-reading it for coherence as well as for what different positions could add or challenge to each other. The evaluation of this is discussed in more detail in Chapter 8.

In terms of the value of this created dialogue, we can see that there is a common anticipation and addressivity to each other's ideas, values and feelings in the various groups. There is an ambivalent movement between official and unofficial views of the organisation.

The unofficial view of management is that they are a bunch of clowns and dead wood at the top, getting in the way of each other ('one manager will say "it's not mine here"...'), slowing things down and introducing change through unnecessary policies and bureaucracy ('the bureaucracy is swamping us'). The management are seen to misunderstand the point of the health care organisation. They have meetings and training rather than actually helping people. The meetings are mockingly referred to as 'fancy meetings', suggesting that they are abstract and divorced from the actual needs of the clients.

Although the corporate team do not hear this carnivalesque view of the organisation, they anticipate it and counter it. They present an official view of a clear hierarchy ('there is a very clear hierarchy'). They appeal to audits and accountability ('there are about seventy thousand people go through casualty'), which is anticipated and acknowledged by a member of the 'mental health team' as a 'paper trail'. This agreement suggests that there is some degree of ambivalence in the carnival genre – with the management decrowned as useless but also given some sympathy. Management also give concrete examples of where they have instigated change, such as deinstitutionalising the mental health services.

The corporate team offers its own unofficial, carnivalesque view of the organisation. In its appropriation of carnival, those at the 'frontline' make millions out of the health system. They are seen to have all the power and control, in contrast to the assertion from the disability team that power and control comes from the top. The self-serving, money-making people need management as a feature of the organisation. There is a suggestion that they would, in fact, invent management if they did not already exist.

Here, within the created dialogue, all the groups give an unofficial, carnivalesque picture of the organisation. For management, it is one where the hierarchy is turned back to front and the front line has the power. For the other groups, it is one where 'dead wood' hovers around at the top and a swamp is created in the middle. It is also one where the professionals help people and the clients suffer due to organisational incompetence.

Overall, we can see that this second created dialogue brings different voices together that address each other as part of their perception of time and space. It is an imaginary act of bringing different pieces of data in contact with each other. In other ways, it very directly highlights the building of turns that is implicit within traditional discourse analysis. As in the previous section, the value of the created dialogue comes into its own when it is considered alongside longer quotations from within the data set. It is to this that I will now turn.

Carnival within a double-voiced quotation

The 'outer' or intergroup polyphony is highlighted through the created dialogue above. We can also look at how this 'outer' polyphony is a broader reflection of a more internal, intra-group polyphony via the use of further quotations from the data set. As in the previous section, building on the created dialogue by turning to real-life quotations helps to analyse the ambivalence, dilemmas and negotiation of the meaning of time and space for the participants.

As the previous quotation was taken from the disability group, here I examine two quotations from the mental health team and corporate team respectively. This is for the sake of completeness.

Extract 2: A discussion around feedback

Joan: There's no feedback

Moderator: How do you mean and what is feedback?

Joan: Feedback as in uhm, how you are performing as opposed to another health board, how you are performing as a unit, you know. You prepare a report, you prepare statistics and you send them into head office and you never again hear about them. And I am not looking for the tap on the back saying 'that was wonderful and well done'

Male: but you

Unknown: but what I would like is you know, 'this is what we are looking for' or you know you don't get any guidelines or you know, you get these obscure requests for information. When you ring up, like 'are you looking for this or, what exactly, are you looking for this' nobody really knows there is so many layers there. And it is like a Chinese whisper by the time the assistant CEO or whoever has made an initial request by the time it gets to me it could have changed ten times so the information that I actually go away and gather mightn't be actually what was looked for initially at all. And nobody knows exactly what is looked for. And the assistant CEO is so far removed that you daren't pick up the phone and say 'look it, is this what you are looking for?' so I mean I find it totally frustrating as well.

This extract usefully brings out the experience of time and space as it is experienced by a member of the administrative team who prepares information. The future is unknown and linear in so far as she does not know what will happen to the information she prepares. Time travels in only one direction here, with no feedback to her as to what uses the information was put. Similarly, the past is also mysterious in so far as nobody seems to know the details of the information that is sought. She works only in the present, disconnected from these other points in time.

This experience is related to the 'layers' of bureaucracy within the hierarchy of the organisation. In terms of her own subjectivity, there is an epic struggle, marked by frustration, against the 'Chinese whispers' and the disconnection from past and future.

The role of direct speech is particularly interesting throughout the extract. This speech works to bring to life the hidden addressee into the group context. The hidden addressee here consists mainly of line managers. Joan says 'I am not looking for the tap on the back saying "that was wonderful and well done"'. Here, she enters into an imaginary dialogue with a manager who congratulates her. This fantasy dialogue with a line manager, who offers a 'penetrative', reassuring word, is not what she is looking for in reality, however. She is looking for a rational reason for spending so much time at it in the first place. The system is not that rational in her experience. Instead, it is a bizarre system.

Similarly, at the very end of the extract, another speaker brings in an imagined conversation with the assistant CEO as part of her talk to the other group: 'look it, is this what you are looking for?' This speaker 'daren't' have this conversation, however, because the manager is so high up and as a consequence so far removed. It is also interesting that although we do not actually even get his reply in this imaginary dialogue, his voice is there as a silent, fearful presence that the speaker addresses in a colloquial way ('look it'). His silent presence structures her discourse. In this sense, it is an 'inside-out' discourse.

What marks this extract as carnivalesque is the familiar, frank interaction with representatives of the official world, who are normally separated by hierarchy and distance. As re-created figures in a micro-dialogue, however, it is possible to abandon official etiquette and interact with them, unencumbered by fear and convention. Here, although framed in terms of what is not possible in reality, the staff are able to ask direct questions, as if they were addressed to a friend; they can get a 'pat on the back' although they may not look for it; they can pick up the phone to the far removed assistant CEO. This carnivalesque world is possible in the focus group context. Management are transformed to 'heros' of the admin staff's world. At the same time, their fearful presence has an independent truth that can structure the discourse of the participants. In this sense, there is an 'outside-in', 'inside-out' struggle within the discourse.

Management also seek to equalise the interaction between members of the organisation from time to time. One further quotation may help illustrate how management bring others' voices into their discourse, to dialogue with. They do this within an idyllic genre. The idyll is marked by a provincial quality, where everyone knows everyone.

The extract begins with John describing the positive 'side' of the organisation.

Extract 3: An idyllic genre

John: I remember just there a few weeks ago the Minister was in North X, the Minister for Health and I was chatting to her name escapes me now, your lady James, the matron of the hospital in TXX, the hospital of the XXX, yeah Mary and she was due to retire within a couple of weeks and we were announcing the new hospital that we had been pushing for for the last five years and it was now coming but she described it as the happiest day of her life right so here was this lady retiring but the fact that there was a new hospital coming she said that the only way that she could describe her feeling was that it was the happiest day of her life so here's this woman at sixty five years of age who so identifies with the services that she's providing, she's going, she's not going to be part of it but it said something about what the service meant to her.

Moderator: And what do you think that says about the HCO in general like its identity, its culture what is that a reflection of? Why did you choose to tell that story?

John: Well I think it kind of captures following the theme of people going the extra mile, people doing what was needed because there was an identification with the region, with its people and a sense of some kind of identity and I suppose you'd wonder is that what's going to be lost at the heart of it or is it that ownership and identification which drives people.

Moderator: Okay but I mean the people who are working on the ground are still going to be the same people who are working on the ground.

Unknown 1: They will increasingly, a point John made earlier about they'll identify with their own hospital and their own unit, that's what will happen I'm sure, more and more that will happen but that has disadvantages as well as that can lead to disintegration if people become totally focused just on their own unit.

Unknown 2: And become more and more like X [the capital city].
Unknown 3: More anonymous.

X: Anonymised data

The sense of community pride in this extract reveals a more idyllic speech genre being employed to describe the organisation. In this genre, the community are serviced by the HCO and people identify with this organisation. It goes beyond financial remuneration as people are doing a community service – going the 'extra mile' – although as we saw with regard to 'vocation', other staff may resent this assumption of going the extra mile.

The 'extra mile' also speaks to an epic echo within the idyll. In the service of the community, the managers 'had been pushing' for the last five years for the creation of a new hospital. This five years of pushing links a future state (achieving the hospital) to the persistence and stubbornness of the managers.

The idyllic 'side' of the organisation, which co-exists with the more ambivalently experienced side of unofficial hierarchy, is vividly brought to life by a key story that one of members of the group relates. He tells of a story of a woman retiring – Mary. Despite the fact that she was retiring, she was still immensely happy about the news of the new hospital. He reports her speech in a dialogical relationship of agreement with it: 'she said that the only way that she could describe her feeling was that it was the happiest day of her life'. This reported speech does give a sense of the reactions of someone 'on the ground', but is overlain with the approving intonations of the manager who subsequently interprets the reported speech as a sign of someone who 'so identifies with the services she's providing'. It is a good example of what we referred to as 'stylisation' in Chapter 3. The other's voice is explicitly brought in to this manager's speech in a 'passive' way.

This extract brings attention to the 'positive' side of the organisational structure. There is a carnivalesque echo within this but not in the sense of decrowning authority. Instead, it is carnivalesque in the sense that carnival involves a non-hierarchical, collective spirit, where individuals are united by common purpose. Throughout the CT's focus group, there is both praise and abuse of other organisational teams. This extract highlights the affirmative quality of carnivalesque ambivalence. As John remarks, it is a 'side of things' that speaks to the admiration the corporate team have for others in the organisation. Possibly, John is bringing attention to this 'side' because much of the discussion previously has focused on the negative side of managing the organisation.

In this 'side' of the organisation, the members are committed to the organisation in so far as they do not want to 'let it down'. Here, the organisation gives people a sense of 'ownership' which drives them on or motivates them. This is another 'folk psychology' around why members 'on the ground' do things. Motivation is theorised not as arising through a sense of ownership alone, however, but also through a desire to improve the system into the future ('they want to make it better'). The system, in turn, is not conceived as a static hierarchy but more as an organically evolving and changing family unit. Everyone believes in the value of it.

The idyll does have its dangers as well. Even in literature, the idyll is always at risk of disruption. Here, it does not come from within the community; instead it comes from outside the organisation in the guise of the national reorganisation. One of the members of the CT states that the identification people have with the regional health service may be lost by integration to a more 'anonymous', more centralised service. The capital city is presented as the symbol of this anonymity and centralisation. As a big city, comparatively speaking, it has less opportunity, it seems, for a personal investment in the services. There is more risk of individualism as people focus on a particular individual hospital rather than with a whole region. With the loss of the idyll, then, comes the possibility of a loss of the positive 'side' of the organisation – the positive motivations for people doing their work. This pleasant psychology may be replaced by a more indifferent and individualistic psychology – one that seeks only to promote limited, individual interests in a reflection of the anonymous structure of the future.

This extract shows how the management do seem to admire and think highly of the people 'on the ground', both in terms of their motivations and in terms of how the organisation is united by a common purpose. It is a side of the organisation that they clearly think well of and are afraid of losing. As we saw earlier, however, this is only a 'side' and other speech genres – particularly irony and parody – show that there are also other sides to the organisation with which the management struggle.

Summary of carnival analysis

The initial project was concerned with how the organisational culture was structured and how integration to a national structure would be managed. Unsurprisingly, then, much of the data relate specifically to these issues. In Table 6.2, I summarise some of key interpretations arising from the created dialogue and analysis of the quotations.

Table 6.2 gives some indication how the organisation is structured and how change is viewed as a consequence. Roughly speaking, in terms of time and space, we can say that there are two complementary experiential realities. The official structure involves a clear hierarchy between management and frontline staff. Decisions move from the top to the bottom of this

Table 6.2 The teams' perception of space and time

Team	Space	Time
CT	Front line angels.	Idyllic, simple time has passed.
	Back room devils.	Change without support.
	Space to make money for some.	Part of machine bureaucracy in future.
	Group of competent people in charge.	
	Communal space of shared purpose.	
MHT	Management divorced from ground.	Little meaningful change.
	Big grey areas.	Not enough time for real work.
	Scary power at top.	
	Swamp of bureaucracy.	
DT	Bureaucracy divorced from front line.	Change with no impact.
	Non-verbal messages come 'from	Some change with impact.
	above'. No communication up.	Change slowed down by clownish
	Too many managers.	management.
	A lot of 'dead wood' in management.	Not enough time for real work.

hierarchy. There is much middle-management in-between as well. This decision-making sometimes leads to change that has an impact on the ground, but other changes have no impact. Either way, there is an uncertain future with the large-scale restructuring of the organisation.

Discussion

Overall, this chapter has been primarily concerned with demonstrating further tools of the dialogical method in dealing with 'double-voiced' discourse. In particular, I used a data set with a high level of double-voiced discourse to illustrate the benefits of creating a dialogue out of sound bites, contextualising them, elaborating the points that arose through quotation and organising the analysis through a research question.

The benefit of the 'created dialogue' lies in being able to take bits of text out of their actual context and to place them in a new context – a context where the implicit and overt criticisms, compliments and imaginary dialogues are responded to by the actual addressee. In doing this, the analysis builds on Bakhtin's (1984) form of literary analysis where he gives the hidden 'other' a viable presence in his reformulation of a dialogue. It also resonates and builds on Norman K. Denzin's (e.g., 2009) influential 'performative' understanding of qualitative analysis. In this understanding, the writer's task is not to reproduce what is real, but to actively create an experiential (emotional, moral, subjective) text that facilitates understanding of what and who is being studied.

This free and irreverent approach to the text brings some of the various voices of the organisation in contact with each other. In this sense, it is a tool of carnival that allows the researcher to create a new, uninhibited space of agreement and disagreement between participants who may otherwise be constrained by social convention. The result of this contact may make for uncomfortable reading for the participants if it were in the form of a final report. However, reading such a report would also offer the opportunity for members of the organisation to critique and understand each other's perspective. Perhaps what they would not dare to say face to face is brought forward, apart from conventional relationships of authority.

On the other hand, this free form of interpretation also brings with it the risk of selecting bits of text that fit into an artificial dialogue that reflects little apart from the researcher's set of intentions. For example, crucial referents of the participants may be lost through literally taking the talk out of its context. Qualifiers, jokes, subsequent denials and complicated elaborations of a terse statement may all be lost in the creation of a new context.

For this reason, the created dialogue is only used as an illustration here of the kind of dialogical interplay and complicated entanglement the participants appear to have in each other's psychology. It is wise to use more traditional methods as a complement to this more free-flowing and creative activity. For example, in this analysis, I also use summary tables to list the different aspects of the organisation that the focus groups referred to – from their 'folk' theories around the psychology of working in the organisation to their understanding of how the organisation is structured. This could also work as different stages of the analysis – a more bureaucratic and a more charismatic stage, with the latter tethered to the former for added credibility.

I also use fuller length quotations as part of my analysis. My key concern is to look at the moment-to-moment exchanges between members of a particular focus group as well as the absent others who manifested a presence through direct quotations. The speech genre – e.g., carnival, folk psychology – is also important in terms of understanding the intonation or emotional attitudes the speakers brought into their speech.

What this analysis hopefully shows is that the discourse is marked by an active engagement of the members with each other and with the concept of the organisation as it changes into the future. While often the discourse swung between extremes of frustration and fault finding as well some degree of admiration for each other's achievements, there was also a sense of working through this ambivalence both with each other as well as with imagined others. No resolution or 'final word' on this was found as one would expect in a dialogical context. This is not to say that individual members of the group do not have settled or strong attitudes, but as a 'group performance' or 'group dialogue', one gets a sense of a polyphony of ideas that acquire different intonations and 'sides' as they are articulated by various members of the group. Meaning making, here, is an ongoing activity.

Similarly, the analysis has also shown how there is no one 'singular' time and space that is experienced in the organisation. Instead, the organisation moves and changes between a clear hierarchy, an involved family, a more unofficial upside-down hierarchy, a swampland, a detached head from its body and a front and back side as well, to mention just a few different experiences of the organisation. What this shows is that the meaning of the organisation as well as its future direction is a changing landscape for the participants.

One way of describing this changing landscape of experience is to say that the organisation is 'polyphonic'. This provides at least one answer to the original question: How do members of the organisation experience their identity amidst organisational change? Yet there is something a little unsatisfactory about this. It raises again the issue of power in a dialogical framework. Ultimately, the corporate team will probably have more say over the official description of the organisation and its response to change than the 'ground' members will. They have more 'sovereign' power. Yet, we have also seen that there is an intensive reflexive relationship to this position of power – e.g., defence from persecution as well as ambivalence towards the motivations of others. They appear to feel and respond to the insinuations of others. Perhaps a report that brings out these criticisms and suggestions in a more frank and open way may allow the management to admit these other voices into their decision-making processes. This is the point at which a 'polyphonic' organisation becomes a prescriptive ideal to be attained rather than a description of what exists.

While this chapter has been concerned with the negotiation of different voices in a complex and diverse organisation, the next chapter will look at relations of distance and closeness in written, academic commentaries on subjectivity and how these can be analysed. Much of the data here also involved informal commentaries on the subjectivity of others, but in the next chapter I look at how the analysis of more formal, written commentaries can proceed.

Further reading

Bakhtin, M.M. (1984 [1929]) *Problems of Dostoevsky's Poetics.* Ed. and trans. C. Emerson. Minneapolis, MN: University of Minnesota Press.

Bruner, J. (1990) *Acts of Meaning.* Cambridge, MA: Harvard University Press.

Denzin, N. (2009) *Qualitative Inquiry under Fire: Toward a New Paradigm Dialogue.* Walnut Creek, CA: Left Coast Press.

Parker, I. (1990) Discourse: Definitions and contradictions. *Philosophical Psychology,* 3(2): 189–204.

Sullivan, P. and McCarthy, J. (2008) Managing the polyphonic sounds of organizational truths. *Organization Studies,* 29(4): 525–41.

Zappen, J.P. (2004) *The Rebirth of Dialogue: Bakhtin, Socrates and the Rhetorical Tradition.* New York: State University of New York Press.

7

ANALYSING COMMENTARIES ON SUBJECTIVITY

In this chapter, I provide some tools for the analysis of commentaries on subjectivity. This is important if one is interested in the freedom open to the 'other'/'hero' of a commentary to disagree, agree or dialogue with the author. It is also important if one is interested in exploring how the 'author' and 'hero' may reconfigure or shift between texts. Finally, it is useful to understand these shifts if one is interested in the potential of the author to transform the subjectivity of the hero, through giving the hero a particular intonation within their own authorial context.

There are different kinds of commentaries on subjectivity. For example, formal commentaries involve specialist, technical language (e.g., an academic writing about an artist from a dialogical perspective). There are also informal commentaries (e.g., discussing what motivates people over a cup of tea). The specific interest, in this chapter, however, lies in developing methodological tools that will enable an exploration of the changing author–hero (self–other) relationship within formal commentaries on subjectivity.

I develop methodological tools to help analyse such commentaries with the help of two contrasting formal, academic commentaries on the experience of 'schizophrenia'. I analyse these commentaries under four headings – genre, chronotope, re-accentuation and authority. Theoretically, I argue that these headings allow us to foreground the changing self–other dialogue within a commentary. Methodologically, I draw out implications for the qualitative analysis of commentaries more generally.

Intertextuality

Commentaries are a form of intertextuality. In this section, I discuss intertextuality to help contextualise and place the role of 'commentaries' in qualitative research more generally. Connecting commentaries to this literature gives more resources for developing tools for the analysis of changes in the author–hero relationship between different texts.

Intertextuality refers to the presence of one text within another. Quotations from other texts may be embedded into the commentary or other texts may be assimilated and absorbed into the commentary through summary. The presence of other texts can also be implicit – where texts with some cultural significance are commentated on through allusion, implicit reference or style. For example, a satire can provide a critical commentary on a culturally significant text without directly referencing it. In this chapter, I focus on explicit commentaries. As we will see, this is because changes in the subjectivity in the participants are easier to identify in these kinds of commentaries.

Intertextuality is a term first coined by Julia Kristeva (1986) to refer to the influence of texts upon each other. She was significantly inspired by Bakhtin's (1981) work on dialogue in doing this. For Kristeva, all texts are a 'mosaic of quotations' (1986: 37). In particular, she argued that all texts are in a network of relationships, not only with the writer and reader, but also with other texts. All texts, to an extent, absorb other texts, reference other texts and recontextualise other texts in a new frame of reference.

In qualitative analysis, Fairclough (1992, 2003) has drawn attention to the importance of intertextuality for understanding features of discourse, including genre. He focuses on the power relationships between genres in intertextual texts. For instance, he has shown how some texts can colonise other texts as a feature of governance. One example of this that he gives is of promotional, marketing genres colonising local authority genres. The language of selling and competition is increasingly used by local authorities attempting to attract investment. This colonisation occurs as a feature of modern forms of capitalism where governments are concerned with introducing competition and flexibility into the public service system.

My focus on self and other and a changing experiential relationship between them makes my reading of 'intertextuality' a little different from both Kristeva (1986) and Fairclough (1992, 2003). These authors draw on Bakhtin to outline a view of intertextuality that is more broadly concerned with the power relationships between texts rather than the author–hero relationship within texts. I do not ignore power relations between texts, but I interpret them in terms of the 'author' 'hero' relationship. In doing this, I am drawing on a reading of Bakhtin that emphasises a phenomenological sense of the searching author. As outlined in more detail in Chapter 1, my interest lies in the shaping activity of the author/self and the responsivity of the other/hero to this. This allows me to examine the 'self–other' dialogue within the text where self and other are considered to have shifting boundaries between different texts.

Analysis of two commentaries on subjectivity

Now that we have seen what commentaries may involve and their place more widely in the literature on intertextuality, I will analyse two formal, written commentaries and examine their relationship to subjectivity. The two texts were selected because they offer significantly different commentaries on 'schizophrenia'. These are both presented below. I discuss these texts under the sub-headings of 'genre', 'chronotope', 're-accentuation' and 'authority'. General methodological points, which emerge from this analysis, are presented in summary form at the end of each section.

The first text (Text A) is an extract from the case study of 'Emilio' from the *DSM-IV-TR: Case Book* (Spitzer et al., 2002). In general, this book is organised by first describing a case study and then explaining how it fits diagnostic categories for mental health problems. Here, Text A1 is an excerpt from a longer summary of Emilio's words and deeds and Text A2 is an excerpt from a longer discussion of these.

The second text (Text B) is a case study of 'The Blairs', a family with a daughter, Lucie, who has been diagnosed with 'schizophrenia' and is an extract from *Sanity, Madness and the Family* (Laing and Esterson, 1964). This book describes a number of case studies of people's unusual experiences but offers an alternative to a clinical perspective. It uses interviews with family members to make sense out of behaviour in 'social-phenomenological terms' (1964: 52). Ronnie Laing and Aaron Esterson try to make sense of Lucie's unusual experiences through linking them to her family context. B1 is a quotation from Lucie describing her relationship to her father and B2 is a commentary on this. Two sample texts are presented below. 'A1', 'A2', 'B1' and 'B2' are my labels for integrated texts – done for ease of discussion.

Text A (Spitzer et al., 2002)

A1 Summary of Emilio

Emilio

Emilio is a 40-year-old man who looks 10 years younger. He is brought to the hospital, his twelfth hospitalization, by his mother because she is afraid of him. He is dressed in a ragged overcoat, bedroom slippers, and a baseball cap and wears several medals around his neck. His affect ranges from anger at his mother ('she feeds me shit ... what comes out of other people's rectums') to a giggling, obsequious seductiveness toward the interviewer.

(2002: 189) (Author's ellipsis)

A2 Commentary on Emilio

'Emilio'

The combination of a chronic illness with marked incoherence, inappropriate affect, auditory hallucinations, and grossly disorganized behaviour leaves little doubt that the diagnosis is chronic Schizophrenia (DSM-IV-TR, p. 312). The course would be noted as Continuous because Emilio apparently never has prolonged remissions of his psychosis. The prominence of his disorganized speech and behaviour, his grossly inappropriate affect, and the absence of prominent catatonic symptoms indicate the Disorganized Type (DSM-IV-TR, p. 315).

(2002: 190)

Text B (Laing and Esterson, 1964)

B1 Lucie quote

But it is my father's apprehension of me, wondering whether I should be kidnapped or some dreadful thing happen to me. It's my own fault. He's got no confidence in me at all. I'm always going to be led away by some crafty, cunning bad man. That sort of thing, you see, he's always like that. He's put that into my mind, my subconscious mind – that I can't be trusted, and I'll always be, you know – the big bad wolf will come after me.

(1964: 62)

B2 Commentary on Lucie

Her identity-for-herself had, therefore, the following structure.

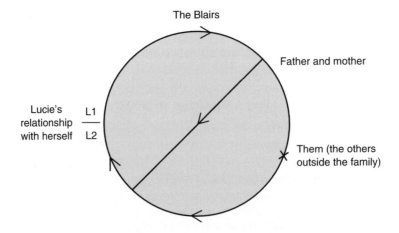

There was no way from L^1 to L^2 (if $L^1 \rightarrow L^2$ represents a direct view of herself), except through the circuit $L^1 \rightarrow F$ or $M \rightarrow L^2$:or $L^1 \rightarrow F$ or $M \rightarrow$ Them $\rightarrow L^2$.

That is, she has difficulty in seeing herself except as her father or mother saw her: or as her father or mother told her 'They' saw her. (p. 63). ... What she hears is either what her father tells her about herself (that she was a slut, a prostitute), or what he tells her 'They' think about her.

(1964: 63) (My ellipsis)

Analysing genre and discourse shifts

Both Text A and Text B are deliberately intertextual, concerned with addressing the reader with an analysis of a 'schizophrenic'. Understanding the shifts in genre and discourse within Texts A and B is useful in helping us to understand the dialogical relationship between the texts, the addressivity within them and the implications that this has for the negotiation of subjectivity.

Text A, 'Emilio', moves from a skilfully told medical drama in A1 to a medical analysis and diagnosis in A2. In doing this, there is a very noticeable shift in language that is characteristic of these different genres. A1 uses colloquial terms that are subsequently transformed to diagnostic labels in A2. So, for example, 'he is dressed in a ragged overcoat, bedroom slippers, and a baseball cap and wears several medals around his neck' in A1 is transformed to 'marked incoherence' and 'grossly disorganized behaviour' in A2. Similarly, the vividly descriptive 'his affect ranges from anger at his mother ... to a giggling, obsequious seductiveness towards the interviewer' of A1 becomes 'inappropriate affect' and then 'grossly inappropriate affect' in A2.

In both A1 and A2, the narrator is omniscient and speaking from a position outside the story (rather than narrating as a character from within the story). This position from outside is known as extradiegetic narration, where 'diegetic' means 'telling' (Gennett, 1982). In both A1 and A2, the extradiegetic narration lends itself to an 'outside-in' discourse. That is, Emilio is rendered in terms of a singular truth in both the medical drama and the medical diagnosis. This takes the form of a reported summary of Emilio's actions and words, leaving Emilio with very little agency to disrupt or challenge the authorial narrative.

More particularly, in A1, this position from outside serves to make sense out of Emilio in dramatic terms as a bizarre, fearful, and dangerous character. His mismatch of clothing stuck together (bedroom slippers and baseball cap) creates a bizarre impression. Later in the case study, this bizarre impression is further reinforced with the comment that he walked with 'exaggerated hip movements' (Spitzer et al. 2002: 189) – not reported above due to space constraints. His mother, we are told, is afraid of him. His mother's fear, for his unknown actions in the past, together with the portrayal of Emilio as different, incoherent and unexpected, resonates with a horror genre.

In A2, the extradiegetic position of the narrator makes sense of Emilio in terms of traditional diagnostic categories. In this genre shift, Emilio, as other, undergoes a metamorphosis from being dramatic and unpredictable to being entirely predictable and even conventional, within a psychiatric framework. As Goffman (1961) points out, psychiatric labels can involve an interpretation of social improprieties as medical symptoms.

Despite the extradiegetic narration, there is some level of freedom given to other voices within these texts. In A1, we fleetingly experience a brief intrusion of Emilio's voice into the drama. His voice appears in parenthesis, with the ostensible effect of evidencing the claims of the author that Emilio's affect involves anger ('she feeds me shit ... what comes out of other people's rectums'). With this intrusion of his voice, a level of double-voicedness is introduced into this discourse. In particular, while it seems that Emilio is in an overall relationship of agreement with the author by evidencing his claims, one could also read the voice in parenthesis in a second, more 'inside-out' sense. It could be a carnivalesque, joking objection to the description of 'inappropriate affect' – e.g., **'but** she feeds me shit...'. Bound up in the summary, the intonation is difficult to assess, but with the introduction of a second voice, liberated from the summary, the possibility arises of reading it in terms of a relationship of disagreement or agreement with the omniscient narrator.

In A2, the reader is addressed as an 'other' whose questions are answered by an expert author regarding Emilio as subject. The author explains to the reader what Emilio's appearance and behaviour actually means. These questions are hidden but structure the discourse: e.g., Reader: what is the diagnosis? Author: 'The diagnosis is...'; Reader: what is the course? Author: 'The course would be noted as...'; Reader: is there any doubt? Author: '...leaves little doubt'. This last answer by the author 'leaves little doubt' also suggests the word with a 'sidewards glance' in the direction of the reader. It is an unnecessary clause that anticipates possible scepticism on the part of the reader.

In contrast to the muffling of Emilio's voice in Text A, in Text B we get a much fuller sense of Lucie's voice. Laing and Esterson (1964) directly report what she says before going on to discuss it. She is given loads of space within this deliberately intertextual text as an author. Text B1, as a quote from Lucie, involves an 'intradiegetic' narrator, telling her story from within the text. Lucie's 'self' and 'other' includes her father and the interviewers. Text B2 involves an extradiegetic narrator, also reporting her story, but from a position outside the text as an omniscient author and non-character. In B2, the other is Lucie, her father, her mother, society around her and the reader. This is a noteworthy narrative shift between the texts and suggests also a genre shift.

If Text A1 can be considered a medical drama, Text B1 can be considered a psycho-drama, within a broadly confessional genre. In this psycho-drama, her father appears as a bullying figure and his voice is freely, indirectly reported 'led away by some crafty, cunning bad man'. The words 'crafty' and 'cunning' are the kinds of words that her father might utter but are fused into Lucie's narration, creating an ambivalent closeness. He says 'that sort of thing', according to Lucie. Equally, when Lucie takes the blame for his lack of confidence in her by saying 'it's my own fault', her father's voice would not be out of place in terms of indirect reporting – e.g., 'he says it's my own fault'. This tone of condemnation coheres with her father's indirectly reported tone of condemnation in B2 (she was a slut, a prostitute).

At the same time, amidst this closeness to her father's voice, Lucie actively works out her own psychological explanation for the effect that he has on her. She says that her father has put into her 'subconscious' mind fears of 'the big bad wolf coming after me'. Her use of the technical term 'subconscious' suggests a psychological sub-genre. It allows a more analytic distance from her father. He becomes predictable – 'he's always like that'. Perhaps this sub-genre also anticipates the reaction of the psychologists who are interviewing her.

The genre moves from a psycho-drama in B1 to a quasi-mathematical description of Lucie's experience in B2. Laing and Esterson present the reader with a diagram, showing sets of relationships, arrows and points in a geometrical space. Below this diagram is a description of what her words could mean. Here, in this description, Lucie's father's voice makes another indirect appearance, although not in quotation marks but in brackets (that she was a slut, a prostitute). The lack of quotation marks are interesting as the words seem to be coming directly from the extradiegetic narrator. This is in contrast to A1 where Emilio's words are both put in brackets and given quotation marks to delineate the author–hero separation.

It is difficult to believe, however, that these words are used as part of Laing and Esterson's mathematical description. In the confines of the brackets, the authors create an ironic distance from Lucie's father's words. As Fairclough (1992) points out, irony involves echoing the words of another but in a blatant mismatch to the original context. The echoing of his words is particularly adept through the use of free indirect reporting within the omniscient narrative. Lucie's father, then, is a presence that shifts from B1 to B2 but moves from an up-close struggle with the author of A1 to a relation of ironic distance from the author of A2.

The genre and discourse shifts from drama to expertise in Text B are reasonably similar to those in Text A. In Text B1, however, Lucie's voice is given a fuller rein. This gives up a little authorial control over the reader response and allows the possibility of a distance between the author and reader. In B2, in contrast, Lucie becomes stuck in a circle, going through others to reach herself. Here, there is a more didactic tone and an assumed affinity between author and reader where the structure of her identity is open to viewing by both from a distance.

In terms of form, there are some similarities between B2 and A2. A2 answers questions didactically and authoritatively from an anticipated reader, e.g.: Reader: what form did her experience have? Author: 'Her experiences had, therefore, the following structure'; Reader: was there any way out for Lucie? Author: 'There was no way out'.

In terms of the content, however, there are some differences between A2 and B2. B2 is concerned with uncovering the structure of Lucie's identity. The circle and mathematical description are a creative representation exclusive to Lucie. It is an exercise in 'abduction'. Shotter (2009) argues that abduction is a form of logic that involves creatively solving problems through 'abducting' them from their original context and creatively placing them in a new context. It can involve bringing a text to an unfamiliar place but a place that orientates to its particularity. This allows us to see possibilities in it that are not possible in its original context.

In Laing and Esterson's (1964) case, they create a distance from Lucie's intense dialogues with her father, neutralising the emotion in them (apart from a faint speckle of irony) and amplifying her own suggestion, in the latter part of A2, that her fears are tangled up with her father and others. In amplifying this side of her dialogue, there is a 'penetrative' word lurking beneath the didactic prose – that her fears are not all her own fault.

In A2, in contrast, there is a much more 'bureaucratic' method of abstraction and a deductive rather than 'abductive' system of logic. The guidelines are followed, the clues are added up and Emilio ends up with a conventional medical diagnosis. This perspective is only of relevance to Emilio, however, as an instance of a wider category.

Methodological implications of studying genre and discourse shifts

These shifts in genre and discourse between texts are important to highlight because they give important clues to the changing relationship between author and hero or self and other. In doing this kind of analysis, the following questions can be asked.

What position does the narrative assume? Here, we have seen that extradiegetic and intradiegetic narration create different sets of relationships with different others. Extradiegetic narration tends towards addressing the reader in a pedagogical relationship of explanation. The other as 'subject' of this explanation, on the other hand, can be reflected upon and discussed at a distance. A hierarchical relationship – of authoring the other from a particular vantage point – is possible in this kind of narration. Meanwhile, the other as reader is drawn into a relationship of closeness with the extradiegetic narration. The reader tends to be addressed as the questioning other who should ultimately understand the answers given. Such a reader is also a 'superaddressee' in Bakhtin's (1981) terms. A superaddresse is an anticipated other who should ultimately understand what is being said. As an anticipated other, they also structure the dialogue, as we saw earlier.

What do the shifts in discourse and genre signify about the self–other relationship? In Text A, the move in genres serves first to create a fearful and unusual subjectivity and then to drain this into a medical category of 'schizophrenia'. In Text B, a psycho-drama, with Lucie as the author/protagonist, moves to an existential commentary on Lucie's entrapment within familial relationships. The point here is that the shifts in genre in intertextual texts mark changes in the kinds of relationship between self and other. The relationship is reciprocally reconfigured in the transition between texts.

What agency does the 'other', as created hero within the text, have to 'answer back' between texts? In both of these cases, the 'other' as 'subject' has little agency in terms of the interpretation that is given. However, Lucie is given a full quotation, where she is able to offer her own theory on her father's relationship which the reader could potentially interrupt Text B with. Equally, although Emilio's voice is much more muffled, his one appearance could be read in a counter-intuitive way (as disagreeing with the author).

Who is the author addressing? Emilio is directly and indirectly reported to the reader as the main protagonist with minimal agency in A1 and A2. He is the subject of an address to the reader. In B1, Lucie is given the position of authorship, addressing a variety of others, including her father, but then, in B2 is moved into the position of authored subject in an address to the reader. Her father's voice makes a transition into this description, through his non-quoted phrases (e.g., prostitute). In doing this, Laing and Esterson, as authors, enter into a relationship of agreement and closeness with the reader and ironic distance from the father. The authors seem to have a more ambivalent relationship with Lucie. In content, they amplify one side of her dialogue, through a penetrative word, but in form, their language creates a distancing abstraction from Lucie's subjectivity.

Overall, from this point of view, the self–other axis is particularly open to examination in deliberately intertextual texts, through shifts in discourse and genre. The variety of 'others', from the reader to the participant, show the shifts in subjectivity of the created participant and the creating author.

Analysing chronotopic shifts

Shifts in time and space underpin the genre shifts in intertextual texts. Alongside a changing subjectivity, there are a variety of time–space configurations that change in interesting ways as the genres shift. These are important to study because they help specify the kind of subjectivity that emerges for both self and other in a changing landscape and in a particular atmosphere.

Perhaps the first thing to note about the extradiegetic narrative of the medical genre in A2 and the academic, existential genre in B2 is the distancing it creates from the protagonists. The language serves to give a shape to their experience that is grounded in evidence. As the omniscient author, 'self' is free to roam through this space and time (Gennett, 1982). For example, in Text A2, the authors can bring in Emilio's previous history, his future course and his present diagnosis together. Equally, in B2, the authors are able to bring Lucie's story into a transformed circular space, move around this and then move out of it to discuss the nature of her identity. It is only the anticipated responses of the reader that impose any restraint on this movement through time and space.

While the self-as-author reveals the freedom of moving around their own created space, the possibilities open to the 'other' undergo a more marked shift between the texts. For Emilio, he first occupies an adventure-space in A1. Here anything can happen through his 'range of affect' – he can inspire intense feelings, such as fear in others, through the force of his personality (his mother is afraid of him) and his unusual and odd clothing give him a sense of mystery and danger. He is also able to confound time by looking younger than he is and by being unaffected by his repetitive contact with the hospital (we are told he has had twelve hospitalisations but are told nothing about any improvement). This lack of interaction between the person and time is typical of adventure space and is nicely described by Bakhtin: the 'hammer of events shatters nothing and forges nothing – it merely tries the durability of an already finished product. And the product passes the test' (1981: 107). In this case, the hammer of events (repeated admissions) serves to confirm the diagnosis of a 'continuous' course of schizophrenia in A2. The diagnosis passes the test. It is also worth noting more generally that as an adventure space, it lacks the markers of place (e.g., where this happened, where he is from, the cultural context) and of biographical time (we are given no sense of what decade this is).

In A2, Emilio moves on to a definite medical path, signposted as 'chronic Schizophrenia', away from an adventure path where anything can happen. On this road, he can travel in only one direction in time. Any 'remission', which may suggest the road back to recovery, is unlikely. This is because the remissions are not 'prolonged', meaning that the course is 'continuous'. One reading of what this means is that Emilio's path in time is travelling towards gradual degeneration. Emilio's subjectivity is universal but he moves from being a universal adventure hero, shaping the world around him to being a universal type that can fit into a designated area in the medical world.

Text B is quite different in terms of the space-time shifts. In B1, Lucie is the intradiegetic narrator and the activity of Laing and Esterson lie in placing this quotation in that particular place in the authorial narrative (and it is worth reading the full case to get a sense of this activity). As the narrator, Lucie reveals a space with the significant figure of her father. She tells us that he fills her space and time with fear and apprehension. At any time, she may be kidnapped, led away and pursued by the 'big bad wolf'. The fear of the future and the atmosphere of apprehension is tied to her father's lack of confidence in her. Her constrained outer space, marked by fear of the world outside the home, reflects her inner psychological relationship with her father marked by lack of confidence and fear.

Despite this intense closeness to her father's psychology, however, the availability of a psychological genre ('my subconscious mind') as we saw earlier, allows a more critical, analytic distance between Lucie and her father. This suggests some level of authorial agency in ambivalently feeling and moving away from her father.

In the switch to B2, Lucie metamorphoses to two points in a circle. She undergoes a division of self. In this division, she moves through time and space as a defined hero with the purpose of connecting herself to herself. This, she is unable to do because she is in a circular space. In this vicious circle, she is unable to see herself properly because she always has to go through her father and mother's perception of who she is as well as their perception of outside others. This is a potentially endless circle, repeating itself through time with no sense of movement outside it. Unlike Bakhtin's ideal view of the 'other' as enriching the self, Laing and Esterson (1964) present a darker view of the other entrapping the self (see Burkitt and Sullivan, 2009, for more on the comparison between Laing and Bakhtin). Like Text A, Text B also lacks specific cultural markers or a sense of the person changing in time.

Methodological implication of chronotopic shifts in intertextual texts

There are a number of methodological implications of chronotopic shifts for the study of intertextual texts. Below, I draw out these implications in terms of specifying the kinds of questions that the analyst can pose to the intertextual text.

What does the author's narrative position allow in terms of movements across time and space? The extradiegetic narrator can move in any way they like, unconcerned with time and space, but the intradiegetic narrator, as we see in A1, is much more bound by the time and space of the world around him or her. This time and space is open to change as the genre changes and as the author–hero relationship changes.

What are the directions of travel for the protagonist? Can the protagonist move back in time (as in 'recovery') or does the protagonist move only in a circle, or towards an ultimate future destiny? What role does the present play? Is it, as in A1 and B1, full of potential or is it the inevitable consequence of past events, as in A2 and B2? How is the reader reconfigured in time and space across intertextual shifts? In the shift from A1 to A2, for instance, the reader is reconfigured from sharing in the drama to possibly judging an analysis.

What agency does the author give the protagonist to both shape and be shaped by time and space across intertextual texts? In other words, is it possible for the 'hammer of events' to change the person in the authorial relationship to that person? In the transition from A1 to A2, the protagonist moves from shaping the world to being shaped by an illness. In everyday life, there is a temptation to author others with an unchanging personality despite what comes their way. In this sense, time and space leave no mark on the personality which is considered to be always the same.

What role does truth play in the constitution of time and space? If there is an uncertain truth (as in, for instance, in B1), then time and space is full of event potential. It is what Bakhtin (1984) refers to as a 'threshold moment'. On the other hand, if the truth lies in a future destiny, then the present is emptied of event potential. Instead, the course of events plays out according to a specified path. In the transition from A1 to A2 and B1 to B2, the uncertainty of the present is replaced by the certainty of the future.

Overall, it is important to bear in mind that the fashioning of time and space in dialogue gives different options for the emergence of the other's subjectivity. It also allows the author (read as self) to traverse across this space and time in different ways in their response to the other.

Analysing accentuation at the word level

Accentuation and re-accentuation is a very dialogical way of referring to the different values that imbue discourse as it passes through different genres. Accentuation is another way of expressing 'intonation', whereas 're-accentuation' refers to the process of overlaying a new value or tone to a previously intoned concept or idea. As we saw in previous chapters, when someone else's words become part of our own, then this involves putting a new value on these words (or re-accentuating them) and in the case of double-voiced discourse, the sound of both these values may compete and sound together simultaneously.

The shifts in genre and chronotope between the different texts show how re-accentuation involves a process of appropriating the reported speech and actions of others and imbuing these with authorial value. In this section, I will look at the re-accentuation of specific words within this context. This re-accentuation helps us to understand the move in levels in intertextual texts from the general to the more specific.

The first word that is accentuated and re-accentuated in Text A is the name of the case – Emilio. Emilio moves from a name of a person in A1 to being enclosed in quote marks to become a denotative of an entire case in A2. In this sense, the quote marks act as a hyper summary of the entire case. In the first accentuation of Emilio, he is authored as an active subject, even if it is within the limited sense of a summary. In the second 're-accentuation', he is authored as an object of symptom display for the reader to scrutinise with the author. As A2 progresses, Emilio does briefly return as a subject with a name, but within the context of 'Emilio', this subjectivity is enmeshed and stuck in technical terminology.

Secondly, the word 'affect' in A1 is first intoned or accentuated as descriptive of Emilio's expression and feeling. The authors, writing a dramatic description, initially intone the word 'affect' dispassionately. Emilio's voice comes in as a subject in putative agreement with the authors, evidencing their claim that he is angry. However, as the description continues in A1, Emilio's 'affect' is described as 'giggling, obsequious seductiveness'. In this sense, the authors more explicitly change the coloration of Emilio's 'affect' with their own judgement or give the affect a new semantic context. 'Obsequious', in particular, is an adverb with a negative connotation. Emilio is brought closer to the authors' personal evaluation, under this description, from a more detached narrative distance.

This authorial evaluation of his 'affect' is amplified in A2. Here, his affect moves to being 'grossly inappropriate'. His 'affect' is re-accentuated from being descriptive with a slight colouring of authorial disapproval to being almost repulsive, clownish and ridiculous. Although Emilio's 'affect' is revealed to the reader, Emilio himself is unable to answer back in any way because in the general context, Emilio has been engulfed by the authorial examination.

In B1 to B2 there are also number of re-accentuations that configure the self–other, author–hero relationship quite differently. In B1, Lucie is the author, addressing the interviewer and in dialogue with a number of absent others, particularly her father. In B2, where Lucie become the other, she becomes abbreviated from a speaking subject to a divided 'L^1' and 'L^2' while her father becomes 'F'. In these abbreviated short-hands, Lucie and Father both become re-accentuated from subjects in an intense psychological inter-action to being points in a circular, geometric relationship. Here, they lose their potential as active heroes, able to dissent or interfere with the autho-rial discourse. Like Emilio, they become shared objects of conversation with the reader. In terms of the content of the re-accentuation, however, as we saw earlier, this re-accentuation amplifies Lucie's own words that her thoughts and fears are inseparable from her father's.

There is also a noteworthy re-accentuation of the word 'they'. The 'big bad wolf' of B1 is the 'They' in B2. The pronoun refers to the dangerous people outside the family. In B2, this word 'They' is ironically put in quote marks and given a capital 'T'. The reader is able to hear the ambivalent sounds of this word through the quote marks – both the father's use of the word to evoke fear and Lucie's ironic 'big bad wolf' interpretation (drawing on another text – 'Red Riding Hood') amidst feeling her father's lack of confi-dence in her. Laing and Esterson also accentuate the 'They' to refer to the exaggerated atmosphere of fear that sustains the vicious circle.

Methodological implications of re-accentuation at the word level

There are a number of features to look out for in terms of re-accentuation at the word level that help give some clue to the mixing between self and other in intertextual texts

The use of quote marks. As we can see in these texts, quote marks are an effec-tive way of re-accentuating words with authorial intonation while the value of the original context is also detectable, including the intonation of a word (e.g., 'They') by the other. Quote marks serve to create a dis-tance from the original context of usage and to invest the word with a new value and meaning in a very deliberate way (see Fairclough, 1992, for more on the use of quote marks).

The use of brackets. Brackets place the other's words inside an authorial context. This also serves to create some distance from the other but gives the other a direct presence within the authorial context. Within this context, however (in brackets), the other is at the mercy of the authorial intonation, particularly irony or using the words out of context to forge a relationship of agreement. Nonetheless, the re-accentuation allows us to establish the contours of self and other.

The use of free indirect reporting. This is much more complicated in terms of the self–other relationship, as Fairclough (1992) also points out. It is a bit more ambivalent where the lines between self and other lie. A good example of this above is Lucie's discourse where her use of 'crafty' and 'cunning' or 'it's my own fault' could be words directly uttered by her father, yet are given her own intonation. Within the one phrase or word, we can detect different tones from different voices.

Perhaps the most important question that a focus on re-accentuation allows is the following:

(Q) What is the emotional orientation of the author to other in intertextual texts?

The way a word is accentuated and re-accentuated helps gives some clue as to the emotional orientation of the author to the hero. Does the re-accentuated word, e.g., 'Emilio' in A2, work to overcome the original intonation through creating an analytic distance from it? Does the re-accentuated word struggle to overcome the original accentuation – as in, for instance, the active agency of Emilio? Does the re-accentuated word work to pass judgement on the original accentuation – e.g., 'affect'?

Above, I have looked at the shifts between words and across texts as the author–hero (self–other) relationship is reconfigured – sometimes with a change of author and of hero (as in B1 to B2). Within the intertextual shifts, the emotional orientation of the author to the other can also be detected as changing through re-accentuated words. In the final section, I will discuss the landscape within which this emotional orientation is grounded by looking at relations of authority between the texts.

From internally-persuasive to authoritative discourses

Bakhtin (1981) draws a distinction between 'authoritative' and 'internally-persuasive' discourse. In the former, it is the authority of a person, tradition or institution that gives a discourse persuasiveness (constituted through a historical relationship with the addressee), whereas 'internally-persuasive' refers literally to the internal persuasiveness of the discourse, e.g., in terms of how internally coherent the reader finds it against other discourses. While in some cases, 'authoritative' and 'internally persuasive' discourses can be quite separate in form, it is possible for discourses to depend on both authority and logical, internal coherence. For this reason, Bakhtin (1981) argues that the same discursive statement may be authoritative for one person and internally persuasive for another or we may move from accepting a position on the basis of its authority and then on its logic.

In the texts above, it is possible to see a move from an internally persuasive discourse in A1 and B1 to a more authoritative discourse in A2 and B2. A1 appears 'internally persuasive' for the authors in so far as they do not claim any outside authority for their interpretations. There is authority, however, in terms of the omniscient narrative voice within the text. This voice moves around a number of different aspects of Emilio – his behaviour, mother, speech, gait and history. They create an internally coherent picture of Emilio as dramatic and odd to the authors. In Text B1, in Lucie's juxtapositioning of the authoritative words tied to her father (I'll always be led away...) against the authoritative tradition of psychology ('subconscious mind'), we can see her working out an internally coherent or persuasive discourse for understanding her relationship to her father and to herself.

These internally persuasive (for the authors) discourses in A1 and B1 shift to a much more authoritative discourse in A2 and B2, respectively. This is not to say that A1 or B1 do not articulate aspects of authoritative discourses e.g., through assuming an omniscient position. Equally, A2 and B2 also seek to persuade through the inner coherence of their claims. The difference from A1 and B1, however, is that A2 and B2 draw much more on authoritative traditions to persuade the reader. A2 explicitly draws on the medical psychiatric tradition, while B2 implicitly draws on the existential and academic tradition (e.g., through diagrams and terminology) to establish persuasiveness.

So far, I have foregrounded the 'manifest' intertextuality – or the presence of texts within texts – but a discussion of history allows us to understand the implicit relationship between these texts and previous historical texts. Below, I will briefly discuss how these traditions are relevant to the constitution of these discourses. This is a brief discussion as the more general focus is on the 'manifest' relationship between self and other.

Foucault (1973) has argued that the rise of psychiatry in the mid-eighteenth century was tied to an Enlightenment discourse of rationality. It is in this context that psychiatry was born. This history is defined by linking rationality to control over the 'immoral' – mainly women, sex workers, beggars and criminals. Using the illness narrative, the morally unacceptable were made sense of and controlled through coercive techniques such as drowning, spinning, electroshock and chemical drugging. In Emilio's case, as we have seen, his diagnosis emerges from a judgement that his affect and behaviour is 'grossly inappropriate'.

Similarly, Goffman (1961) shows that diagnostic labels can be viewed as interpretations of social improprieties. The difficulty, however, is that some improprieties some of the time result in a diagnostic label, while others do not. What diagnosis is given is a matter of interpretation more than method and this interpretation often depends on chance – including the wishes of the family, the interpersonal relationship with the doctor and the proximity to an institution. In Emilio's case, the wishes of his mother as well as the social improprieties he commits (such as odd dress and gait) subsequently result in a medical diagnosis.

What is of interest here is how the medical discourse is used unquestionably by the authors in A2. The only question that arises is the specific diagnosis that should pertain to Emilio. Occasionally, a sprinkling of uncertainty can be detected in terms of the appropriate diagnosis as we saw earlier (e.g., 'little doubt') but the paradigm itself is unquestioned. The medical discourse is used authoritatively, resting upon tradition. The citation of the colloquially known 'psychiatric bible', i.e., DSM-IV-TR, is used to lend further authority to the diagnosis.

Text B is historically in direct dialogue with Text A. It is a text of the anti-psychiatry movement and therefore in a dialogical relationship of disagreement (this is explicitly made clear early on in the book). This movement, rooted in Romanticism, resists the medical linkage of behaviour to a personal illness. Instead, it focuses on the person's relationship to significant others. In B2 the authors interpret Lucie's experience in terms of her relationship with her family rather than as an individual illness. It uses the authority of a diagram, quasi-mathematical notation and confident prose ('therefore') to persuade the reader. Underpinning this analysis is the authority of the existential tradition with its emphasis on alienation and individual freedom.

The shift from an 'internally persuasive' discursive tendency to an 'authoritative' discursive tendency illustrates a changing relationship between self and other through a prism of authority. In internally persuasive discourses, the other (including the protagonist and reader) has more opportunities to move within the authorial discourse, while in authoritative discourse, the author attempts to exert more control over the other's range of possibilities and movements. This is not necessarily negative. A 'penetrative word' for instance, can be uttered with authority and be quite helpful. I will briefly discuss some methodological implications of authority in the self–other dialogical relationship below. I will do this in terms of stating a number of questions the analyst can pose to intertextual texts.

Methodological implications of internally-persuasive and authoritative discourses

What are the historical values that underpin a text? Identifying these involves doing background reading on the discourses. This, as we also saw in earlier chapters, is vital in understanding the landscape within which self and other are placed. It also helps to identify relations of agreement and disagreement across diverse perspectives, and to understand how they have historically been in contact with each other. Here, it has allowed us to identify the broader dialogical relationship between Texts A and B.

How are particular genres appropriated by the authors? A discourse is 'authoritative' or 'internally persuasive' depending on how it is appropriated. If a discourse is echoed, with little questioning, then one could argue that it is authoritative for the author. If it is actively questioned or appeals to logical coherence, which in turn can be open to question, then it is more likely to be 'internally-persuasive'. Nonetheless, these are fluid boundaries and discourses do shift between 'authority' and 'internal persuasiveness'.

What level of authority is evident in the text? The 'anti-psychiatry' movement assumes authority on the basis of a phenomenological, existential tradition, partly as a means of resisting the authority of the psychiatric tradition, but also as a means of producing a romantic subjectivity. This, in turn, has encouraged further interpretative frameworks for understanding unusual experiences. The psychiatric tradition, rooted in authority, is also very reassuring for many people. As Morson (2004) points out, when an authoritative discourse becomes authoritarian or intolerant to any questioning, it can lead to coercion and oppression. This depends on the particular appropriation of a discourse in space and time.

Discussion

In this chapter, I have examined the self–other dialogue through the prism of commentaries on experiences of 'schizophrenia'. I have argued that intertextual texts are useful in showing reciprocal reconfigurations in the self–other dialogue as a changing 'author–hero' relationship. In particular, I have focused on a dramatic summary followed by a medical commentary and of a quotation followed by an existential commentary. These two texts, however, are just indicative of the kinds of changing dialogues that can take place across the same intertextual text. For example, if one wanted to do a fuller analysis of intertextual shifts in understanding 'schizophrenic' experience, then it would be very important to examine first-person accounts of these (see, e.g., Ruth Chandler and Mark Hayward, 2009). With these, new sets of intertextual relationship, often outside mainstream approaches, are used to author and make sense of these experiences in different ways.

There are many other domains where the analysis of shifts in subjectivity across intertextual texts could be open to a dialogical analysis. This is particularly the case with manifestly intertextual texts that reflect on the speech and actions of another, for example, in policy documents, diary analysis and newspaper reporting.

This kind of analysis may also be useful as a reflective tool for practitioners (e.g., therapists, research psychologists) who wish to examine their treatment of the other as a subject of their written reports. What freedom is the other allowed? How does the other shift in emotional orientation from the pages of a transcript to the pages of a report with a particular readership in mind? These are pertinent questions for a reflective practitioner. It allows the practitioner to reflect upon their own relationship with the protagonists of their reports (see Michael Guilfoyle, 2001, for more on developing reflective tools of analysis in therapy).

Approaching both texts academically, my sympathies lie much more with B2 – mainly because I find the inclusion of the other's voice to be important. I also find the method of 'abducting' subjective experience from its original context and imagining another way of representing it to be adventurous in spirit and enlightening in promise. In contrast to this, the deductive method of identifying the most appropriate, pre-existing category for subjectivity appears to move subjectivity into a realm where voices become exemplars of a pre-given, totalising system. Here, the particular stories of an individual's life seem unimportant. I say this in recognition of the diversity of views and experiences in the mental health field.

My preference for voice and creative transformation of experience brings me more generally to the question of evaluation. How do we evaluate a dialogical analysis? It is to this issue that I will turn in the next chapter.

Further reading

Burkitt, I. and Sullivan, P. (2009) Embodied ideas and divided selves: Revisiting Laing via Bakhtin. *British Journal of Social Psychology*, 48(3): 563–77.

Chandler, R. and Hayward, M. (2009) *Voicing Psychotic Experiences: A Reconsideration of Recovery and Diversity*. Brighton: OLM Pavilion.

Fairclough, N. (1992) *Discourse and Social Change*. Cambridge: Polity Press.

Gennett, G. (1982) *Figures of Literary Discourse*. Trans. Alan Sheridan. New York: Columbia University Press.

Guilfoyle, M. (2001) Problematising psychotherapy: The discursive production of a bulimic. *Culture and Psychology*, 7(2): 151–79.

Kristeva, J. (1986) Word, dialogue and novel, in T. Moi (ed.) *The Kristeva Reader*. Oxford: Basil Blackwell. pp. 34–61.

Laing, R.D. and Esterson, A. (1964) *Sanity, Madness and the Family*. London: Penguin.

Shotter, J. (2009) Bateson, double description, Todes, and embodiment: Preparing activities and their relation to abduction. *Journal for the Theory of Social Behaviour*, 39: 219–45.

Spitzer, R.L, Gibbon, M., Skodol, A.E., Williams, J.B.W. and First, M.B. (2002) *DSM-IV-TR: Case Book: A Learning Companion to the Diagnostic and Statistical Manual of Mental Disorders* (4th edition). Arlington, VA: American Psychiatric Association.

8

EVALUATION

This chapter is concerned with establishing a set of evaluation criteria for a dialogical approach to qualitative analysis. I do this through an examination of the linkage between time, space and causality, drawing extensively from Rom Harré and Edward Madden's (1975) and Brent Slife and Richard Williams' (1995) discussion of various types of causality and their relationship to evaluation in the social sciences. I argue that qualitative research involves a high level of intertextuality through the insertion of quotations and data into the text. This intertextuality can be thought of as being open to a variety of time–space configurations. Out of this discussion, I develop some specific criteria for evaluating a dialogical approach to qualitative analysis.

In writing this chapter on evaluation, I am in danger of 'scratching where it does not itch' (Kvale, 1995: 37) and fostering an attitude of distrust in my reader as a consequence. Perhaps the research and the dialogical approach can be judged as it is presented? Maybe there are no criteria for judging research quality when we hold a romantic view of research – that research is an interpersonal encounter between text and subject? What I am getting at here is that in a postmodern framework, with contested meanings of what is 'good' and 'valuable', deciding on criteria to evaluate research is a tricky problem.

My strategy is to link the evaluation of a piece of research to the relationship between events in time and space, as these are conceptualised by any particular research method. This may sound confusing so I will elaborate with a brief example before delving in to the more academic justification of this argument in the following section.

To move away from the qualitative focus of the book for a moment, for illustrative reasons, let us say your study is interested in establishing the relationship between social behaviour and alcohol. Now, you could design an experiment for this. It may involve administering alcohol and then watching (through a one-way mirror) how the participant reacts to a stranger suddenly walking into the room where the participant is. You may find that the participant becomes animated.

To evaluate this study would involve invoking a number of assumptions around time and space. One is that the two events should be close in time (alcohol wears off) and in space (if the alcohol was administered in the pub, the person may already be primed to be social in the laboratory). You would also need to make sure that there is a reliable relationship between these events to make sure that the events are related (this would involve doing the same experiment regularly and with different participants and even different experimenters). You would also need to isolate out other possible events getting in the way of the relations (such as gender differences).

The evaluation of the study depends on the assumption that one event should come before the other, that they should be close in space and that they should be repeatable (reliable) across time. These are useful assumptions for this kind of experiment. This is only one possible configuration of time and space that is used in research, however. In the next section, I will discuss other configurations of time and space and their implications for the evaluation of research.

Traditional evaluation criteria

The most common evaluation criteria in psychology are the traditional concepts of 'validity', 'reliability' and 'generalisability'. These are the three traditional linchpins of quality control. These are complicated concepts but at their most basic they ask the following questions of research: Does the study measure what it purports to measure (validity)? Is it replicable if the study were to be done again (reliability)? Are we able to extrapolate to the world at large from the sample (generalisability)? These criteria make sense when the theory of knowledge (epistemology) assumes that, although open to errors of measurement, the world is stable, causes lead to effects and parts represent wholes.

In our hypothetical experiment above, these assumptions lead to scientists reading significance into repeating the experiment, isolating out all other extraneous events to make sure that only the two events are in relationship, and generalising to the outside world (linking alcohol to sociability). These assumptions underpin a 'scientific realism' (Madill, Jordan and Shirley, 2000) and is strongly influenced by the philosopher David Hume. Hume argued for a model of 'efficient causality'. In this model, causes come before effects and are close to them in space (contiguous). Most quantitative approaches in psychology assume this level of 'realism' and as Madill, Jordan and Shirley (2000) note, such a framework can be used, although adjusted, in qualitative approaches as well.

Harré and Madden (1975) and Slife and Williams (1995) illustrate that this model of time and space is not the only one. They draw on an Aristotelian view of time, space and causality, and show how these are relevant to the social sciences. As well as 'efficient causality', Aristotle also includes a number of other kinds of causality. One is 'formal causality'. Here events are simultaneously in relationship with each other (e.g., being sociable and being in the pub may go together and the more one is in the pub, the more sociable one may become). There is also 'final causality' or teleology, where events in the future 'cause' events in the present (e.g., getting paid as a future event 'causes' events in the present such as being at work). Finally, there is 'material causality'. Here properties of material cause events (e.g., a wood sculpture is partially 'caused' by the properties of wood). I put 'cause' in inverted commas because an efficient, singular 'cause' has come to dominate our common-sense understanding of the word. Aristotelian 'causality' refers to a broad understanding of 'cause' to mean the sets of relationships between events in different organisational arrangements of time and space. Moreover, an event cannot be reduced to one single cause but there are many types of cause for an event.

These sets of relationships between events are not mutually exclusive but different forms tend to dominate to different degrees in different kinds of research. For instance, Slife and Williams (1995) argue that structural models of identity, such as Marxism and Freudianism, consider structures (such as the structure of the the class system or the unconscious) as co-existent in time with the effects (such as class inequality or defence mechanisms). Moreover, these effects can reciprocally impact on the structure (the class system may change, for better or worse, in response to the effects of inequality; the unconscious may become more potent in response to the effects of strong defence mechanisms).

Material causality tends to dominate much of biology, psychology and psychiatry. This assumes that the material of one event (e.g., the grey matter of thinking) is in some sense a cause of another event (e.g., mental illness through a chemical imbalance in the grey matter). The two events co-exist, although one is considered to be the cause of another, in so far as the effect is contingent on a particular type of material. In 'final causality', an ultimate cause that lies in the future can be partially responsible for actions in the present. For instance, in a Piagetian model of child development, each stage is seen as moving towards a 'formal operational' stage in the future. This is known as a teleological cause – one that lies in the future but that the present moves towards.

The different ways in which causes and effects are theorised have implications for the confidence researchers can have in their findings. There are many layers of explanation for why an effect may occur (from the past, in the future, from events around it) which raises the question for quantitative

Table 8.1 The relationship between events and evaluation

Causality	Time and space of events	Examples of relevant methods	Evaluation questions
Efficient	One event comes before another event in time and is close to it in space.	Experimental research.	Have all other events been ruled out as interfering with the relationship under study?
Formal	One event is in a simultaneous relationship with another event in time and space.	Structural analysis in general (e.g., psychoanalysis, Marxism).	How does the structure exert its influence and how is it influenced by its effects? Where is the evidence?
Teleological	Events in the future precipitate events in the present.	Some models of childhood development. Some models of evolution.	Where are the stages that lead to a final state? Can these be recognised across different examples?
Material	Permanent properties of events create other events.	Some biological, psychological, and medical methods.	What the effects of material properties? Are these effects the same across events?

psychologists of how they know they have measured the relationship between events that they thought they had measured. The future, past and present can be seen as interlinking and intermixing in counter-intuitive ways. To complicate matters, as Ian Hacking (1995) has pointed out, humans interact with causal explanations. For instance, linking mental illness to a chemical imbalance in the brain may lead people to interpret their experience in this way, as opposed to class inequality or traumatic experiences. The latter interpretation would suggest there is no 'illness' in the sense of a material imbalance in the brain but that the person can participate, perhaps through political engagement, in their own recovery.

A summary of these different relationships is presented in Table 8.1. It is a rough summary for the purposes of illustration. Many methods incorporate aspects of all of these types of causality.

Evaluation criteria in qualitative research

In this section, I discuss the relevance of these views of time and space to qualitative research. From here, I move on to discuss the specific relevance to a dialogical methodology.

In qualitative research, the research takes the form of an intertextual product – the quotation (or data) and the treatment of the quotation by an authorial, academic text via an interpretation or analysis. Here, the criteria for evaluation also depend on an epistemological framework, including the theorisation of time and space. Madill, Jordan and Shirley's (2000) discussion of grounded theory and discourse analysis is particularly useful to understand these configurations.

In 'scientific realist' grounded theory (and in my view, some classic versions of phenomenology and narrative analysis), triangulation of the findings and consistency of interpretation is considered to be possible, although not to the same extent as it is in a statistical test. In the sense of recovering the meaning, the researcher assumes that the quotations/data are a cause of the interpretation. In other words, the interpretation is an effect of the antecedent set of texts that came before it and this resonates with an efficient model of causality. Evaluating this kind of research is possible through checking that the interpretation is generally the same across time and validated by other interpreters, including academics and also participants. The same texts (causes) should lead to the same academic interpretation (effects).

According to Madill et al. (2000) a 'contextualist' approach to grounded theory (and in my view, some versions of phenomenology and narrative methods) foregrounds the relationship between the context (including the interests of the reader, the analytic style of the researcher and the circumstances of the data collection) and the text. Here, the local and provisional quality of the quotations, including the subjectivity of the researcher in producing and categorising them, are seen as part of the overall intertextual product. To put it in other terms, the effect (the final analysis) and the cause (the original data and quotations) are in simultaneous relationship with each other and with the reader. This is a type of formal causality. This leads to ongoing, changing interpretations but is welcomed within the approach as having the potential to offer rich analytic descriptions of phenomena that change with the context.

Evaluating this kind of research is a matter of understanding how different perspectives, analytic styles and readings offer 'completeness' rather than 'convergence' (Madill et al., 2000: 12). There is no expectation that a singular reality will be revealed through the interpretation. Instead, the contradictions and biases of the author and reader are seen as constitutive of the intertextual product so that its meaning may change across space (different personal and cultural contexts) and time. There is an expectation, however, that the analysis will be rigorous, coherent and grounded in the participants' accounts.

In discourse analysis, material causality has a much greater prominence than other approaches in terms of the relationship between the interpretation and the quotations/data. 'Discourse analysis' means analysis of the stuff of discourse. It is out of the theorised material properties of discourse in general (e.g., that it constructs a reality; that it expresses power relations; that it contains voices) that any particular interpretation is based (e.g., the identification of 'extreme case formulations', 'turn-taking', 'institutional discourses', 'dialogue'). Of course this material is non-physical and in many ways, an interpretation of what the 'stuff' of discourse is. We have already seen in Chapter 2 that there are conflicting understandings of what the properties of discourse are, what it does and reflects. What is important to consider here, however, is that the relationship between the event of interpretation and event of the original data is marked by the perceived 'stuff' of discourse, whatever framework that may involve.

In terms of evaluation, there is a theoretical clash to be overcome with material causality. The material relationship between the interpretation and the original quotations/data is difficult to evaluate in a scientific realist way – for instance, by triangulating or doing repeated interpretations. This is because the nature of the material (discourse) makes this very problematic. The analysis, as further discourse, is vulnerable to the same effects of rhetoric, power and conflict as the material it analyses. Any successful triangulation would only confirm the same vulnerability to discursive effects.

Nevertheless, in practice, as Willig (2001) shows, different forms of discourse analysis tend to adopt similar criteria for evaluating the research. These mainly include 'coherence', in various guises, and 'persuasiveness'. Coherence refers to how well the final intertextual product fits together both internally and with other studies. There should be some internal correspondence between what the analyst interprets from the quotation and the quoted material. There should also be some evidence that what the analyst claims for one quotation can be credibly seen in other quotations as an identified coherent pattern.

However, if there is an exception, where the analysts' claims are not applicable to a particular quotation, then this also offers the opportunity to evaluate the quality of the analysis. More technically, this is known as 'deviant case analysis'. Through 'deviant cases', the limits of the interpretation can be assessed. It can also be used as a means of adding nuance to an interpretation. Alexa Hepburn and Jonathan Potter's (2007) study of the 'practice of crying' in the context of a child protection helpline is a good example of the use of deviant case to add nuance to the interpretation.

Coherence creates controversy for discursive approaches when it refers to the linkage between the data and the theory. This type of coherence is referred to as 'participant orientation'. Potter and Wetherell (1987), for instance, point out that there should be continuity between how the participants orientate to the talk (e.g., treating a question as an 'accusation') and how the analyst treats the same phenomena (they are justified in speaking of it as an 'accusation' in this context). In this view, it is incoherent with the data to link it to theoretical constructs (such as invisible power relations) unless it is orientated to in this way by the participants. However, Foucauldian, psychoanalytic and also a dialogical approach would argue that to be coherent with the data means to identify features of the discourse that the theoretical framework allows them to see, regardless of whether the participants orientate to these features as well. This general controversy reflects the difficulty in achieving standard evaluation criteria outside particular frameworks.

The evaluation criteria for different discursive approaches tend to be united again, however, under 'persuasiveness'. This is a very pragmatic criterion and refers to how well the study generates further debate, questions, generates new insights and methods of doing things or is 'fruitful', in Potter and Wetherell's (1987) terms. Under this criterion, discourse analysis of all varieties has been very valid and emerges out of an evaluation quite well. It is also worth noting that this criterion suggests a relationship between a future event (how useful the interpretation will turn out to be) and the current event (the interpretation). As such, this is an evaluative criterion based on teleology or final causality.

What is particularly striking about these evaluative criteria is their relationship to more general moral standards. Svend Brinkmann (2007) illustrates some more moral qualities that easily map on to discursive research as criteria for evaluation. He shows how a 'good' qualitative researcher needs to be sensitive to nuance, seeks to improve the world in some way through the application of their research findings and is able to allow the participants to 'object' to their descriptions. Epistemology and ethics are explicitly intertwined in qualitative research. In discursive research, being sensitive to nuance could be read as establishing coherence, allowing the other to object as 'deviant case analysis' and seeking to improve the world as 'fruitfulness'.

These criteria, grounded in ethics, are a little vague and it is difficult to know, when doing a discourse analysis, if one has indeed been virtuous or not. It is very helpful then to turn to what a poor analysis looks like. Charles Antaki, Michael Billig, Derek Edwards and Jonathan Potter (2003) have outlined what a poor analysis does. It: (1) summarises the data; (2) takes sides; (3) over-quotes or under-quotes; (4) identifies discourses with mental constructs; (5) uses false survey or generalises beyond the context of the study; (6) simply spots features. As we have seen in previous chapters, however, a dialogical approach can be guilty of summary, spotting features, under-quoting and identifying discourses not with mental constructs, but with subjectivity. To this, I shall return later.

So far, I have approached the issue of evaluation of qualitative research in general from the point of view of time–space, where evaluative judgements tend to be based on how well the quotations create the desired type of intertextuality: (a) one where the quotation is seen as leading to the surrounding interpretation – in a type of efficient causality; (b) where the quotation is in a simultaneous, ongoing relationship with the surrounding interpretation – in a type of formal causality; and (c) where the interpretation results from the material of the quotation – in a type of material causality. Table 8.2 summarises the relationship between causality, qualitative methods and evaluation criteria.

Table 8.2   The relationship between causality, qualitative method and evaluation criteria

Causality	Method	Evaluation
Efficient	Classic grounded theory, phenomenology, narrative.	The event of the data should lead to the event of the interpretation in the same way over time.
Formal	Contextualist versions of grounded theory, phenomenology, narrative.	No single correct interpretation. The interpretation as a living relationship between interpreter and interpreted.
Material	Discourse analysis.	The material features of discourse should form the basis of the interpretation, although the interpretation is vulnerable to discourse.

This categorisation is not meant to be black and white. Instead, these types of time–space relations are just tendencies of the different methodologies and in practice many exhibit all four models of causality. For example, discourse analysis is concerned with how one 'turn' follows from a previous 'turn' (efficient causality) and anticipates the next turn (final causality) within a particular context, including sets of power relations (formal causality). Nevertheless, it is the constructive material of the language/conversation itself that most clearly defines the intertextual relationship between interpretation and quotation. This material is theorised as open to identification and therefore to evaluation.

In the next section, I will assess how we can begin to evaluate a dialogical approach, bearing these previous points in mind. I will address this as a problem around evaluating an intertextual product as a dialogical relationship between quotations/data and interpretation. In doing this, I will turn back again to Antaki et al.'s (2003) and Potter and Wetherell's (1987) set of evaluative criteria. I will dialogue with these criteria, agreeing with some and disagreeing with others.

Evaluative criteria for a dialogical approach

From a dialogical point of view, a good intertextual product (analysis) strives to be 'polyphonic'. What this means is that distinct voices are put into contact with each other by the interpreting, authorial voice. Similar to contextual types of inquiry, there is a formal or reciprocal relationship between the quotations and the interpretation, the authorial voice and the reader, as they enter into dialogue with each other. The quoted text and the authorial voice are seen to simultaneously give meaning to each other in a type of 'formal' causality. This is the first major type of space and time that forms the background to any evaluation.

This contact means more than a passive recognition of subjectivity or the open potential of qualitative research. It is a much more active, even Romantic, conception of the interaction. The participants are considered to be 'heroes', testing a truth within the text (e.g., their outlook on art, the role of bureaucracy in an organisation) through their lived experience and against the values and judgement of others – real and imagined. The responsibility of the author/analyst lies in creating intertextuality from a position of 'outsideness' that allows a 'truth' to acquire a polyphony of sounds as it passes through the voices of the heroes.

Spatially, the author or analyst is 'outside' the text in so far as they actively shape the intertextuality from their own point of view and with their own accentuation (voice). This is not to say that a narrating confessional voice within the text is not possible as yet another voice. This 'voice' too, however, would need to be authored from a point 'outside' the text, as we draft and redraft our narrative to make it coherent. What unites the reader, authors and participants in a dialogical approach is the engagement with the polyphonic sounds of the 'truth' as it passes through different voices. The reader is invited to evaluate this by also participating through testing the ideas against other voices (perhaps, in this context, other academic discussions of the same topic as well as their own experience).

Good and poor examples of 'polyphony' are possible to identify. To return to Chapter 7, for instance, the 'Emilio' example was less polyphonic than the Lucie example. This is because Emilio's voice was more muffled than Lucie's voice. There was only one short quotation in brackets, interrupted by an ellipsis. This made it more difficult for Emilio to escape from outside the author's intonation and for the reader to establish a dialogue with Emilio. Lucie, in contrast, was given a full quotation and a subsequent interpretation. This interpretation was quite authoritative in authoring 'Lucie'. This, in itself, is fine – interpretations do try to be authoritative – but her voice hovered above the interpretation. In this sense, the reader was given the possibility of interacting with Lucie's 'truth', Laing and Esterson's 'truth' and even her father's 'truth' and evaluating these against each other.

While 'polyphony' is one criterion for evaluating the research, the second main criterion concerns how well the interpretation is tethered to the material of the discourse. In this case, such material includes direct and indirect speech, ellipses, speech genres, intonation and the chronotope. From this material, the resultant interpretation draws attention to aspects of subjectivity such as transformative experience, doubt, uncertainty, distance and closeness to others, and wrestling with the other. The identification of what I consider to be general discursive features tied to subjectivity leads to the possibility of a 'bureaucratic' approach, 'key moments' and 'summary tables'.

In principle, both 'polyphony' and 'material' features of discourse should be open to evaluation in two general senses. One is in terms of 'checking'. Kvale (1995) points to 'checking' as a form validation tied to 'craftsmanship'. Both self and others should be able to check the summary tables and interpretations against the corpus of data and the key moments. This is with the proviso, of course, that the evaluator shares the more fundamental epistemological 'belief' that the author is one genuinely seeking truth.

The other general sense of evaluation arises from Madill et al.'s (2000) discussion of different analytic styles, within a contextual approach, that can give complementary detail of the same data. In other words, someone else may also arrive with different 'key moments' and descriptions of 'time–space' configurations that can complement as well as create a space to 'test' the first interpretation – through seeing the overlaps and working out the differences between different interpretations.

So, 'polyphony' as a reciprocal relationship between author and hero forms the backbone of one set of criteria. How much space the hero is given in the text is an important feature of this criterion. The more material relationship between features of discourse and the interpretation forms the backbone of the other main criterion. The evaluator can 'check' and 'add' to the interpretation from their point of view. Yet, underpinning this evaluation is a more general belief in a dialogical subjectivity that is intertwined with language and that can be interpreted in better and worse ways. Table 8.3 summaries these two evaluation criteria.

Polyphony and the identification of discursive features are both quite broad criteria. In the section below, I suggest more specific criteria, within this remit, that can be used to evaluate the approach. I will also highlight

Table 8.3 **The relationship between causality and evaluation in a dialogical approach**

Criteria in a dialogical approach	Causality	Evaluation
Polyphony.	Formal.	Check level of interaction with participant voices.
Identifying features.	Material.	Check the identification of material features in the data.

how the feedback process from colleagues is vital to evaluation by giving specific examples of feedback I received on writing earlier data type chapters (from John McCarthy and Anna Madill). In this sense, the process of evaluating the research should start within the writing by asking for the views of outside others – as well as casting an evaluative eye over the interpretations oneself. This is what Kvale (1995) refers to as 'communicative validity'. This is very consistent with the dialogical perspective that the other supplements and adds to our own point of view on the world, which is bounded by the unique place we occupy in space and time.

How well has the researcher(s) established the research question?

This criterion is a very important one for judging the quality of a dialogical approach. Burman (2004: 6) puts it stridently, in the context of some comments on Antaki et al.'s (2003) criteria of evaluation: 'The most uninteresting and weak examples of discourse work that I have encountered principally founder through the failure to specify why this analysis is being done, and is worth doing.'

In a dialogical analysis, the question plays a key role in terms of striving towards a polyphonic authorship. It allows the author to delimit the boundaries of the text and shapes the interaction between the author and the 'heroes'. The question can be posed both within the text through the analysis and outside the text in the data collection phase. What is particularly interesting from a dialogical point of view is how the different participants respond to the question (e.g., what is the significance of the Romantic and the Professional genre for the artist's lived experience of making art?).

In a dialogical approach, the answers are not treated as if the participants represent a sample, as happens in quantitative research – e.g., '30 per cent of the authors used a Romantic genre'. This represents a more abstract, theoretical position reflective of 'pravda' or an abstract truth, discussed in previous chapters. Instead, the aim is to create a dialogue between different voices. The truth we are seeking is based on 'istina' or the lived experience of complex truth rather than pravda (abstract truth). This is particularly suited to moral questions or questions around identity and the existential search for meaning (as I have discussed in this book). The goal here is not cognitive understanding alone, but also a more visceral understanding of the relationship between particular contexts, people's experiences and the ways in which their world of meaning is felt and thought through. This understanding depends on entering into dialogue with the participants from one's own point of view.

On a very practical level, establishing the question allows the identification of key moments. A 'key moment', as we saw in Chapter 4, is akin to an 'utterance' and refers to moments in time where the researcher makes the judgement that they can respond to an utterance – academically and/or personally. It is of variable length but knowing a general question allows the researcher to judge which parts of long texts best respond to the question and in turn can be responded to.

In this interaction with the data, the initial question may evolve and change as the analysis progresses. In the example below, I include a sample of some feedback I got from Anna Madill. I got this feedback after doing the analysis. It meant I had to rethink what exactly I was asking and why.

Example 1

In Chapter 5, I initially wrote the following:

> I started off with the general question: 'How do the members of the organisation make sense out of their place in the organisation?'
> and Anna responded with the following feedback:
> Not clear why this question

I viewed this question as more than just an issue around information. Instead, it prompted me to think again about why I had chosen this question and how it related to what I had actually analysed. I knew I had chosen this out of a personal interest and also because I knew that much of the data dealt with the issue. With this feedback, however, I also knew that I had analysed much more than how the members made sense out of their place in the organisation.

So I rephrased it in the writing to:

> (Q)   I settled on the general question: 'How do members of the organisation experience their identity amidst organisational change?'

Anna's feedback came after the initial draft was done and this new sense of the question seemed to capture much better what had come up in the analysis. The turn of phrase 'settled' is admittedly misleading. It suggests that I settled on this question and then used this wording to approach the data. Instead, I settled on the question after the analysis was done. Yet the alternative 'the question turned out to be "x" from the replies I got to a different question', works against conventional time-sequence reporting of events.

This example is illustrative of how the question can evolve and change while the final product (the written-up analysis) tends to be presented as an inevitable time-sequence of events. This is not to say that the final 'question' here is the best possible one, but rather that the understanding of the question may shift and change as one interacts with the data and other people.

What space is given to participant voices in the text?

This criterion relates to the level of intertextuality that is possible in the text. How much presence can we give to the participants' voices? Unfortunately, there is simply not enough space in many journals, books or practitioner reports to accommodate the number of quotations or extracts for analysis as the researcher would generally wish. I have used summary tables along with quotations, sound bites and created dialogues in an effort to introduce as much intertextuality as possible.

This use of summary, however, is explicitly forbidden by Antaki et al.'s (2003) criteria for evaluating discursive research. They make the important point that the summary will lose the subtlety of the original texts and also hide the set of motivations through which the researcher approaches the text. It obscures this data from the gaze of the evaluator (and appendices with raw data would be voluminous).

In its use of summary tables, the method here moves significantly away from traditional discourse analysis. The motivation for using these summary tables is an ethical as well as aesthetic one. Ethically, I adopt the viewpoint that the data set deserves a presence of some shape, even if it is a summary. If one does not summarise the rest of the data set, one is at risk of falling into the other flaw of discourse analysis identified by Antaki et al. (2003) which is 'under-analysis through isolated quotation'. In the context of a large data set, any quotation in the final analysis will be isolated from the rest of the data set.

Aesthetically, in terms of coherence, the summary can contextualise and frame the subsequent 'real-life' quotations and their analysis. Summary tables can aid the intonation, sound and texture of the participants as they come alive in the quotation and are given a presence in the text. They are in a 'formal' relationship with the interpretation in so far as they are seen to give evidence for the interpretation while the interpretation emerges in part from the summary. Stylistically, summary tables are a form of 'reported speech' and the quotation seeks to bring this reported speech to life.

In terms of evaluating the use of a summary table, the raw data set needs to be available. However, this is often impossible due to practical constraints on space in the final publication. Within the analysis, a collaborator or colleague may give an indication as to how useful the summary is. Once it is published, the evaluation of the summary tables can be best done through relating them to the more substantial extracts that are made available.

While summary tables are useful but unsatisfactory in terms of giving a presence to the participant voices, a slightly more satisfactory device in this regard is the use of 'sound bites'. This is a bit of a trick to allow further intertextuality. It is an example of an 'under-quotation'. Yet, in the context of examining the self–other relationship as it plays out in the data, it is an important addition. What the participants say in an interesting line or two may help to accentuate points that other participants' make or reinforce a longer quotation that has been included. Moreover, as we saw in Chapter 6, they can also be used quite creatively in terms of allowing different participants to dialogue with each other directly, through the guiding hand of the author. I will discuss this in more detail under the fourth criterion below.

Within the process of the analysis, these sound bites can be written out in a separate document for potential inclusion in the final document. At this point they can be evaluated by a collaborator or by self in terms of how they connect to subjectivity and other pieces of the text. Once it is published, they can be evaluated in terms of their linkage to the surrounding analysis and to other, longer quotations.

Undoubtedly, however, while these two devices (summary tables and sound bites) help with creating intertextuality, it is the quotation itself which is most helpful in this regard. It is a very good opportunity for the reader of the interpretation to discern the links (or jumps) the author is making between the original text and the interpretation. These links need to be strong and the process of re-reading and redrafting is very helpful here. Nevertheless, it often takes another perspective, hopefully at a draft stage, to spot weaknesses here. Example 2 is a good illustration of this.

Example 2

Regarding an interpretation of a quotation of an artist talking about their love of steel, I originally wrote:

> Instead of being precious, it allows him to involve his whole personality in shaping it without worry of destroying it. This enjoyment of shaping and getting his whole personality involved in the material is also expressed poetically in the interviews

Here, John underlined 'whole personality' (appearing twice) and wrote in the margin:

Where in the extract?

This prompted me to look again at the extract and my interpretation. My interpretation of 'whole personality' related to the language of embodiment that he was using. The choice of words 'whole personality' went a little beyond this, however. It stretched the linkage between the extract and the interpretation. There was no evidence, in fact, that his 'whole personality' was involved. For this reason, in the next draft, I deleted this comment and redrafted the paragraph to focus on the language of embodiment.

Overall, in the evaluation of the intertextuality of the analysis, it is important to move continually between the interpretation and the quotation to check to see if there is continuity between them and a justifiable coherence in terms of the overall analytic framework. This is the main linchpin in terms of quality control. Sound bites and summary tables are particularly vulnerable to being taken out of context and manipulated by the author. So is the quotation, but at least it allows an evaluator to explicitly 'defend' the quoted voice from this manipulation or to constructively suggest a helpful addition/deletion. The quotation also allows the evaluator to check the summary tables and sound bites against their own reading of the participants' lived experience.

How well does the analysis draw attention to the discursive organisation of subjectivity?

The two criteria discussed so far specifically refer to the relationship between the 'data' and the interpretation as each simultaneously gives meaning to the other. The questioning voice of the author and the voices of the participants enter in dialogue with each other within the arena of the written-up analysis. The next criterion, however, refers much more to the material relationship between features of the discourse in general (such as chronotope, genre, direct and indirect speech) and the interpretation around changing subjectivity that it gives rise to.

We have seen that Antaki et al. (2003) draw attention to the difficulties of simply 'spotting' features of the discourse and calling it 'analysis'. Yet, in terms of approaching a full data set, systematic 'spotting' can be an important first step in understanding the range of different voices and extracts, not all of which can make it into the final analysis. For this reason, a very 'material' type of analysis of the 'key moments' at an early stage in the analysis process is beneficial. It allows the researcher to make a judgement around the time–space qualities of the discourse (chronotope), the emotional connection the authors have with what is being said, the possible genres, and direct and indirect speech.

This 'spotting' process does not lend itself to frequency tables because, consistent with the emphasis on '*istina*' and lived experience, the goal is not to 'generalise' the findings outside the sample. However, such spotting does allow an early first point of evaluation. The data can be reviewed to see if the material properties identified as being part of the discourse are coherent with the data. Other people can be invited to check the systematically 'spotted features' against the raw data. This may be difficult because, while time and space can be organised along pretty well-established paths (e.g., creating distance from the other, moving closer, promising future reward, constructing a bygone age), the genres can involve a mix of different sources, interconnect in unusual ways and relate to both subject (e.g., art) and form (e.g., Professional genre). Nevertheless, by constructing the tables, one can test one's own reading of the time–space dimension and genres against that of colleagues and collaborators.

In terms of the actual analysis, the more 'charismatic' and perhaps more difficult process is to link the 'spotting' that has come into the first part of the analysis to the kind of subjectivity that emerges. Also, Antaki et al. (2003) warn against linking discourse to mental constructs. Yet, linking the discourse to mental constructs is difficult to avoid, as Burman (2004) points out. As well as this, the conceptualisation of discourse as living voices involves an explicit link between discourse and a dialogical subjectivity.

In the example below, taken from Chapter 6, Anna points out a difficulty between linking a spotted feature to subjectivity. It relates to Extract 3. In this extract, one of the managers speaks of 'pushing' to build a new hospital within the context of community pride. In the initial draft, I had linked the 'idyll' to this sense of community pride.

Example 3

I had initially written:

> The idyll is marked by a provincial quality, where everyone knows everyone and time has a slow, viscous quality. Here, it took five years of pushing for any significant change to happen – the building of a new hospital.

To this, Anna had circled both 'slow viscous quality' and 'five years of pushing' and written:

> Are you relating these? Are they not different in value?

This question prompted me to think again. Why had I made this connection? Was it out of a desire to substantiate the 'idyll' and link it to transformative experience – in this case 'five years of pushing'? Yet, the idyll suggests routine and repetition more than working over years for a goal. One possibility was that perhaps there was no idyll at all in this extract. After thinking again, however, I tried to take a more measured approach to the data. Perhaps the 'five years of pushing' linked a future state (achieving the hospital) to the character of the managers – persistence and stubbornness. I thought this suggested more of an epic than an idyll.

In the end, I wrote the following:

> The 'extra mile' also speaks to an epic echo within the idyll. In the service of the community, the managers 'had been pushing' for the last five years for the creation of a new hospital. This five years of pushing links a future state (achieving the hospital) to the persistence and stubbornness of the managers

I thought that the expression 'epic echo' in particular created a sense that there could be a mix between genres. As part of this new analysis, I borrowed a part of the original quotation – 'going the extra mile' and 'had been pushing' – and embedded it into the interpretation as a means of justifying a new link to the epic.

This example shows an informal side of 'triangulation' through 'checking'. It is the outside other (in this case, Anna), who is able to read the material and the interpretation and make a judgement. This is possible in the context of a material connection between the original text ('pushing') and the interpretation ('the idyll'). It is possible for someone to evaluate the connections that are being made within the framework used – in this case the dialogical framework. The evaluation itself, however, can also be interpreted in different ways and has the pragmatic potential of improving the analysis through engaging with the different possibilities that it offers.

How well does the author use syncrisis and anacrisis?

This is another criterion that relates to more 'formal' relational causality. 'Anacrisis' and 'Syncrisis' are terms that Bakhtin (1984 [1929]) uses to describe the Socratic dialogues. He argues that Socrates is a master of both. 'Anacrisis' is a process of getting others to express their point of view on a subject in terms of how it connects to their lived experience. 'Syncrisis' is a process of juxtaposing different points of view together.

The entire dialogical project involves interpreting the assumptions, beliefs and viewpoints of the participants by means of reflecting on the data (bringing out their point of view through anacrisis) and juxtaposing different quotations against each other (syncrisis). Both syncrisis and anacrisis can be judged in terms of 'coherence' with the data and 'persuasiveness'.

Creating a dialogue between different sound bites is one way of establishing anacrisis and syncrisis. This presupposes a general research question that serves as point of organisation for the created dialogue. It also presupposes that the various participants will have conflicting and perhaps even conflicted views.

It is difficult to evaluate the created dialogue. The dialogue needs to appear coherent and yet use the actual words of the participants. The goal is to foreground the addressivity of different participants to each other. It involves a constant evaluation in terms of coherence. The key test to evaluate this is the question: Does it sound as if the participants are replying to each other? Fillers are inserted to help this coherence.

In terms of content, it is important to establish relations of agreement and disagreement with each other. This is important in terms of achieving syncrisis or juxtaposing different viewpoints against each other. It is also important in terms of achieving anacrisis or the expression of (or search for) a viewpoint against the anticipated judgements of others. In the created dialogue, this involves bringing indirect engagements with others through qualifications, jokes and allusions to a very direct, head-to-head dialogue. This will inevitably involve a lot of redrafting.

Outside this 'internal' evaluation, 'outside evaluation' is also possible for the created dialogue and its interpretation. In the comment below, John assesses an interpretation of the second 'created dialogue' in Chapter 6:

Example 4

After the created dialogue, I had originally written:

> We can see that the unofficial view of management as a bunch of clowns and dead wood at the top, getting in the way of each other, is countered by the corporate team through an appeal to audits and accountability.

To this, John had inserted the comment:

> More than that, I think e.g., see the turn on casualty by a CT* person and the turn on the acute side of mental health services. I skimmed all of the CT contributions in this extract (ignoring the others in between) and I think they offer a richer counter than you suggest through quite a deep account of what their role is, how they see the organisation and implicitly what their values are.

*Corporate Team

This comment illustrates that the 'created dialogue' can be evaluated on a turn-by-turn basis or by looking only at one set of contributions apart from the others. The interpretation can also be evaluated in terms of how well it brings out the synrcrisis and anacrisis of the 'created dialogue'.

John's comment allowed me to re-read the extract with a new sensibility to the CT point of view, including their values and lived experience. After much redrafting, I settled on the following, with some help from John's comment:

> ...They appeal to audits and accountability ('there are about seventy thousand people go through casualty'), which is anticipated and acknowledged by a member of the 'mental health team' as a 'paper trail'. This agreement suggests that there is some degree of ambivalence in the carnival genre – with the management decrowned as useless but also given some sympathy. Management also give concrete examples of where they have instigated change, such as deinstitutionalising the mental health services.

This, I felt, brought out better the complexity and presence of the CT view. In a way, the fact that John was able to discern this depth from the created dialogue also acted as a form of positive evaluation for the created dialogue – that the quotations that were selected and put together could offer the reader something against which to evaluate the interpretation.

Another way of evaluating the created dialogue and surrounding interpretation is to adopt a more body-centred approach than a cognitive one alone. John, for example, asked the telling question earlier in the chapter:

Example 5

As an aside, were your sympathies with the MHT* and DG** groups? I thought they were on a couple of occasions

*Mental health team
**Disability group

This comment is a form of anacrisis in itself, in that it helps me to reflect on my own 'point of view'. It led me to think about how the goals of syncrisis and anacrisis could be reconciled with my own analytic style and whether a 'confession' might be appropriate in the text. After much deliberation, however, I decided against this. This was mainly because I did not know where my sympathies lay and I doubted that any confession on my part would prevent a subsequent misreading of the text or may even led to an interpretation of authorial egomania. Instead, I reviewed the extracts again and tried to make sure that I was giving as complex and as deep a reading of the different viewpoints as possible. I wanted to avoid 'straw manning' any of the viewpoints. From doing this, I found, perhaps inevitably, that I had sympathy with all of the different groups in different ways or could find value in the different viewpoints.

This visceral reaction to the viewpoints could also be an evaluation criterion for syncrisis and anacrisis. Cromby (in press) makes the point that qualitative analyses implicitly favour rationality and control, through their privileging of language alone. The visceral response of sympathy moves beyond such a traditional privileging. Allowing oneself to feel sympathy may create opportunities to find value in the complexity of the different viewpoints, even if some are more convincing than others.

Discussion

Overall in this chapter, I have sought to establish evaluative criteria for a dialogical approach that can be used both for the researchers and for the readers. Evaluation is a process that needs to take place at every stage of the analysis, from interpreting the initial data set, to writing and to re-writing the analysis. In this sense, evaluation is an ongoing participatory activity.

We have looked at some thorny issues in this review, such as causation and the time–space relationship between events. From this, I have argued that in so far as a dialogical analysis identifies features of the discourse, then it shares a practice of material-based interpretation with other forms of discourse analysis. This is with the important caveat, however, that like these other forms of discourse analysis, the material is identified from a theorisation of what the 'stuff' of discourse consists of (i.e., the self–other axis). While this framework is limited by the values it ascribes to discourse (an author seeking truth; a dilemmatic subjectivity), it is as limited as other theoretical readings of what the 'stuff' of discourse could be (unconscious, institutional, strategic).

These boundaries of the framework help us to understand the specific evaluative criteria that may be appropriate to it. This is a more general point that is well made by Madill et al. (2000) and Willig (2001). Research should be evaluated from within its own theoretical framework. This is just as well from a dialogical point of view because it would otherwise count as a poor analytic procedure according to Antaki et al.'s (2003) argument. Yet, as Burman (2004) points out, Antaki et al.'s (2003) criteria are also open to interpretation and amendment. In the case of dialogism, amending these criteria involves bringing a discourse analysis closer to a more traditional 'contextualist' approach to grounded theory that looks at the discourse in terms of lived experience.

This move away from the material of discourse alone towards linking it to a dialogic subjectivity introduces a more 'formal' causality to the interpretation, where the relationship between the analysis and the data is ongoing and responsive to each other (as in, for instance, the changing set of questions one poses to a data set). Within this, the discursive features become important not in terms of how they construct a particular social reality, but more in terms of how they illuminate the working out of subjective experience through dialogue with the other. This too, however, can be subject to 'checking' and 'adding' by others.

Despite these differences, what a dialogical framework does share with other discursive frameworks in terms of evaluation is the emphasis on 'coherence' and 'persuasiveness' (as a goal). These are very broad criteria, however. Here, I have argued for the coherence between the data and the interpretation to be systematic or bureaucratic from the outset. However, the 'style' of the researcher, or the charisma, is not open to reproduction by others, but it is open to 'checking' and a more 'communicative validity'. Here, I have tried to illustrate this communicative validity with reference to examples of the kind of feedback that helps the analysis to improve. This is not only judged by a cognitive sense of coherence, but also by a much visceral sense of coherence – where the value of different viewpoints can be experienced, through, for instance, feeling 'sympathy' even if one disagrees with the viewpoint as a whole.

Overall, while in this chapter I have been at pains to establish a set of evaluative criteria that can be usefully applied to a dialogical approach, in the next chapter I will turn to wider issues around how useful this general framework is, what the limitations and difficulties of it are and how it can add to other approaches. In particular, I will argue that a dialogical approach is useful when it comes to addressing questions that place lived experience, emotion and an existential search for meaning at its core. In other words, I am keen to emphasise that it is an approach with reasonably clear boundaries. It can be evaluated in terms of its specific goals and framework.

Further reading

Antaki, C., Billig, M., Edwards, D. and Potter, J. (2003) Discourse analysis means doing analysis: A critique of six analytic shortcomings. *Discourse Analysis Online*, 1(1). Available online at: http://extra.shu.ac.uk/daol/.

Brinkmann, S. (2007) The good qualitative researcher. *Qualitative Research in Psychology*, 4: 127–44.

Burman, E. (2004) Discourse analysis means analysing discourse: Some comments on Antaki, Billig, Edwards and Potter, 'Discourse analysis means doing analysis: A critique of six analytical shortcomings'. *Discourse Analysis Online*. Available online at: http://extra.shu.ac.uk/daol/.

Harré, R. and Madden, E.H. (1975) *Causal Powers: A Theory of Natural Necessity.* Totowa, NJ: Rowman & Littlefield.

Kvale, S. (1995) The social construction of validity. *Qualitative Inquiry*, 1(1): 19–40.

Madill, A., Jordan, A. and Shirley, C. (2000) Objectivity and reliability in qualitative analysis: Realist, contextualist and radical constructionist epistemologies. *British Journal of Psychology*, 91(1): 1–20.

Potter, J. and Wetherell, M. (1987) *Discourse and Social Psychology: Beyond Attitudes and Behaviour.* London: Sage.

Slife, B.D. and Williams, R.N. (1995) *What's Behind the Research? Discovering Hidden Assumptions in the Behavioural Sciences.* London: Sage.

Weinert, F. (2009) *Copernicus, Darwin and Freud: Revolutions in the History and Philosophy of Science.* Chichester: Wiley Blackwell.

Willig, C. (2001) *Introducing Qualitative Research in Psychology: Adventures in Theory and Method.* Buckingham: Open University Press.

9

DISCUSSION

As we have seen in this book, the dialogical approach to qualitative analysis has strengths and weaknesses. It is suitable for some research questions more than others. In particular, it is well suited to questions around lived experience, identity and the interpretation of action. It is arguably less suited to questions around political participation, encouraging change or analysing general power imbalances. In this chapter, I take a reflective look at both the theory and method of a dialogical approach to help delineate some of these boundaries of the dialogical approach in more detail. In the process, I summarise some of the key theoretical and methodological points of a dialogical approach. This is not intended to be an exhaustive summary, but rather a stroll through some of the features that particularly stand out. In the final part of the chapter, I suggest some of the ways in which the boundaries of the dialogical approach can be extended in future research.

Theoretical reflection

The theoretical foundations of a dialogical method rest upon Bakhtin's writings on identity and social life. However, there are many different readings of what Bakhtin said, what he meant by what he said and if indeed he said what he said, with a number of disputes around what he authored. Here, I have developed a very particular reading of Bakthin's dialogism that rests upon a set of values that are primarily aesthetic and romantic. In doing this, I have been influenced mainly by North American appropriations of Bakhtin's work, including Morson and Emerson (1990) and Holquist (2002). Below, I set out what these foundations have led me towards, their relationship to other theoretical approaches in qualitative research and their limitations. I do this as a reflection on the previous chapters so will refer to these as part of the overview.

The moral organisation of time and space

This point emerges from the use of the chronotope in the data analysis. The chronotope refers to the organisation of time and space in language. What we have seen, here, is that this organisation reflects different values that make contact with people in different ways. For instance, the Romantic and Professional genres that underpin the experience of artists organise time and space differently. Passion, intuition and absorption give the art experience a high value – something to strive towards, to enjoy in the moment, to reflect upon afterwards. The Professional genre reflects a more strategic subjectivity, negotiating the exigencies of the outer world, feeling pressures and ambivalence, pricing an aesthetic value. Equally, in the 'Health Care Organisation' (HCO), the organisation could alternate in terms a carnivalesque space of abuse, idiocy and endless ineffectual, irrational change to more family-based genres of vocation, reasonable hierarchy, a shared past but with some traces of alienation and pride.

What is useful about the chronotope, as a methodological concept, is that it draws attention to the responsive and shifting experiences of time and space. Other qualitative approaches tend to underplay this dynamism. Phenomenological approaches and 'constructionist grounded theory' are very good at showing what people think and feel about their social world, while discursive approaches are very good at revealing the changing constructions of the social world. What is understated in these analyses, however, is how the organisation of time and space is linked to moral truths and particular subjectivities.

One possible reason for this lack of attention to the chronotope may be because it is a little unclear when it comes to debates around the individual's agency. Indeed, in doing the analysis, it is sometimes difficult to establish whether someone can simply speak a genre and organise a time and space (e.g., come along to an institution and make everyone an epic hero in a moment) or if the organisation of particular places is already constituted by various historical and social forces over which the individual has little or no control. There is a contextual side to this as well. In some contexts (e.g., when talking to friends), it can be easier to change the time and space (such as poking someone in the ribs as a carnival act of 'praise-abuse') than in other contexts.

Outside the interpersonal context, there is also a more sociological reading of carnival available. With set 'carnival' times through history (set in the calendar, sanctified by authority), carnival could be viewed as an emancipatory institution that liberates selves from official convention. Peter Stallybrass and Allon White (1986), for instance, draw attention to the sociological aspect of carnival. Carnival can be read as a collective performance that allows the collective release of steam. Time and space change in such festival times as part of a collective desire. This 'safety valve' reading brings us on to some shaky ground. 'Good power' is pitched somewhat reductively against 'bad power'.

In this book, I have shied away from a sociological reading of carnival. Instead, a dialogical analysis, as I am reading it, is much more interested in how carnival, as a sense of time and space, interacts with subjectivity or becomes embodied. Carnival, in my reading, is a genre, a way of viewing and interacting with the world.

My intersubjective reading of carnival also has its limitations. In all of the case studies I have drawn on, the participants speak from within a world where time and space are already largely constituted. For instance, Kevin's irritation at the art galleries and the power they have over prices is an established historical feature of the art world (Becker, 1984). The capacity of Kevin to dialogue this feature of the art world out of existence is limited. These weaknesses of the dialogical approach are perhaps best expressed by Hirschkop:

> As we all know too well, the picking and choosing of language forms takes place not on a level playing field, but in an unevenly structured linguistic world, in which some speakers and institutions have a great deal more influence than others. And that is why historical becoming, in actuality as opposed to Bakhtin's philosophy, consists of violent struggle as much as verbal give and take: because its narratives, *pace* Bakhtin, are made by turning points and decisions which are often enforced on *others* by fiat rather than presented to them as a gift.
>
> (1999: 263)

Hirschkop (1999) makes a telling point and one that would be very familiar to critical theorists sensitive to power, economics, ideology and violence. Such power transcends and constitutes the landscape of the self–other dialogue.

One way of approaching this critique is to focus on the role of consciousness. The self–other approach exalts the role of consciousness in bringing power dynamics under intense analysis and reflection. So in the case of the art world, what is of immense interest is the artist's capacity to reflect upon (cognitively and emotionally) these power imbalances. Similarly, in the HCO, there is an intense level of reflection, and irritation, around the organisation of the bureaucracy. There is even some resistance to authorial control, at a literary level, by Emilio and Lucie in Chapter 7. These participants may not be able to change anything through conscious reflection alone, but they can talk about power and make sense out of it and perhaps even give it a carnivalesque flavour from time to time.

What we have seen in the case studies here is that the mundane, everyday analysis of power relations involves an emotional as well as a cognitive, abstract reflection. Such everyday analyses become 'lived' in terms of the struggles and pleasures of bringing the abstract to conscious attention. In bringing these power relations to the attention of others, moments of 'calibration' between chronotopes are possible, as is a political consciousness (Holquist, 2002). For example, in Chapter 7, Lucie's sudden psychological analysis of her father's relationship with her allows her to calibrate with an authoritative psychological tradition. In Chapter 6, the parodic and imaginary dialogues with management allow a mundane, carnivalesque sensibility to permeate the official hierarchical organisation. It is these moments that the dialogical approach tends to highlight and even celebrate rather than the drowning out or the violent effacing of the person who is tangled up in the web of these systems.

From this point of view, Hirschkop's critique stands, but is softened by the potential of consciousness to see, analyse and respond to the imposition of a world by fiat. This is an arena of personal crisis, where the self tries to make sense out of experience with and against concrete and imaginary, anticipated others. What comes into focus, when one does this, is the figure of the Romantic hero, living ideas through his or her life and understanding these through others. They learn from the other experientially and bodily as much as cognitively. The principles of these ideas (such as patriarchy, economic oppression, the moral imposition of time and space) blur into the background as the *istina* or abstract side of the ideas and it is the *pravda*, or the fusion of the ideas with the Romantic hero, that are brought sharply into relief.

The focus on the Romantic hero, engaged with and responsive to others' ideas, brings me to the next main theoretical reflection – self and other as the dialogical axis of language.

The self–other axis

Self and other constitute the main theoretical axis of language in a dialogical approach. This is a structural assumption of the approach. Just as the psychoanalytic emphasis on the 'unconscious' or the Focuauldian reliance on 'power' are the poles around which the fabric of discourse hangs, in a dialogical approach, discourse dissolves into the self–other distinction. Pragmatically, this assumption allows the analyst to speak of changing boundaries, voices and the seeking author. It also leads to a focus on intonation or the emotional and moral connection to what is said.

At its broadest, 'self' is interpreted as the active 'author' and 'other' as the responsive addressee. Yet, what falls into the category 'other' and 'self' is not necessarily static but potentially open to change. We saw one example of this movement between 'self' and a variety of 'others' in Chapter 7. We examined a number of 'reciprocal reconfigurations' between 'self' and 'other' as the addressee changed, and the capacity to allow the other to 'speak' and interfere with the process of authorship also changed across texts. Similarly, in Chapter 5 we saw that the self–other distinction is sometimes a permeable boundary. For example, the artist, Ina, questioned her own motivations. Here, self is divided between the questioning, conscious self and the intuitive, unconscious, feeling self – either of which or both could be addressee and/or author at different points in her relationship with the objects.

More generally, understanding what constitutes 'self' and 'other' may change across time and space. The many examples of ironic re-voicing and micro-dialogues in the focus groups illustrate the variety of ways of engaging with the other across different chronotopes. In a fantasy micro-dialogue, a carnivalesque version of the other may appear. Similarly, in parody, the other's intonation may be detectable from within the authorial intonation. This reflects the distinction between 'outside-in' discourses where the authorship is grounded in the certainty of the authorial discourse and more 'inside-out' discourses where the other's discourse ambivalently interferes with and changes the authorial discourse.

The trusting assumption of an author vulnerable to crisis involves a radical re-evaluation of the traditionally conceived strategic aspects of language, such as the 'extreme case formulation' or the 'disclaimer'. In a dialogical view, these are considered as 'sore-spots' and the 'word with a loophole'. The author is not only a calculating agent or a conduit to their inner world, but is also viewed as open to uncertainty, being bombastic at times, responsive, afraid and deeply anticipative of others' replies. This also means that we cannot simply trust that what the author says gives access to a phenomenological experience. There are too many caveats and anticipation of others' judgements to treat the content of what is said in isolation from the form.

The anchorage of language to the self–other axis does create some theoretical and methodological difficulties. Theoretically, it means that self and other are conceptualised as indigent. This is a foundational assumption of dialogue that gives it a flavour of realism. Yet, like other qualitative approaches, it is an assumption that rests on an outlook and a value. It is an orientation towards the world rather than any empirical observation. This means, like any other value system, that it is difficult to find counter-evidence. Absolution for calculating, unscrupulous action comes in the form of an introspective, conflicted self and/or a self seeking to author the other and dependent on the other's response as a consequence. For instance, the corporate team, as the face of management in Chapter 6, ambivalently relate to their position of power, at least as viewed through a dialogical lens. Indeed, what emerges from this analysis is that there is no Machiavellian participant but rather that the anticipation of Machiavellian others runs through and structures much of their experience.

Methodologically, the ambivalence around who is self and other means that the identification of 'self' and 'other' is often unclear. For this reason, the methodological tools outlined here tend to focus on the identification of different kinds of discourse (e.g., 'outside-in'; 'inside-out'), genre, and the emotional register. From these, we can draw dotted lines to the identification of self and other, but even so, this does involve a degree of creative authorship on the part of the analyst. Within the analysis, the participants are transformed into 'others', with relatively congealed boundaries that may well be alien to them. Ultimately, however, the aspiration of a dialogical method is to aesthetically enrich the 'other' by entering into dialogue with what they have to say.

Lest the reader leave with a somewhat edifying concept of dialogue where absolution lies in the assumption of indigency, I will now turn to the third theoretical theme that emerges from this book which is the dark side of dialogue.

The dark side of dialogue: anticipated others

While Bakhtin's dialogical approach focuses on the self–other dialogue at the expense of discovering the veins of power, this does not necessarily mean that the pedagogical opportunities of a dialogical encounter are always to be relished. I have already alluded to the crisis-ridden subject of a Bakhtinian dialogue. Here, I will expand briefly on this to show how the variety of 'others' in dialogue casts a dark shadow over the more innocent interpretation advanced thus far.

A key distinction in dialogue is between 'anticipated' and 'real' responses. A 'real' or 'anticipated' response does not have to be from a person – it may come from art material, for instance. I argued throughout the book that the anticipation of others' judgements can be reflexively reworked into the structure of discourse. We saw this in particular detail in Chapter 6. Here, each of the different focus groups anticipated each other's judgements so much so that we could bring these allusions together in a created dialogue. Leaving aside this methodological tool, however, it is noteworthy that the anticipated 'other' can exacerbate, embellish and exaggerate the 'sore-spots', paranoia and suspicion with which selves approach each other.

It is worth quoting Emerson here to appreciate this dark side of the dialogical encounter:

> Read Bakhtin carefully, and you will see that nowhere does he suggest that dialogue between real people necessarily brings truth, happiness, or honesty. It brings only concretization (and even that is temporary), and the possibility of change, of some forward movement. Under optimal conditions, dialogue provides options. But there can still be mutual deception, mountains of lies exchanged, pressing desires unanswered or unregistered, gratuitous cruelty administered on terrain to which only the intimate beloved has access. By having a real other respond to me, I am spared one thing only: the worst cumulative effects of my own echo chamber of words.

(1997: 152–3)

Consciousness, as Bakhtin (1984 [1929]) puts it, can be 'terrifying'. The capacity of the anticipated response to torture and to amplify the worst paranoid imagining of an active consciousness is immense. The 'real' response only allows a moment of finalisation and contour giving to the 'echo-chamber' of anticipated responses. Of course, this 'finalisation' may be extremely hurtful or exaggerate and amplify an existing sore-spot. Nevertheless, it is encapsulated in another's utterance and allows the possibility of approaching it from the 'outside' or from a distance. Equally, the penetrative word of another may drag us away from the worst imaginings of anticipated judgements. In both cases, the task facing the author is to listen and respond both to what is said and the tone in which it is said. An alternative temptation is to use the 'real' response only as a jumping-off point to an intense internal dialogue with the anticipated, imagined replies of others.

To be unsettled and changed by otherness is an extraordinary achievement, involving the Romantic struggle outlined in the previous section. It is extraordinary considering the power of the anticipated response over the genuine response. In this regard, there is a prescriptive undercurrent to dialogue. It urges us to linger over the responses of others, particularly in moments of crisis.

Nevertheless, there are moments when a self-confident authorship of a variety of others does not have to be so crisis-ridden. We saw some examples of this in Chapter 5 with the example of Donna's art-making. Her dialogue with the glass and her art involved a transformation and elevation of material into sublime experience. Equally, the expert narratives around 'schizophrenia' in Chapter 7 could be remarkably sure and confident in their authorship of others. Even here, however, both of these self-confident discourses depended on a somewhat malleable other that could yield to and be shaped by such self-confidence rather than meaningfully resist the form-shaping activity of its authorship.

Methodologically, the possibility of anticipated interlocutors spilling out and into our dialogues with concrete others is missing or understated in other qualitative approaches. In discursive approaches, the 'other' tends to be primarily considered as the immediate interlocutor or the obvious audience of a public address. In more phenomenological approaches, the 'other' tends to be the interviewer or the subjects of an address. The benefit of the dialogical approach is that through its focus on double-voiced discourse, it admits the possibility of a multi-levelled experience with a diversity of sometimes competing addressees and replies – often to the more self-confident, authoritative words of others.

This emphasis on the anticipated other means that there are a potential unlimited number of addressees to an utterance with the capacity to structure the shape of the utterance. Methodologically, this introduces quite a degree of uncertainty into the analysis of discourse. Ultimately, however, it does not matter who the various 'others' are that structure a discourse as long as the creation of experience through dialogue is brought into relief. This brings me to the more concrete reflections on the methodological boundaries of the approach.

Reflections on method

One of the biggest challenges of qualitative research is to work out a set of methodological tools that can systematise theoretical principles. Here, I have relied extensively on the identification of key moments, genres, discourse types, emotional register and chronotope.

The use of key moments

The use of 'key moments' or 'key utterances' is helpful as part of a preliminary engagement with the data set, alongside re-reading and note-taking. It is possible to do an analysis without using them but they can be a helpful route into the data.

The use of these moments makes the dialogical approach different from those approaches that rely on an exhaustive coding of the entire set (either line by line or thematically) or the exhaustive analysis of turn-taking in discourse. These other methods are also useful as a means of familiarisation with the entire data set and building up an analysis. The use of 'key moments', however, is particular suited to a dialogical epistemology. This is because it is consistent with the focus on the 'utterance' as the basic unit of communication. An 'utterance' is that which the addressee feels capable of responding to. This gives a level of flexibility in terms of focusing the analysis on key parts of the data set. As such, it may be useful for large data sets. Moreover, as the reading and re-reading of the data set continues and the possible questions evolve and change, then the boundaries of the 'key moments' and the number of 'key moments' may also change.

One of the limitations of the 'key moment', however, is that it is an inconsistent unit of analysis in terms of length. The advantage of other qualitative approaches is that standardised units of analysis give the analyst confidence that they are systematic. With a 'key moment', it is quite different. At one level, entire pages of text may seem to be relevant to a key moment while other 'key moments' may only be a few lines long. Much data may not even make it as a key moment but rather end up on the editing floor.

For example, in Chapters 5 and 6, the number of key moments was significantly reduced as the analysis went on. Each of these was a different length and sometimes the boundaries of the key moment were revised with re-reading. Moreover, as we saw in Chapter 7, an entire analysis was built around four 'key moments' in a written text, while in Chapters 5 and 6, there was more than twenty key moments to each participant. This may seem messy and inconsistent against the light of other qualitative approaches. This is a consequence of placing the 'response' and the 'utterance' at the forefront of the data analysis.

Making the analyst's response to the data into a first step of analysis may lead to a kind of interpretative omnipotence or a monological, singular reading of the text. Other approaches also have this danger to a certain extent, as the questions they pose shape what they see in the data. To guard against this, I have been keen to stress, in Chapters 5 and 6 in particular, that different participants' experiences, articulated through different genres, can be put in dialogue with each other. For instance, in Chapter 5, we looked at two quite different key moments from each artist – one relating to the Romantic genre and the other relating to the Professional genre. Similarly, in Chapter 6, we looked at 'key moments' from each of the different participants to help give some equality to the number of 'key moments' across participants.

Perhaps the best method of guarding against interpretative omnipotence, however, is the use of collaborators in research. Here, I have stressed the informal, creative aspect of such collaboration. Others' perspectives can help identify and challenge the use of key moments as well as their significance. Saying this may appear odd considering that this is a single-authored book. However, as Chapter 8 hopefully made clear, collaboration and feedback from colleagues has been a feature of the interpretations and indeed one of the limitations of the analyses is that this kind of dialogical activity is not even more present throughout the analysis.

These measures are not guaranteed to prevent a monological, academic insistence on the structure of experience. However, the aspiration is to put a variety of different experiences in dialogue with each other through the prism of the question that is posed to the participants, as well as collaborating with others outside the text.

The identification of discursive features

The identification of discursive features introduces a systematic or bureaucratic flavour into a dialogical analysis. As we saw in Chapter 4, it involves taking all of the 'key moments' and identifying the genre and discourse type, the emotional intonation, the chronotope and the context in which the utterance is said. These can be collated in the form of a table.

This level of systematisation could be viewed as another form of coding the data. The codes are structured around four different avenues into the data (genre, discourse, emotion, chronotope). The codes, in this sense, work as a matrix of different possibilities for viewing the same piece of data. This offers quite an amount of guidance to the analyst in terms of what to look for in a particular text. This may be particularly useful to students who struggle to rephrase and go beyond what the participants say in qualitative coding exercises.

In practice, however, it can also be quite difficult to effectively use these methods of interpretation meaningfully. In the case studies I have discussed, while I talked about discursive features, it was sometimes a struggle to come up with appropriate types. For instance, much of the interview data with the artists could be viewed as a form of confession – where they reveal their thoughts and feelings. This is a very broad category of genre. Yet, narrowing down the genre also means that one could be left simply with the repeated words and phrases of the participants. Striking a middle course between these is not easy. Identifying discourses is also difficult, although helped by the conventional interpretation of different genres – i.e., epic genres tend to be 'outside-in' while parodic genres tend to be more 'inside-out'. Similarly, the identification of 'chronotopes' in terms of how time and space are organised is also difficult, depending on what the assumptions of the talk are – e.g., assuming a final goal or idyllic past.

Writing up the analysis

Writing up the analysis is perhaps the most charismatic or creative part of the method. It involves actively linking the groundwork done in the analysis of the data set to the lived experience and subjectivity of the participants.

The form that this takes is primarily constituted by the research question, which itself is open to change.

One of the key aspects of a dialogical approach is its recognition of the contradictory desire on the part of the analyst to include as much of the lived experience and voices of the participants as possible and also to do justice to the entire data set. For this reason, I have used the method of combining summary with quotations and sound bites. I have shown in Chapters 5 and 6 in particular that the balance between these is iterative. That is, as the drafts of the analysis progress, more quotations will have to leave, be reduced to a sound bite and/or become assimilated to a more general summary. The benefit of this is that there is some scope for a comprehensive engagement with the question from various parts of the data set. However, the summary, as we saw in Chapter 7 in the case of 'Emilio', can work to muffle alternative readings of the data. For this reason, it is important that as many of the participants' voices as possible are included without damaging the authorial engagement with the question.

The use of sound bites is particularly interesting. They are an explicit recognition of the tendency of qualitative approaches, including some discourse and phenomenological approaches, to refer to bits of extracts that are not included in the quotation that is being analysed. In 'interpretive phenomenological analysis', Jonathan Smith (2010) refers to 'utterances that shine' as 'pearls' and 'gems'. Sound bites are like this.

However, if recorded as part of the analysis, they can also be used to 'create' a dialogue on the basis of the anticipated responses. Doing this brings the method significantly beyond other qualitative approaches where there is a focus on doing as much as possible to bring in the context as part of the analysis. The 'created dialogue', on the other hand, gives a more literary sensibility to the write-up than other qualitative analyses. It is particularly suited to highly double-voiced discourse and may be less useful for other types of data. It can also be embedded in a more traditional context of quotations and summaries so that the creative leanings of the analyst remain tethered to the actual structure of the participant discourse.

Ethics

The importance of tethering the analysis to the participant discourse touches on ethics. The participants may well expect that their own voice, perspective and thoughts will be favourably represented by the analyst. Yet, no matter how favourable the analyst is, the task of qualitative research is to create a new text, albeit an intertextual one, and in a sense, what the participants say will become re-accentuated in many different ways as part of the impulse to answer a particular research question. Most, if not all, qualitative approaches do change the shape of the participants' discourse in one way or another and in some cases it may be (creatively) bent out of all recognition.

In qualitative research, in general, much care is taken around securing informed consent (outside public domain material). However, if the analysis adopts a general attitude of suspicion, the participants may not like it – if they get to see it. Likewise, even if the analysis approaches the discourse from the point of view of 'trust' and sympathy, but interprets 'sore-spots' along the way, the participants may not like it either. This does create an ethical dilemma. Do we take the analysis back to the participants and potentially hurt their feelings because they possibly have a right to know, or do we rely on initial informed consent and anonymise the data?

A third possibility is to explain, as part of the informed consent procedures, that although they might like the resulting interpretation, there is also a chance that they may not like it – although it can be anonymised to protect their identity. Moreover, once the interpretation is in the public domain, it may receive further interpretations that the participants may or may not like. Working out the full implications of handing over their words to someone else may be worth spending some time on at the beginning of the data collection process as part of a general discussion around the potential value of the research (see Hollway and Jefferson, 2000, for more on this).

Similarly there are also some pros and cons to bringing the results of an interpretation back to the participants as part of a validation exercise. Some recent research with Anna Madill (Madill and Sullivan, in preparation) has illustrated the potential benefits and difficulties with these kinds of exercises, for both researchers and participants. Such exercises can be uncomfortable and challenging, from the point of identity, sense of self and the quality of the analysis. Within general ethical guidelines, the extent to which one engages with the participants before and after the study is a judgement call that the author needs to make based on the particularity of their study.

Future directions

Now that I have briefly reflected on the dialogical approach to qualitative analysis, I will speculate upon the future directions of this approach. Although I have been at pains to outline what a dialogical approach means and how it can be systematised in doing qualitative data analysis, I wish to end in a more open spirit. The methodological and theoretical tools outlined here are just one possible approach to data analysis. They can be followed but the greater challenge lies in improving them, dialoguing with them and adding to them.

For example, this book has been rooted in the writings of Bakhtin and a particular interpretation of these writings. In the process, much energy was expended in carving out a dialogical territory in the vast landscape of qualitative theory and practice. This was important for this book because of the tendency for Bakhtin to be added to general discursive, phenomenological and narrative approaches. Broadly conceived, his work teeters between the concern with form in discourse analysis and the concern with lived experienced in phenomenological methods of analysis. He adds to all of this literature but he also has the potential to offer something quite different from traditional appropriations of his work.

In the future, I think there is scope to adopt a less reverential approach to his work than I have generally adopted here, and to interrogate different interpretations of this work from a different vantage point. In particular, I see much potential in looking at the overlaps, parallels and distinctions between his work and other theorists, such as Lacan, Heidegger, Dewey and Foucault, in terms of the analysis of qualitative data. In doing this, the challenge is to think of the concrete implication this dialogue would have in terms of modifying existing methodological tools within qualitative analysis.

In terms of content areas, there are a number of possibilities for the application of a dialogical methodology. In this book, I have used case studies of artists, a public sector organisation and intertextual texts on schizophrenia. These case studies have all been united by questions that are interested in the lived experience of the 'idea-hero' and the difficulties and capabilities of the dialogical exchange.

There are other applications of this approach to qualitative analysis. In recent years, for example, family therapists such as Tom Anderson (1991) have examined how the utterance involves the whole person responding emotionally, cognitively and sensuously to the utterance of the other. Similarly, 'Cognitive Analytic Therapy' (e.g., Ryle and Kerr, 2002) is concerned with the dialogical encounter between therapist and client. This kind of therapy work could be usefully complemented by a research focus on the intertextuality of the transcripts and the kinds of authoring that takes place between clients and therapists.

Health research more generally is particularly appropriate for a dialogical analysis. While traditionally phenomenological approaches and varieties of grounded theory tend to be used most in this kind of research, a dialogical approach also has much to offer. In particular, people's experience of time and their negotiation of changed identities resonate deeply with the dialogical emphasis on transformational experiences and the impact that these have on perception of the social world.

It is finally worth mentioning that qualitative analysis is used more and more in internet-based research (see, e.g., Gough, 2007; Hurley, Sullivan and McCarthy, 2007). This is interesting from a dialogical point of view because of the possible time frames of reply (instant, prolonged), the investment of self in a virtual medium and the possibilities available for changing identity or authoring different selves. More generally, the address to a wide audience and the anticipation of their replies foregrounds the role of the 'generalised other', or 'superaddressee' in Bakhtinian (1981) terms. This is a particularly interesting feature of communication on which more theoretical and methodological work could be done.

There are many other areas and applications of this methodology. Each application has the potential to extend, modify and enrich the approach. The qualitative analyst's own concerns, ideas and style can supplement and add to the theory and method of this approach. In other words, the approach can be prescriptive but it does not need to be. It is intended as an open rather than a closed set of possibilities for analysing data or even as a starting point into dialogical theory. We saw in Chapter 1, for instance, that other methodological appropriations of Bakhtin's dialogical work are possible (e.g., Hicks, 2002; McCarthy and Wright, 2004).

There are academic interests and political agendas for which a dialogical approach, as I have outlined it, may not be suited. For example, action research and agendas to encourage positive change in society may well flounder with a dialogical approach (e.g., see Nicole Asquith, 2008, for an excellent example of the use of discourse analysis in hate speech). With its focus on reflective consciousness, a dialogical analysis seeks to equalise all of the participants on a plane of existential reflection. This may be too innocent and naïve a methodology to helpfully engage with these kinds of questions. Then again, it may surprise us – perhaps it can be used with a bit of imagination and/or modification.

To speak of imagination, surprise and modification may be a good way to end this chapter. I think these words sum up the spirit as well as the open potential of a dialogical methodology for qualitative analysis in the future.

Further reading

Anderson, T. (1991) Part One. The reflecting team, in T. Anderson (ed.) *The Reflecting Team: Dialogues and Dialogues about the Dialogues*. Kent: Borgmann Publishing. pp. 3–71.

Asquith, N. (2008) *Text and Context of Malediction: A Study of Antisemitic and Heterosexist Hate Violence*. Saarbrucken: VDM Verlag.

Emerson, C. (1997) *The First Hundred Years of Mikhail Bakhtin*. Princeton, NJ: Princeton University Press.

Gough, B. (2007) Coming out in the heterosexist world of sport: A qualitative analysis of web postings by gay athletes. *Journal of Gay and Lesbian Mental Health*, 11(1/2): 153–74.

Hicks, D. (2001) *Reading Lives: Working-Class Children and Literacy Learning*. New York: Teachers' College Press.

Hirschkop, K. (1999) *Mikhail Bakhtin: An Aesthetic for Democracy*. Oxford and New York: Oxford University Press.

Hurley, A., Sullivan, P. and McCarthy, J. (2007) The construction of self in online support groups for victims of domestic violence. *British Journal of Social Psychology*, 46(4): 859–74.

McCarthy, J. and Wright, P. (2004) *Technology as Experience*. Cambridge, MA: MIT Press.

Sullivan, P. and McCarthy, J. (2007) The relationship between self and activity in the context of artists making art. *Mind, Culture and Activity*, 14(4): 235–52.

BIBLIOGRAPHY

Anderson, T. (1991) Part One. The reflecting team, in T. Anderson (ed.) *The Reflecting Team: Dialogues and Dialogues about the Dialogues*. Kent: Borgmann Publishing. pp. 3–71.

Antaki, C., Billig, M., Edwards, D. and Potter, J. (2002) Discourse analysis means doing analysis: A critique of six analytic shortcomings. *Discourse Analysis Online*, 1(1). Available online at: http://extra.shu.ac.uk/daol/.

Asquith, N. (2008) *Text and Context of Malediction: A Study of Antisemitic and Heterosexist Hate Violence*. Saarbrucken: VDM Verlag.

Austin, J. (1962) *How to do Things with Words*. Cambridge, MA: Harvard University Press.

Bakhtin, M.M. (1981) *The Dialogic Imagination: Four Essays*. Trans. C. Emerson and M. Holquist, ed. M. Holquist. Austin, TX: University of Texas Press.

Bakhtin, M.M. (1984 [1929]) *Problems of Dostoevsky's Poetics*. ed. and trans. C. Emerson. Minneapolis, MN: University of Minnesota Press.

Bakhtin, M.M. (1986) *Speech Genres and Other Late Essays*. Trans. V.W. McGee, ed. C. Emerson and M. Holquist. Austin, TX: University of Texas Press.

Bakhtin, M.M. (1990) *Art and Answerability: Early Philosophical Essays by M.M. Bakhtin*. Trans. V. Liapunov, ed. M. Holquist and V. Liapunov. Austin, TX: University of Texas Press.

Bakhtin, M.M. (1993) *Toward a Philosophy of the Act*. Trans. V. Liapunov, ed. M. Holquist and V. Liapunov. Austin, TX: University of Texas Press.

Bamberg, M. (2006) Stories: big or small. Why do we care? *Narrative Inquiry*, 16(1): 139–47.

Barthes, R. (1977) The death of the author, in S. Heath (ed. and trans.) *Image, Music, Text*. London: Fontana. pp. 142–8.

Becker, H.S. (1984) *Art Worlds*. Berkeley, CA: University of California Press.

Berlin, I. (1999 [1965]) *The Roots of Romanticism*. Ed. H. Hardy. London: Chatto & Windus.

Bernard-Donals, M.F. (1994) *Mikhail Bakhtin: Between Phenomenology and Marxism*. New York: Cambridge University Press.

Billig, M. (1987) *Arguing and Thinking: A Rhetorical Approach to Social Psychology*. Cambridge: Cambridge University Press.

Billig, M. (1999) *Freudian Repression: Conversation Creating the Unconscious*. Cambridge: Cambridge University Press.

Branney, P. (2008) Subjectivity, not personality: Combining discourse analysis and psychoanalysis. *Social and Personality Psychology Compass*, 2(2): 574–90.

Brinkmann, S. (2007) The good qualitative researcher. *Qualitative Research in Psychology*, 4: 127–44.

Bruner, J. (1990) *Acts of Meaning*. Cambridge, MA: Harvard University Press.

Buber, M. (1970) *I and Thou*. Trans. W. Kaufman. New York: Touchstone.

Burck, C. (2005) Comparing qualitative research methodologies for systemic research: The use of grounded theory, discourse analysis and narrative analysis. *The Association for Family Therapy and Systemic Practice*, 27: 237–62.

Burkitt, I. (2008) *Social Selves: Theories of Self and Society* (2nd edition). London: Sage.

Burkitt, I. (2010) Dialogues with self and others: Communication, miscommunication, and the dialogical unconscious. *Theory and Psychology*, 20(3): 305–21.

Burkitt, I. and Sullivan, P. (2009) Embodied ideas and divided selves: Revisiting Laing via Bakhtin. *British Journal of Social Psychology*, 48(3): 563–77.

Burman, E. (2004) Discourse analysis means analysing discourse: Some comments on Antaki, Billig, Edwards and Potter, 'Discourse analysis means doing analysis: A critique of six analytical shortcomings'. *Discourse Analysis Online*. Available online at: http://extra.shu.ac.uk/daol/.

Burman, E. (2009) Resisting the de-radicalization of psychosocial analyses. *Psychoanalysis, Culture and Society*, 13: 374–8.

Burr, V. (1995) *An Introduction to Social Constructionism*. London: Sage.

Chandler, R. and Hayward, M. (2009) *Voicing Psychotic Experiences: A Reconsideration of Recovery and Diversity*. Brighton: OLM Pavilion.

Charmaz, K. (2006) *Constructing Grounded Theory: A Practical Guide through Qualitative Analysis*. London: Sage.

Clark, K. and Holquist, M. (1984) *Mikhail Bakhtin*. Cambridge, MA: Harvard University Press.

Cromby, J. (2004) Between constructionism and neuroscience: The societal co-construction of embodied subjectivity. *Theory and Psychology*, 14(6): 797–821.

Cromby, J. (in press) Feeling the way: Qualitative clinical research and the affective turn. *Qualitative Research in Psychology*.

Crossley, M. (2000) *Introducing Narrative Psychology: Self, Trauma and the Construction of Meaning*. Buckingham: Open University Press.

Csikszentmihalyi, M. (1990) *Flow: The Psychology of Optimal Experience*. New York: Harper & Row.

Czarniawska, B. (2004) *Narratives in Social Science Research*. London: Sage.

Denzin, N. (2009) *Qualitative Inquiry under Fire: Toward a New Paradigm Dialogue*. Walnut Creek, CA: Left Coast Press.

Edwards, D. (1995) Two to tango: Script formulations, dispositions, and rhetorical symmetry in relationship troubles talk. *Research on Language and Social Interaction*, 28(4): 319–50.

Elsbree, L. (1982) *The Rituals of Life: Patterns in Narrative*. Port Washing, NY: Kennikat Press.

Emerson, C. (1983) The outer word and inner speech: Bakhtin, Vygotsky and the internalisation of language. *Critical Inquiry*, 10(2): 245–64.

Emerson, C. (1994) Getting Bakhtin, right and left. *Comparative Literature*, 46: 288–303.

Emerson, C. (1997) *The First Hundred Years of Mikhail Bakhtin*. Princeton, NJ: Princeton University Press.

Fairclough, N. (1992) *Discourse and Social Change*. Cambridge: Polity Press.

Fairclough, N. (2003) *Analysing Discourse: Textual Analysis for Social Research*. London: Routledge.

Foucault, M. (1973) *Madness and Civilisation: A History of Insanity in the Age of Reason*. Trans. R. Howard. New York: Vintage.

Gadamer, H.G. (1989) *Truth and Method*. Trans. J. Weinsheimer and D.G. Marshall. New York: Continuum.

Gardiner, M. (1992) *The Dialogics of Critique: M.M. Bakhtin and the Theory of Ideology*. London: Routledge.

Garfinkel, H. (1967) *Studies in Ethnomethodology*. Englewood Cliffs, NJ: Prentice-Hall.

Gee, J.P. (2005) *An Introduction to Discourse Analysis: Theory and Method* (2nd edition). London: Routledge.

Geertz, C. (1973) *The Interpretation of Cultures*. New York: Basic Books.

Gennett, G. (1982) *Figures of Literary Discourse*. Trans. A. Sheridan. New York: Columbia University Press.

Gillespie, A. and Cornish, F. (2009) Intersubjectivity: Towards a dialogical analysis. *Journal for the Theory of Social Behaviour*, 40(1): 19–46.

Giorgi, A. (1985) Sketch of a psychological phenomenological method, in A. Giorgi (ed.) *Phenomenology and Psychological Research*. Pittsburgh, PA: Duquesne University Press.

Giorgi, A. (2009) *The Descriptive Phenomenological Method in Psychology*. Pittsburgh, PA: Duquesne University Press.

Glaser, B.G. and Strauss, A.L. (1967) *The Discovery of Grounded Theory: Strategies for Qualitative Research*. Chicago, IL: Aldine.

Goffman, E. (1959) *The Presentation of Self in Everyday Life*. New York: Anchor.

Goffman, E. (1961) *Ayslums*. New York: Anchor.

Goffman, E. (1981) *Forms of Talk*. Philadelphia, PA: University of Pennsylvania Press.

Gough, B. (2004) Psychoanalysis as a resource for understanding emotional ruptures in the text: The case of defensive masculinities. *The British Journal of Social Psychology*, 43: 245–67.

Gough, B. (2007) Coming out in the heterosexist world of sport: A qualitative analysis of web postings by gay athletes. *Journal of Gay and Lesbian Psychotherapy*, 11(1/2): 153–74.

Guilfoyle, M. (2001) Problematising psychotherapy: The discursive production of a bulimic. *Culture and Psychology*, 7(2): 151–79.

Habermas, J. (1984) *Theory of Communicative Action* (Vol. 1). Trans. T. McCarthy. London: Heinemann.

Hacking, I. (1995) The looping effect of human kinds, in D. Sperber, D. Premack and A.J. Premack (eds) *Causal Cognition: An Interdisciplinary Approach*. Oxford: Oxford University Press. pp. 351–83.

Halliday, M. (1994) *An Introduction to Functional* Grammar (2nd edition). London: Edward Arnold.

Harré, R. and Madden, E.H. (1975) *Causal Powers: A Theory of Natural Necessity*. Totowa, NJ: Rowman & Littlefield.

Harré, R., Moghaddam, F.M., Cairnie, T.P., Rothbart, D. and Sabat, S. (2009) Recent advances in positioning theory. *Theory and Psychology*, 19(1): 5–31.

Henriques, J., Hollway, W., Urwin, C., Venn C. and Walkerdine, V. (1984) *Changing the Subject: Psychology, Social Regulation and Subjectivity*. London: Methuen.

Hepburn, A. and Potter, J. (2007) Crying receipts: Time, empathy and institutional practice. *Research on Language and Social Interaction*, 40: 89–116.

Hermans, H.J.M. (2001a) The dialogical self: Toward a theory of personal and cultural positioning. *Culture and Psychology*, 7(3): 243–81.

Hermans, H.J.M. (2001b) The construction of a personal position repertoire: Method and practice. *Culture and Psychology*, 7(3): 323–66.

Hermans, H.J.M. (2002) The dialogical self as a society of mind. *Theory and Psychology*, 12(2): 147–60.

Hicks, D. (1996) Contextual inquiries: A discourse-oriented study of classroom learning, in D. Hicks (ed.) *Discourse, Learning and Schooling*. New York: Cambridge University Press. pp. 104–41.

Hicks, D. (2000) Self and other in Bakhtin's early philosophical essays: Prelude to a theory of prose consciousness. *Mind, Culture and Activity*, 7(3): 227–42.

Hicks, D. (2002) *Reading Lives: Working-Class Children and Literacy Learning*. New York: Teachers' College Press.

Hirschkop, K. (1999) *Mikhail Bakhtin: An Aesthetics for Democracy*. Oxford and New York: Oxford University Press.

Hollway, W. (1984) Gender difference and the production of subjectivity, in J. Henriques, W. Hollway, C. Urwin, C. Venn and V. Walkerdine, *Changing the Subject: Psychology, Social Regulation and Subjectivity*. London: Methuen. pp. 223–62.

Hollway, W. and Jefferson, T. (2000) *Doing Qualitative Research Differently: Free Association, Narrative and the Interview Method*. London: Sage.

Holquist, M. (2002) *Dialogism, Bakhtin and His World* (2nd edition). London: Routledge.

Hurley, A., Sullivan, P. and McCarthy, J. (2007) The construction of self in online support groups for victims of domestic violence. *British Journal of Social Psychology*, 46(4): 859–74.

King, N. and Horrocks, C. (2009) *Interviews in Qualitative Research*. London: Sage.

Kress, G. (2001) From Saussure to critical linguistics: The turn towards a social view of language, in M. Wetherell, S. Taylor and S. Yates (eds) *Discourse Theory and Practice: A Reader*. Milton Keynes: Open University Press. pp. 29–47.

Kristeva, J. (1986) Word, dialogue and novel, in T. Moi (ed.) *The Kristeva Reader*. Oxford: Basil Blackwell. pp. 34–61.

Kvale, S. (1995) The social construction of validity. *Qualitative Inquiry*, 1(1): 19–40.

Kvale, S. (1996) *Interviews: An Introduction to Qualitative Research Interviewing*. London: Sage.

Laing, R.D. and Esterson, A. (1964) *Sanity, Madness and the Family*. London: Penguin.

Landau, M. (1991) *Narratives of Human Evolution*. New Haven, CT: Yale University Press.

Langdridge, D. (2007) *Phenomenological Psychology: Theory, Research and Method*. Harlow: Prentice Hall.

Langdridge, D. and Hagger-Johnson, G. (2009) *Introduction to Research Methods and Data Analysis in Psychology* (2nd edition). Harlow: Prentice Hall.

Lodge, D. (1990) *After Bakhtin: Essays on Fiction and Criticism*. London: Routledge.

Madill, A. (2010) Realism, in L.M. Given (ed.) *The Sage Encyclopedia of Qualitative Research Methods*. London: Sage.

Madill, A. and Doherty, K. (1994) 'So you did what you wanted then': Discourse analysis, personal agency and psychotherapy. *Journal of Community and Applied Social Psychology*, 2: 261–73.

Madill, A., Jordan, A. and Shirley, C. (2000) Objectivity and reliability in qualitative analysis: Realist, contextualist and radical constructionist epistemologies. *British Journal of Psychology*, 91(1): 1–20.

Madill, A. and Sullivan, P. (2010) Medical training as adventure-wonder and adventure-ordeal: A dialogical analysis of affect-laden pedagogy. *Social Science and Medicine*, 71(12): 2195–203.

Madill, A. and Sullivan P. (in preparation) Participant validation as a dialogical exercise.

McCarthy, J., Sullivan, P. and Wright, P. (2006) Culture, personal experience and agency. *British Journal of Social Psychology*, 45(2): 421–39.

McCarthy, J. and Wright, P. (2004) *Technology as Experience*. Cambridge, MA: MIT Press.

McCarthy, J. and Wright, P. (2007) *Technology as Experience*. Cambridge, MA: MIT Press.

Morson, G.S. (2004) The process of ideological becoming, in A.F. Ball and S.W. Freedman (eds) *Bakhtinian Perspectives on Language, Literacy and Learning*. New York: Cambridge University Press. pp. 315–33.

Morson, G.S. and Emerson, C. (1990) *Mikhail Bakhtin: Creation of a Prosaics*. Stanford, CA: Stanford University Press.

Ní Chonchúir, M. and McCarthy, J. (2007) The enchanting potential of technology: A dialogical case study of enchantment and the internet. *Personal and Ubiquitous Computing*, 12(5): 401–9.

O'Connell, D. and Kowall, S. (1995) Basic principles of transcription, in J.A. Smith, R. Harré and L. van Langenhove (eds) *Rethinking Methods in Psychology*. London: Sage. pp. 93–104.

Parker, I. (1990) Discourse: Definitions and contradictions. *Philosophical Psychology*, 3(2): 189–204.

Parker, I. (1992) *Discourse Dynamics: Critical Analysis for Social and Individual Psychology*. London: Routledge.

Parker, I. (1994) Reflexive research and the grounding of analysis: Social psychology and the psy-complex. *Journal of Community and Applied Social Psychology*, 4(4): 234–9.

Parker, I. (1997) Discourse analysis and psycho-analysis. *British Journal of Social Psychology*, 36: 479–95.

Parker, I. (2002) *Critical Discursive Psychology*. Basingstoke: Palgrave.

Parker, I. (2005) *Qualitative Psychology: Introducing Radical Research*. Buckingham: Open University Press.

Parker, I. (2010) *Lacanian Psychoanalysis: Revolutions in Subjectivity*. London: Routledge.

Poole, B. (1998). Bakhtin and Cassirer : The philosophical origins of carnival messianism. *South Atlantic Quarterly*. Vol. 97(3/4), 537–578.

Potter, J. (2001) Wittgenstein and Austin, in M. Wetherell, S. Taylor and S. Yates (eds) *Discourse Theory and Practice: A Reader*. Milton Keynes: Open University Press. pp. 39–47.

Potter, J. and Wetherell, M. (1987) *Discourse and Social Psychology: Beyond Attitudes and Behaviour*. London: Sage.

Potter, J. and Wetherell, M. (2005) Postscript to Chinese edition of 'Discourse and Social Psycholgoy: Beyond Attitudes and Behaviour'. Available at: http://www.staff.lboro.ac.uk/~ssjap/JP%20Articles/Potter%20Wetherell%20new%20DASP%20postscript%202005.pdf.

Propp, V. (1968) *Morphology of the Folktale*. Austin, TX: University of Texas Press.

Ratner, C. (2008) Cultural psychology and qualitative methodology: Scientific and political considerations. *Culture and Psychology*, 14(3): 259–88.

Ricoeur, P. (1973) The hermeneutical function of distanciation. Trans. D. Pellauer. *Philosophy Today*, 17: 129–41.

Ricoeur, P. (1981) *Hermeneutics and the Human Sciences: Essays on Language, Action and Interpretation*. Ed. and trans. J.B. Thompson. Cambridge: Cambridge University Press.

Roberts, J.M. (2004) Will the materialists in the Bakhtin Circle please stand up?, in J. Joseph and J.M. Roberts (eds) *Realism Discourse and Deconstruction*. London: Routledge. pp. 89–111.

Ryle, A. and Kerr, I.A. (2002) *Introducing Cognitive Analytic Therapy: Principles and Practice*. Chichester: Wiley.

Searle, J. (1969) *Speech Acts: An Essay in the Philosophy of Language*. Cambridge: Cambridge University Press.

Shotter, J. (1975) *Images of Man in Psychological Research*. London: Methuen.

Shotter, J. (1993) *Cultural Politics of Everyday Life*. Milton Keynes: Open University Press.

Shotter, J. (1997) Dialogical realities: The ordinary, the everyday and other strange new worlds. *Journal for the Theory of Social Behaviour*, 27(2/3): 345–57.

Shotter, J. (2009) Bateson, double description, Todes, and embodiment: Preparing activities and their relation to abduction. *Journal for the Theory of Social Behaviour*, 39: 219–45.

Shotter, J. and Billig, M. (1998) A Bakhtinian psychology: From out of the heads of individuals and into the dialogues between them, in M. Bell and M. Gardiner (eds) *Bakhtin and the Human Sciences: No Last Words*. London: Sage. pp. 13–30.

Silverman, D. (1993) *Interpretive Qualitative Data: Methods for Analysing Talk, Text and Interaction*. London: Sage.

Slife, B.D. and Williams, R.N. (1995) *What's Behind the Research? Discovering Hidden Assumptions in the Behavioural Sciences*. London: Sage.

Smith, J.A. (1996) Beyond the divide between cognition and discourse: Using interpretive phenomenological analysis in health psychology. *Psychology and Health*, 11: 261–71.

Smith, J.A. (2010) 'We could be diving for pearls': The value of the gem in experiential qualitative psychology. Key Note. *Qualitative Methods in Psychology*, X(X): xx–x.

Smith, J.A., Flowers, P. and Larkin, M. (2009) *Interpretive Phenomenological Analysis: Theory, Method and Research*. London: Sage.

Spitzer, R.L, Gibbon, M., Skodol, A.E., Williams, J.B.W. and First, M.B. (2002) *DSM-IV-TR Case Book: A Learning Companion to the Diagnostic and Statistical Manual of Mental Disorders* (4th edition). Arlington, VA: American Psychiatric Association.

Stallybrass, P. and White, A. (1986) *The Politics and Poetics of Transgression*. New York: Cornell University Press.

Starks, H. (2007) Choose your method: A comparison of phenomenology, discourse analysis and grounded theory. *Qualitative Health Research*, 17(10): 1372–80.

Strauss, A. (1987) *Qualitative Analysis for Social Scientists*. Cambridge: Cambridge University Press.

Strauss, A. and Corbin, J. (1990) *Basics of Qualitative Research: Grounded Theory Procedures and Techniques*. London: Sage.

Sullivan, P. (2007) Understanding self and other through 'spirit' and 'soul'. *Culture and Psychology*, 13(1): 105–28.

Sullivan, P. (2008) Our emotional connection to truth: Moving beyond a functional view of language in discourse analysis. *Journal for the Theory of Social Behaviour*, 38(2): 193–207.

Sullivan, P. and McCarthy, J. (2005) A dialogical account of experience-based inquiry. *Theory and Psychology*, 15(5): 621–38.

Sullivan, P. and McCarthy, J. (2007) The relationship between self and activity in the context of artists making art. *Mind, Culture and Activity*, 14(4): 235–52.

Sullivan, P. and McCarthy, J. (2008) Managing the polyphonic sounds of organizational truths. *Organization Studies*, 29(4): 525–41.

Sullivan, P. and McCarthy, J. (2009) An experiential account of the psychology of art. *Psychology of Aesthetics, Creativity, and the Arts*, 3(3): 181–7.

Taylor, C. (1984) Foucault on freedom and truth. *Political Theory*, 12(2): 152–83.

Urwin, C. (1984) Power relations and the emergence of language, in J. Henriques, W. Hollway, C. Urwin, C. Venn and V. Walkerdine, *Changing the Subject: Psychology, Social Regulation and Subjectivity*. London: Methuen. pp. 262–320.

Walkerdine, V. (1981) Sex, power and pedagogy. *Screen Education*, 28: 14–23.

Walkerdine, V. (1987) No laughing matter: Girls' comics and the preparation for adolescent femininity, in J.M. Broughton (ed.) *Critical Theories of Psychological Development*. New York: Plenum Press.

Walkerdine, V. and the Girls and Mathematics Unit (1989) *Counting Girls Out*. London: Virago.

Weber, M. (1947) *The Theory of Social and Economic Organization*. Trans. A.M. Henderson and Talcott Parsons. Glencoe, IL: The Free Press.

Weinert, F. (2009) *Copernicus, Darwin and Freud: Revolutions in the History and Philosophy of Science*. Chichester: Wiley Blackwell.

Wengraf, T. (2001) *Qualitative Research Interviewing: Narrative and Semi-Structured Methods*. London: Sage.

Wertsch, J.V. (1991) *Voices of the Mind: A Sociocultural Approach to Mediated Action*. Cambridge, MA: Harvard University Press.

Wertsch, J.V. (1998) *Mind as Action*. New York: Oxford University Press.

Wetherell, M., Taylor, S. and Yates, S. (eds) (2001) *Discourse Theory and Practice: A Reader*. Milton Keynes: Open University Press.

White, H. (1973) *Metahistory: The Historical Imagination in Nineteenth Century Europe*. Baltimore, MD: Johns Hopkins University Press.

Wilkinson, S. and Kitzinger, C. (eds) (1995) *Feminism and Discourse: Psychological Perspectives*. London: Sage.

Willig, C. (2001) *Introducing Qualitative Research in Psychology: Adventures in Theory and Method*. Buckingham: Open University Press.

Zappen, J.P. (2004) *The Rebirth of Dialogue: Bakhtin, Socrates and the Rhetorical Tradition*. New York: State University of New York Press.

INDEX

'abduction' as a form of logic 130, 141
accentuation and re-accentuation
    135–7
anacrisis 159–62
Anderson, Tom 177
Antaki, C. 150, 153, 155, 158, 162
anthropological approaches to analysis
    8–10
'anticipated' and 'real' responses 170
Aristotle 144
'art world', the 94, 96, 99, 167
Asquith, Nicola 178
audit trail procedure 64–5, 80
Austin, John 10, 27
'authoritative' discourse 137–40

background reading 84–6, 94
Bakhtin, Mikhail 1–6, 13–18, 30–4, 43–62,
    68–9, 78–9, 111, 119, 124, 131–4,
    137–8, 159, 165, 170–1, 177–8;
    biography of 6–8
Bakhtin, Nikolai 7
'Bakhtin Circle' 5–6
Bamberg, M. 12
Barthes, R. 25, 29
Becker, Howard 94
Berlin, Isaiah 85
Billig, M. 53–5, 69
'blank' subjectivity 21–3, 26, 28–30;
    relationship of dialogue to 30
'bracketing' 38–9
brackets, use of 137
Branney, Peter 30
Brinkmann, Svend 149
Bruner, Jerome 12
bureaucracy, 'ideal type' of 65
'bureaucratic' approach to qualitative
    research 64–80; used with dialogic
    methods 67–80
Burkitt, Ian 56 59, 63, 133, 141
Burman, E. 153, 158, 162
Burr, V. 33
Bush, George W. 48–52, 62

carnival genre 104, 111–20, 166–7
causality: and evaluation 152; types
    of 143–51
'charismatic' approach to research 64–7,
    78–80
Charmaz, Kathy 11, 40
chronotopes 46–7, 61, 75–6, 166, 174
chronotopic shifts 132–4
cognitive analytic therapy 177
coherence of research 148–9
collaboration in research 173–4
commentaries on subjectivity 123–41
'complex' subjectivity 30–1, 36–41;
    in relation to dialogue 37
'contextual inquiry' 18
Cornish, F. 16
'created dialogue' 103–13, 160–1, 170,
    175; analytic value of 107–8; benefits
    of 119
critical discourse analysis 31–2
critical narrative analysis 12
critical realism 5–6
Cromby, John 23, 162
Czikszentmihalyi, Mihaly 89

data analysis, bureaucratic 74–8
data preparation, bureaucratic 68–74
'death of the author' 25–6
Denzin, Norman K. 119
deviant case analysis 93, 148–9
Dewey, John 18
'dialogic unconscious' 59
dialogical approach to qualitative analysis
    1, 7–8, 13–17, 32, 62, 153, 163, 165,
    167, 170, 172, 175; bureaucracy in
    67–80; charisma in 78–80; evaluation
    criteria for 143–62; future prospects
    for 176–8; limitations of 101; theoret-
    ical foundations of 165–72
'dialogical self' theory 17
dialogue: meanings of 2–6; methodologi-
    cal readings of 17–18
'disclaimers' 14, 54–5

discourse: aesthetic view of 43–4; *direct and indirect* 16; as a methodological tool 43; *outside-in* and *inside-out* 44–53, 91, 101, 169–70, 174; relationship of genre to 45–7; rhetorical features of 60; *see also* 'double-voiced' discourse
discourse analysis 9, 12–14, 21–33, 37, 50, 71, 147–9, 155–6, 162; *fine-grained* and *large-scale* 22–5, 41, 67
Doherty, Kathy 26
Dostoevsky, Fyodor 56–8, 78–9
'double-voiced' discourse 16, 45, 53–6, 60, 62, 91, 96–100, 103, 135, 172, 175; carnival genre in 111–19
Duquesne school 11

Edwards, D. 25, 28
'efficient causality' 143–4, 150
Elshree, Langdon 12
Emerson, C. 34, 46, 58, 171
emotional attitudes of different methodologies 8–13
epic discourse 48–50, 61
epistemology 4, 25–6, 144, 147
epochè see 'bracketing'
Esterson, Aaron 125, 128–33, 151
ethics 175–6
ethnomethodology 27–8
evaluation criteria for a dialogical approach 143–62; and causality 150
'extreme case formulation' 14, 59

Fairclough, N. 32, 46–7, 124, 129, 137
family therapy 177
focus group data 103–21, 170
folk psychiatry 104–11
Foucault, Michel 31–6, 138
free indirect reporting 137

Garfinkel, Harold 28
Gee, J.P. 69, 71
generalisability of psychological studies 144
genres 45–50, 61, 83–4, 87; dialogue between 93–4
Gillespie, A, 16
Giorgi, A. 11, 38
Glaser, Barney 39
Goffman, Erving 10, 49, 65, 128, 139
Gough, B. 33
grounded theory 8–13, 39–40, 66–7, 147, 162

Hacking, Ian 146
Hagger-Johnson, G. 69–70

Halliday, Michael 31–2
Harré, Rom 143, 145
Hepburn, Alexa 148
Hermans, Hubert 17
'hermeneutic circle' 82
hermeneutics 9
Hicks, Deborah 18, 61
hidden dialogue 56–9
Hirschkop, Ken 7, 167–8
Holquist, M. 60–1
Hook, Derek 32
Hume, David 144
Husserl, E. 38–9

identity, sense of 3
informed consent 176
'internal critic' concept 54–5, 69
'internally-persuasive' discourse 137–40
internet-based research 178
interpretive phenomenological analysis 1, 11, 13, 38, 42, 175
intertextuality 123–4, 140–3, 147, 150–1, 155–7
intonation 41, 44, 49, 56, 61–2, 100, 168
Istina 3, 8, 153, 157, 168

Jefferson, Gail 69
Jesus Christ 65
Jordan, A. 66, 78, 144, 147

Kant, Immanuel 85
'key moments' from data 72–7, 83, 100, 172–4
Kress, Gunter 25
Kristeva, Julia 124
Kvale, S. 151, 153

Lacan, Jacques 33–6
Laing, Ronnie 125, 128–33, 151
Landau, Misia 12
Langdridge, Darren 12, 69–70
language: aesthetic pleasure from 65; involvement of power relations in 31–3; as strategic action 26–7; as a transparent medium 38–9; as unconscious desire 33–4
langue 24
'life-world' concept 38
linguistics, structural 23–4
Lodge, David 46
'loopholes' in discourse 59, 62

McCarthy, John 13, 18, 20, 51, 70, 74, 81, 102, 103, 122, 153, 178, 179

Madden, Edward 143, 145
Madill, Anna 26, 66, 68, 72, 75, 78, 144, 147, 151, 154, 162, 176
Marxism 5–6
Matusov, Eugene 17–18, 70
micro dialogues 58–9, 169
Mishler, Eliot 68
Morson, G.S. 46, 58, 140

narrative analysis 9, 12–13, 61, 67, 147
Nixon, Richard 65
'novel' genre 60–1

ontology 5, 25, 34
'other' as distinct from 'self' 3–4, 16

Parker, I. 21, 23, 26, 30–3, 37–40
parody 50–3, 55, 169
parole 24
'participant orientation' 148–9
participant voices in text 155–7
personal position repertoire 17
phenomenology 8–11, 13, 38, 67, 147, 166, 172
'polyphonic' organisations 121
polyphony of voices and ideas 7, 108, 113, 121, 150–1
Potter, Jonathan 23–4, 27, 148–50
power relations 31–2, 167
pravda 15, 153, 168
'Professional' genre 94–100, 166
Propp, Vladimir 12
psychiatry 138–40
psychoanalysis 33, 39

quotations (data extracts) 87–95, 100
quote marks, use of 136

reflective practitioners 141
reliability of psychological studies 144
research questions 82, 153–5
'reverse engineering' of grounded theory 39
Ricoeur, Paul 9–12, 45
Romanticism 85–9, 93–4, 98–9, 167–8

Saussure, Ferdinand de 23–6, 44
'scientific realism' 144, 147
Searle, John 27
self–other distinction 168–70
selfhood, senses of 3–4
Shirley, C. 66, 78, 144, 147

Shotter, John 5, 15, 22, 130
'sidewards glances' in discourse 53–6, 59–61
Slife, Brent 143, 145
Smith, Jonathan 11, 175
social constructionism 5, 33
social convention 111
Socratic dialogue 159
'sound bites' from data 73–4, 79, 86–8, 94–5, 105, 156–7, 175
speech act theory 27–8
'spotting' of features in discourse 157–8
Stallybrass, Peter 166–7
Strauss, Anselm 39–40
'stylisation' in discourse 52–3, 117
subjectivity in data 1, 21–43, 157–9; types of 21; *see also* 'blank' subjectivity; commentaries on subjectivity; 'complex' subjectivity; 'uncomplicated' subjectivity
summaries of analysis 83–4, 110, 120, 155, 157
'superaddressees' 56, 59, 109, 131–4, 178
syncrisis 159–62

Taylor, Charles 32, 42
'teleological causes' 145
transcription of data 66–71
triangulation 11, 147–8, 159
'trusting' attitude to discourse 10–11
truth-claims 10

'uncomplicated' subjectivity 38–41; benefits and difficulties of 40; relationship of dialogue to 41
utterances 172–3

validity of psychological studies 144
'voice', concept of 44–7, 62; *see also* participant voices in text

Walkerdine, V. 34–7
Weber, Max 64–5
Wertsch, James 17
Wetherell, M. 23–4, 27, 148–50
White, Allon 166–7
White, Hayden 12
Williams, Richard 143, 145
Willig, C. 148, 162
Wright, Peter 18
writing-up of analysis 81–101, 174–5